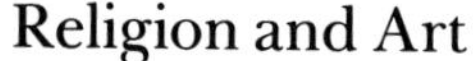

Religion and Art

RELIGION AND ART

by Richard Wagner

TRANSLATED BY
William Ashton Ellis

University of Nebraska Press
Lincoln and London

Manufactured in the United States of America

First Bison Book printing: 1994
Most recent printing indicated by the last digit below:
10 9 8 7 6 5 4 3 2 1

The paper in this book meets the minimum requirements of American National Standard for Information Sciences—Permanence of Paper for Printed Library Materials, ANSI Z39.48–1984

Library of Congress Cataloging-in-Publication Data
Wagner, Richard, 1813–1883.
[Literary works. English. Selections]
Religion and art / by Richard Wagner; translated by William Ashton Ellis.
p. cm.
Originally published: London: K. Paul, Trench, Trübner, 1897.
(Richard Wagner's prose works; v. 6)
ISBN 0-8032-9764-5 (pbk.)
1. Music—Philosophy and aesthetics. I. Title.
ML410.W1A1273 1994
780'.1—dc20
94-28469 CIP
MN

Reprinted from the original 1897 English translation of Volume VI (*Religion and Art*) of *Richard Wagner's Prose Works,* published by Kegan Paul, Trench, Trübner & Co., Ltd., London. The University of Nebraska Press is grateful to the Sherrod Library, East Tennessee State University, for loaning a copy of the book for reproduction.

ERRATA.

Page 26, line 6, *for* "answers" *read* "answer."
,, 138, ,, 5 from bottom, *for* "aad" *read* "and."
,, 139, last line, *for* "wandschaften" *read* "wandtschaften."
,, 157, line 11, *for* "wisskt" *read* "winkt."
,, 231, ,, 9 from bottom, *for* "blood" *read* "bread."
,, 303, ,, 5, *for* "mystich" *read* "mystisch."

CONTENTS

TRANSLATOR'S PREFACE.

HE obvious title for the present volume is that of its principal essay "Religion and Art," with whose main idea almost every article in the book is more or less connected, and its latter half exclusively so. The contents are identical with those of the tenth volume of Richard Wagner's *Gesammelte Schriften*, with three exceptions, two of omission and one of addition. The omissions are the article entitled "What is German?," already published in Vol. IV. of the present series, and the drama of "Parsifal," excluded for the same reason as all the other finished stage-works. The addition is a very small one, namely the fragment "On the Womanly in the Human Race," which I felt obliged to publish in this connection, as the author meant it to complete the circle of his thoughts upon "Regeneration"; it will probably have to figure again, however, with the other posthumous publications to appear in the eighth and concluding volume of this series.

In his prefatory note to the tenth volume of the *Ges. Schr.* (1883) the editor, Freiherr Hans von Wolzogen, remarks: "The publication of the present volume fulfils a wish expressed by the master in the last months before his death. His own intentions, together with the chronologic sequence adhered to in the previous volumes, have been the guiding principles in the arrangement of these writings." For my own part, I could have wished that the chronologic sequence had been still more strictly adhered to, instead of the majority of the shorter writings being made to form the commencement of the book; for there are certain important passages in these minor "Introductions" etc., that lose their due significance through dislocation. However, a radical re-arrangement of these first forty pages, with a distribution of their shorter papers among the longer works, would have much confused the Anglo-German student who might desire to compare the translation with the original; therefore I have retained the order given to the essays by their German editor.

As far as I am aware, none of the contents of this volume have been rendered into English prior to the translation now laid before the reader, with the solitary exception of "Religion and Art" (including its first supplement, "What boots this knowledge?"). Of the latter offence I must confess to having been personally guilty in *The Meister* for 1889, two years before the present attempt to translate the whole of Richard Wagner's prose was even thought of. To-day it is inconceivable to me how I then could have had the temerity to storm a work whose peculiarities of style demand at least a long and close acquaintance with the master's mode of thought, to say nothing of a systematic pursuit of his ideal through all the essays which that treatise crowns; for the rendering of "Art and Revolution" in the preceding issues of *The Meister* was mere child's-play by the side of such a task. As an act of penance I feel compelled to quote its first two sentences, now represented by the opening sentence on page 213 *infra*: "One might say that when Religion becomes artificial it is the opportunity for Art to save the spirit of Religion. She gives physical worth to the mythical symbols which the former would force on our belief in their abstract sense, and, by an ideal portrayal of these symbols, reveals their hidden truth." This is by no means the worst example I could have selected from my earlier translation, but I have chosen it to illustrate the folly of trying to make a complex sentence more readable by splitting it into two—a course which should be absolutely forbidden to the translator unless he can vindicate it by very good reasons indeed; here it strikes a false note at the very commencement of the essay, and therefore obscures the meaning of the whole work. Whether the English rendering offered in the present volume be an improvement on the style of the older one, or the reverse, it is not for me to judge; all I can say is, that scarcely four consecutive words will be found identical in the two versions.

With an apology for the above digression, I must now proceed to a review of the circumstances in which the various articles embodied in the present volume were written by their author.

It will be noticed that an interval of three years occurs between the first article, that on Spohr's "Jessonda," and the period of renewed literary activity which begins with the Introduction to the earliest number of the Bayreuther Blätter. To tell the truth, that interval must be extended for another two years back, making five in all, to arrive at any similar epoch in the author's life. In the spring of 1872 Richard Wagner had left the calm and quietude of Tribschen for what might at first appear the equally pronounced seclusion of Bayreuth; but, just as the last year of his retirement on the lake of Lucerne had been broken by the constant necessity of journeys in furtherance of his Festspiel scheme, so he was allowed but little peace and rest after the first few months of his removal to the Franconian town. In Volume V. we were given the fruits of that brief respite, in the shape of the essay on "Actors and Singers" and the various minor articles concluding with the "Letter to an Actor" of November 1872. Then another round of business-visits to various German towns and cities had to be undertaken, lasting till the end of April 1873, saving for temporary returns to Bayreuth; in one of which was written the "Glance at the German Operatic stage of To-day" (Vol V.), which may itself be regarded as a sort of diary of that tour of inspection.

Meanwhile the building of the Festival-house was proceeding apace, so that on August 2, 1873, the topmost beam could be set in place with fitting ceremony. Yet the master's troubles were by no means ended. Subscriptions to the building-fund were flagging terribly, and in the autumn of that year it seemed that the Bayreuth enterprise would after all collapse for lack of financial support. In October, accordingly, a meeting of the Patronat-Verein was assembled at Bayreuth, attended by Friedrich Nietzsche among others. As outcome of this convocation, an Appeal drawn up by Dr A. Stern, of Dresden, was issued to four thousand book and music sellers: result—a few thalers from two or three students!

Had it not been for Wagner's personally pledging his credit for the work, the Bayreuth Bühnenfestspielhaus must there and then have been abandoned. But at the beginning of the year 1874 King Ludwig came forward to its rescue, and plans for the performances could be entertained once more, though it proved necessary to postpone their date until 1876 instead of 1875, as previously contemplated.

In the spring of 1874 the "Villa Wahnfried" was at last ready for habitation, and the master was able to move into it from his lodgings in the Dammallee. The principal singers gathered round him in July for a preliminary study of their rôles; the final touch was put to the orchestration of *Götterdämmerung*, Nov. 21; and the year was closed by a trip to Leipzig, in search of singers to fill the still remaining gaps.—The first article in this volume is the echo of that flying visit, in the same way as the "Glance at the German Operatic Stage" had been the record of the longer tour of two years back.

Even this, however, did not end the master's peregrinations. In the spring of 1875 a fresh cycle of concerts in aid of the Bayreuth enterprise had to be conducted in Vienna, Pesth, Berlin etc., leaving him but two months rest before the commencement of the major rehearsals of July and August of that year. These were followed by a stay of two or three weeks at Teplitz, for bodily and mental recuperation. Returning to Bayreuth before the end of September, he had to make trial of his new-found "Siegfried," Herr Unger, and to draft a comprehensive scheme of rehearsals for the summer of 1876, to enable his singers to arrange betimes with their various employers. No sooner was this circular despatched, than he set out for Vienna, to fulfil an engagement to superintend the rehearsals for "uncut" performances of *Tannhäuser* and *Lohengrin*, involving another interruption of almost two months.

The double festival of Christmas and Frau Wagner's birthday was once more spent in Wahnfried. The new year, 1876, brought with it the composition of the Centennial March for the United States of America, and another excursion to Vienna and Berlin, this time to conduct a performance of *Lohengrin* for the benefit of the opera-chorus, in the first-named city, and to prepare *Tristan und Isolde* for representation in the second.

At last the master was able to settle down again in Bayreuth for the final rehearsals and performances of his tetralogy. As he has given a fairly full account of these in his "Retrospect" (page 95), I may pass over that world-historical event as beyond the compass of my hasty chronicle.

After all the exertions of that arduous time we next find Richard Wagner, with all his family, on a pleasure-trip to Naples and Sorrento at the end of September 1876, returning by way of Rome and Bologna, in both of which cities festivities awaited him. Christmas again is spent at Bayreuth. On January 1, 1877, he issues the circular of page 15, suggesting the formation of a new Patronat-Verein, and by the middle of September the prospectus of a so-called "School" at Bayreuth (page 19). Between these two appeals occurred the visit to London, to direct the Wagner Festival at the Albert Hall, with a view to wiping off the very large deficit on the Bayreuth Festival of 1876. Though the immediate financial result of this visit to our shores was practically nil, it is not to be doubted that its moral effect contributed most appreciably to the ultimate insurance of the Bayreuth enterprise, long after the master's death.—The deficit itself was finally liquidated by an arrangement with the Munich Court-theatre, whereby the *Ring des Nibelungen* was permitted to be given there in full and Wagner's "royalties" were pledged for gradual repayment of the debt.—

The text of *Parsifal* had meanwhile been written; completed on February 23, 1877, in December of that year it appeared in print. With January 1878 arrived the first number of the Bayreuther Blätter. The *Ring des Nibelungen* had begun its journey round the world, impelled by fate, and even the plan of "exercises and practices" at Bayreuth had been compulsorily abandoned. Thus nothing remained for Richard Wagner, but to educate his "public" and patiently await the time when it should be possible to present it with his last great work, complete in tone and action. Parallel with the composition of the music for *Parsifal* we therefore have the series of articles for the Bayreuth journal which constitute the bulk of the present volume. The *Parsifal* music was begun in the autumn of 1877, and its 'sketch' concluded on April 25, 1879; its fully instrumented overture was performed in Wahnfried on Christmas-day of 1878. The literary works commence at the end of 1877, and are continued, with hardly a break, down to November 1879.

But a change of scene had now become imperative. To the master himself it must have been a perpetual agony to look at that playhouse standing silent on its hill, that supreme effort of his life accomplished after a quarter-of-a-century's endeavour, and called to realisation for so brief a span. There seemed no immediate prospect of the theatre being opened again, for postponement after postponement had been decreed by lack of funds. Would its walls resound once more in his lifetime? A constant care and eyesore must it have been to him; small wonder that he wished to blot the sight out for a while, escape where he could win the ideal atmosphere wherein to orchestrate his most ideal of dramas. Illness, too, necessitated a total change of climate and surroundings. At the end of December 1879 we therefore find Richard Wagner departing with his family for the south of Italy. On Jan. 3, 1880, he reaches Naples, and remains there till the middle of the summer, driven back at last by the heat and a recurrence of his old complaint, facial erysipelas. He slowly makes his journey northward, spending some weeks at Sienna and a month or so in Venice, reaching Munich on October 31, and Bayreuth on the 17th of November. During his long absence, of nearly eleven months, the instrumentation of *Parsifal* had progressed apace, and the treatise upon "Religion and Art" been written. At Bayreuth he added the supplement, "What boots this knowledge?" and almost simultaneously announced the resumption of the Stage-festivals in 1882.

"Know thyself" was written in the early part of 1881, followed by another period of active arrangements for the representations of 1882, trials of scenery, rehearsals with the principal singers and so forth. In September "Hero-dom and Christendom" appeared, and the instrumentation of the third act of *Parsifal* was commenced, at Bayreuth; but the longing for a sunnier sky soon gained the upper hand, and at the beginning of November the Wahnfried household departed for Palermo. It was here that Richard Wagner gave the finishing touch to his last dramatic work, January 13th, 1882. In April he left Sicily for home, and arrived at Bayreuth the middle of May for the final preparations for the new Stage-festival, with which may be coupled the letters to Hans von Wolzogen and Friedrich Schön, of March and June.

Almost immediately after the festival the master set out once more for Italy (Sep. 14, 1882), never to return alive to German soil. Proceeding direct to Venice, he stopped for a week at the Hotel Europa, and then removed to the suite of apartments he had hired in the Palazzo Vendramin, on the Grand Canal, where he died on February 13th, 1883, from the heart-complaint he long had suffered under. The future of "Bayreuth" had been ensured by the unequivocal success of the *Parsifal* performances in the previous summer, and that embodiment of energy might fitly sink to rest.

I have been obliged to relate the outward events of our author's life at greater length than in previous volumes, because they are so intimately connected with these writings. But there are many important matters which space forbids me to dwell upon—such as the gradual formation of that "Bayreuth colony" which must needs have exercised some influence upon the master's cast of thought, however much he towered above his surroundings. It has been said that a man learns more by teaching, than his pupils can ever acquire by being taught; but, apart from generalities, the circle of men and women who gathered round Richard Wagner at Bayreuth from time to time was more than ordinarily intellectual. Perhaps the most positive influence then exercised on Wagner by a living personage was that of Count Gobineau, a French scholar and diplomatist armed with the widest knowledge of the world and its inhabitants, won from years of travel in every quarter of the globe. Only second to the influence of Gobineau came that of Friedrich Nietzsche; for a very brief period indeed, and in quite a negative direction. A great deal in the articles of 1878-1880 may be considered as an answer to Nietzsche's "*Menschliches, Allzumenschliches*"—"Human, All-too-human"—the first volume whereof appeared in May, 1878. In fact, it is so impossible not to recognise a literary duel in the writings of these two men at that epoch, that I am obliged to reopen a question which I had hoped to have disposed of in my preface to Volume V.

Since writing that preface I have had the opportunity of studying the second volume of "Nietzsche's Life," published by his sister in the interval, as also a very large portion of Nietzsche's own voluminous works. In not one respect have I found cause to alter the opinion derived from a more cursory glance at this mass of literature; on the contrary, I now am able to substantiate my theories, in Nietzsche's regard, by facts of which I then was ignorant. The only difficulty is to select the most characteristic and important, from such a vast array. I therefore must return to the commencement of this remarkable and wellnigh tragic friendship.

In the first volume of Frau Förster-Nietzsche's * Life of

* F. Nietzsche's only sister, Elisabeth, married a staunch adherent of the master's, Dr Bernhard Förster, whom she accompanied in 1886 to Nueva Germania, a little colony which her husband had founded in Paraguay according to the suggestions made by Richard Wagner in his "Religion and Art" and its appendices. Dr Förster died in 1889, and his widow

her brother (pubd. 1895) we were taken no farther than the young man's meeting with Wagner at the house of the master's sister, Frau Brockhaus (Leipzig, November 8, 1868), and his appointment to a professorship at the University of Basle. In the second volume, published this year, Frau Förster gives us a full and most interesting account of the beginning, course and termination of this friendship between her brother and a man just five months older than their father († 1849); the story is told without any animus against Richard Wagner, and with such a naïve candour of detail, that even the master himself would probably have been able to throw no further light upon the causes of this great sorrow that befell him, the secession of so beloved a friend and erewhile stout a champion as F. Nietzsche.

When Nietzsche took up his residence at Basle in April, 1869, he was no more than 24½ years old, and his appointment to a professorship at so youthful an age is sufficient evidence of his precocious talent. On the other hand, he was at the very time in life when romantic attachments are most often formed, attachments none too frequently of an enduring character. Before he had been five weeks at Basle an irresistible attraction drew him to seek out Wagner in his sanctuary at Tribschen, near Lucerne—a journey of about three hours. He paid his call, and was rewarded by an invitation to spend Whit-monday there. This is how he records the impression, in a letter to his friend Erwin Rohde: "Wagner is all that we had hoped of him; a great and lavish mind, an energetic character, and an entrancingly amiable man." Other visits quickly followed the first, and at the end of August young Nietzsche writes to another friend, Freiherr von Gersdorff: "I have found a man who, as no other, reveals to me the likeness of what Schopenhauer calls 'the genius.' This is no other than Richard Wagner, about whom you must believe no judgment that appears in the press, the writings of musical pedants, and so forth. *No one* knows him, or can judge him, for all the world stands on another fundament and is not native to his atmosphere. In him there reigns so unconditional an ideality, so deep and touching a humanity, so sublime an earnestness of life, that near him I feel myself in neighbourhood

returned to Germany soon afterwards, to tend her brother in his mental illness, and to superintend the publication of his works,—in both of which devoted tasks she is still engaged.—W. A. E.

of the divine." And a week or so later, to Erwin Rohde: "I have my Italy, like you; only that I cannot fly there oftener than on the Saturday to Sunday. Its name is Tribschen, which already is quite a home to me. Latterly I have been there four times over, and hardly a week elapses without a letter taking the self-same route. What I learn, see, hear and understand there, is indescribable. Schopenhauer and Goethe, Æschylus and Pindar, are still alive, believe me." Again, in March 1870, to Gersdorff: "The incredible earnestness and German profundity in Wagner's world- and art-philosophy. . . . How glad I am that you are busy reading *Oper und Drama*. . . . When you come and see me, we must go to Tribschen. It is an infinite enrichment of one's life, to meet such a genius at close quarters. For me, everything that is best and loveliest is knit with the names of Schopenhauer and Wagner."

And so it went on, until Wagner finally left Tribschen for Bayreuth in April 1872. Meanwhile Nietzsche had written his *Geburt der Tragödie* (pubd. January 1872). To anyone reading that work without further information—as we all had to read it until the recent publication of Nietzsche's preliminary sketches—it would seem that he was a thick-and-thin believer in Wagner's musico-dramatic principles; take pages 148-50 of that work, for instance, where he deals with the third act of *Tristan und Isolde*. But in these preliminary sketches, of 1870-71, we find expressions so extraordinarily at variance with the master's scheme as the following: "Wagner bears the same relation to Grand Opera as Schiller to French Tragedy. The fundamental error remains, though within it everything is filled with German ideal radicalism. . . . Wagner is unconsciously striving for an art-form in which the root-evil of Opera is [i.e. shall be] overcome: namely the *very grandest symphony*, whose principal instruments sing a song that can be rendered to the senses (*versinnlicht*) by an action. . . . I believe we must do away with the *singer* altogether. For the dramatic singer is a chimera. Or we must place him in the orchestra. But no longer must he interfere with the music, simply work as *chorus*, i.e. as human voice in combination with the orchestra. The restitution of the *Chorus*: beside it the pictorial world, the *Mimus*. The ancients have the right relation: only through an excessive preponderance of the Apollinic principle did their Tragedy go to ground: we must return to the pre-Æschylic stage" (Nietzsche's *Schriften*, Vol. IX. pages 151, 152 and 156). The editor of these Sketches presumes that the author suppressed those passages, and many like them, "out of consideration for Richard Wagner." As that would involve a great insincerity in Nietzsche's publication of his opinion that Wagner's art was "the re-awaking of the Dionysic spirit and the re-birth of Tragedy" (*Geb. d. Trag.*, p. 142), and as, despite some amateur attempts, the author was not a productive musician, a dramatist, or in fact a creative artist at all, we may be allowed to place Nietzsche in the humbler position of having been convinced by Wagner that his half-fledged views were false.

However, those views return with double force in January 1874, when we find Nietzsche expressing himself in certain unpublished "Thoughts about Wagner" as follows: "Wagner assembles every *effective* element, in an age that needs very coarse and potent stimuli because of its own density. The magnificent, intoxicating, bewildering, the grandiose, the terrible, strepitous, ugly, convulsive, neurotic,—each finds its place. Enormous dimensions, stupendous means. . . . The intoxicating, sensuous, ecstatic, the sudden, the emotional at any cost—terrible tendences! . . . There is something comic in it: Wagner cannot persuade the Germans to take the theatre seriously. They remain cold and easy-going — he waxes hot, as if the Germans' welfare hung upon it. . . . These vague impulses without an object, this ecstasy, this despair, this tone of suffering and desire, this accent of love and fervour. Seldom a blither sunray, but much witchcraft of lighting. . . . A total contradiction: a quite specific expression of [the musician's] feeling as music, quite definite—and beside it the drama, a parallel expression of quite definite feelings, of the dramatis personæ, by word and motion. How can these ever combine? . . . Excesses of the most reprehensible kind in Tristan, for instance the outbursts at the end of the second act. Immoderation in the cudgelling scene of the Meistersinger. . . . Wagner's *adherents*? Singers, who became interesting as dramatic figures [etc. etc.]—Littérateurs with all sorts of hazy longings for reform" (Vol. X., 398, 400, 403, 405, 409, 412).

Now, one would scarcely have expected that at the very time when Nietzsche was jotting down these thoughts a new edition of the "Birth of Tragedy" was being prepared for the press (printed in Feb. '74), and that he altered nothing in its eulogy of Wagner though he made several minor alterations in respect of style etc., — among other things, replacing Isolde's dying words, as sung, by their very slightly different version in the *Ges. Schr.* One's doubts of Nietzsche's sincerity are beginning to increase.

But what had taken place in the relations of the two men between April 1872 and January 1874? Frau Förster tells us. Her brother goes to Bayreuth for the laying of the foundation-stone, and finds himself in the seventh heaven, the circle of friends then being "small and homogeneous." He offers to give up his professorship and become a wandering lecturer to the various local Wagner-vereins on the master's art and theories; Wagner will not permit him to sacrifice his career in such a way, and very wisely induces him to abandon the plan. Upon one or two minor occasions Nietzsche breaks a spear for his "friend and leader"; but, the magnetic current once broken, Nietzsche begins to be mistrustful: for all the master's affectionate letters to him, he weighs their words to see if they come up to the former standard of warmth. A meeting at Strassburg in the autumn of 1872 puts everything on the old footing for a while; but the younger man cannot arrange to spend Christmas at Bayreuth: Wagner seems to be vexed, and Nietzsche imagines himself suspected of cooling down. At Easter 1873, however, Nietzsche accepts an invitation, goes to Bayreuth, and is delighted. In October of that year he attends the Patronat meeting and submits a draft-circular; the meeting rejects it, much to Wagner's own disgust. Prospects are looking black at Bayreuth, and Nietzsche returns to Basle much depressed, despairing of the festival ever coming off.—It must be remembered that his health had been undermined when doing ambulance work for a few weeks in the Franco-German war, and ever since that time he had been a victim to periodic attacks of optic neuralgia, violent headaches and severe dyspepsia. Wagner, who himself suffered at times in a somewhat similar way, calls him a "hypochondriac" in one of his letters. Perhaps, then, we may ascribe those written "thoughts" of 1874 to what is known in the vernacular as "a fit of the blues"; if that were the case, they should have been destroyed on the first return of brighter mental weather—but?

In Feb. 1874 Nietzsche is overflowing with joy at the news that

King Ludwig has guaranteed 100,000 thalers for the completion and equipment of the Festspielhaus. In June he receives an invitation to visit Wagner in his newly-entered home; busy writing his "Schopenhauer," he postpones the visit until August. And now occurs a remarkable episode, which throws a flood of light on the mood in which Nietzsche had taken to regard his intimacy with Wagner: I will relate it in Frau Förster's words, presupposing that my readers are already acquainted with the master's dislike of Brahms' music, and reminding them that Nietzsche, a man of barely thirty, was the *guest* of a famous artist past his sixtieth year. Frau Förster writes (*Das Leben F. N.'s*, Vol. II. p. 180): "My brother and I had heard the 'Triumphlied' of Brahms in the Basle cathedral. It was a splendid performance, and pleased Fritz very much. When he went to Bayreuth in August he took the pianoforte-arrangement with him, apparently in the naïve belief that Wagner would like it. I say, 'apparently,' for upon later reflection it has occurred to me that this red-bound 'Triumphlied' was meant as a sort of goad, and therefore Wagner's prodigious wrath seems to have not been altogether groundless. So I will leave the continuation of the tale to Wagner, who had an exquisite fashion of satirising himself: 'Your brother set this red book on the piano; whenever I went into the drawing-room the red thing stared me in the face—it exasperated me, as a red rag to a bull. Perhaps I guessed that Nietzsche wanted it to say to me: See here, another man who can turn out something good,—and one evening I broke out, with a vengeance!' Wagner had a hearty laugh at the recollection. 'What did my brother say?'—I asked in alarm. 'Nothing at all,' answered Wagner, 'he simply blushed, and looked at me in astonishment and modest dignity. I would give a hundred-thousand marks to have such splendid manners as this Nietzsche, always distinguished, always well-bred; it's an immense advantage in the world.' That story of Wagner's came back to my mind at this moment [Spring 1875]. 'Fritz,' I said, 'why didn't you tell me that tale about Brahms' Triumphlied? Wagner related the whole thing to me himself!' Fritz looked straight before him, and held his tongue; at last he said, beneath his breath: 'Lisbeth, then Wagner was not great.'"

I may leave this story to expound itself, for the present. It is notable, however, that Nietzsche had come to be rather a wet blanket, somewhat too "superior" in fact: in the troublous times of 1873 he found that "Wagner's greatness of soul was shewn the plainest in hours of seriousness and sorrow," but "the merry, joking Wagner was not quite to his taste," and Wagner noticed it, as Frau Förster tells us (p. 216 *ibidem*): "Wagner once said to me, 'Your brother is often quite tiresome in his gentle superiority, especially as he cannot conceal his thoughts from one; sometimes he is positively ashamed of my jests—and I can't help pushing them all the farther.'"—O that Nietzsche, also, could have stood on his head on the sofa! It *ought* not to have horrified his disciples.

But whatever change may have been coming over Nietzsche's feelings with regard to Wagner, the master's love remained undiminished. Countless were the invitations to visit Wahnfried again; not one of them was accepted. Even from the grand rehearsals of the *Ring des Nibelungen* in the summer of 1875 Nietzsche stayed away, though many of his friends were trooping there. It is true that he was very unwell all that summer, but his sister tells us (p. 236) "that, as Wagner very correctly perceived, he made use of every pretext to delay, or entirely obviate, a meeting." Meanwhile his "Richard Wagner at Bayreuth" was under way. From the preliminary draft—though very much more favourable to Wagner's art than had been those Thoughts of Jan. 1874—I may quote the following: "In the last few years I have two or three times felt within myself the ridiculous doubt, whether Wagner really has a musical gift at all" (X. p. 418). As to the work itself, I have already shewn, in my last preface, how it was begun in Feb. 1875, laid down in May, resumed in Sept. and set aside in Oct. of that year, and how, at the last moment, its last three chapters were added to it in two days of June 1876. Never was such a panegyric addressed to a living artist, never such an excess of hyperbole. From among the more sober passages I instance the following: "It seems that not only a new art, but Art itself has been discovered. . . . In the Ring des Nibelungen I find the most ethical music that I know. . . . As philosopher, he not only has passed through the fire of various philosophic systems without fear, but also through the steam of science and of pedantry, and kept faith with his higher self. . . . Between Kant and the Eleates, between Schopenhauer and Empedocles, between Æschylus and Richard Wagner there are such affinities that one can almost feel the relativity of all ideas of time. . . . Wagner has an *astringent* force: in that he belongs to the really great powers of culture. . . . Does it not almost seem an act of magic, that brings us such an apparition in the present day? Must not those who here are privileged to help, to look, be even transformed and renewed themselves, and henceforth carry this transformation and renewal into other walks of life? . . . The absolutely free artist, who can no else than think in all the arts at once, the reconciler and mediator between seemingly-sundered spheres, the restorer of unity and totality in the artistic faculty *etc. etc.* . . . It is more than a figure of speech, to say that he has surprised Nature with his gaze, that he has seen her naked. . . . And so at last we have the advent of the greatest magician and benefactor among mortals, the dithyrambic dramatist" (Vol. I. pp, 500, 505, 514, 515, 516, 519, 540, 544, 545).

This "Richard Wagner in Bayreuth" appeared in the first ten days of July. Nietzsche followed it to Bayreuth, with the intention of staying for all the final rehearsals and performances; at the end of the rehearsals he rushes away, and allows his sister to arrive ungreeted in the rooms whence he had fled. The reason for his sudden departure he himself tells us in an unpublished sketch, dating from the year 1878 (XI. 126): "My fault was in coming to Bayreuth with an ideal: I had to experience the bitterest undeception," and in a similar note of 1880 or 1881 (p. 400 *ibid.*): "When I lauded Schopenhauer as my educator, I had forgotten that not one of his dogmas had resisted my misgivings for a long time previously; but it troubled me little how often I had underlined his sentences with 'imperfectly proven,' or 'undemonstrable,' or 'over-stated,' for I was thankful for the potent impression which Schopenhauer himself [in his writings] had made on me for a whole decad, far and away above the things [he said], and even against them. When, later on, I paid my tribute to Richard Wagner on a festal occasion, I again had forgotten that all his music had shrunk into a few hundred bars, for me, from here and there"; against which passage we may set another from this selfsame period: "Music as a continuous accompaniment is distracting under any circumstances, and the best music too often a weariness" (*ibidem*, p. 350).

Nietzsche returned to Bayreuth for some of the *Ring* performances, however, and must have made himself rather a nuisance. His sister informs us that "he had not the smallest occasion to feel offended. Wagner in fact displayed the utmost eagerness to honour and distinguish him in every respect; but Fritz withdrew from these marks of esteem, wherever he could; this loud and noisy praise of Wagner's was repugnant to him." Not unnaturally, as will be gathered from the following little anecdote: "It was a visible torture to him, when admirers wished to talk with him about his 'Richard Wagner in Bayreuth.' A lady of keen discernment asked me, 'Why is your brother so unwilling to hear us speak about his latest work?' When I repeated the question to him, he cried: 'Oh, if people would only leave the old tale alone!' 'But,' I said in amazement, 'it appeared exactly five weeks since.' 'Five years, it seems to me,' said Fritz." Frau Förster also quotes a long passage from an article by the well-known author E. Schuré, in the *Revue des Deux Mondes* of August 1895, premising that "Mons. Schuré was an excellent observer, but his conclusions are quite false." This passage tells us how Schuré met Nietzsche at Bayreuth, and gives a description of his manner and appearance, from which I will select a sentence or two: "Rien de plus trompeur que le calme apparent de son expression. L'œil fixe trahissait le travail douloureux de la pensée. C'était à la fois l'œil d'un observateur aigu et d'un visionnaire fanatique. Ce double caractère lui donnait quelque chose d'inquiet et d'inquiétant, d'autant plus qu'il semblait toujours rivé sur un point unique. Dans les moments d'effusion, ce regard s'humectait d'une douceur de rêve, mais bientôt il redevenait hostile. . . . Devant les prodiges d'art qu'il [Wagner] accomplissait chaque jour sous nos yeux, nous avions tous, non pas, Dieu merci! les sentiments, mais quelque chose des étonnements de Mime en face de Siegfried qui reforge l'épée brisée de son père après l'avoir réduite en limaille et fondu au creuset. L'orgueil de Nietzsche souffrait-il de cette infériorité? Sa sensibilité suraiguë se blessa-t-elle de certaines rudesses familières du maître? . . . Dans sa première intimité avec Wagner, Nietzsche s'était placé avec son maître sur un pied d'égalité. Il lui avait dédié son premier livre comme 'à son sublime lutteur d'avant-garde.' Il se figurait peut-être la réforme de l'Allemagne comme une école de philosophie, d'esthétique et de morale dont Schopenhauer serait l'ancêtre vénéré, Wagner l'artiste et le metteur en œuvre, mais dont lui, Nietzsche, serait le prophète et suprême législateur." Space forbids my making a longer extract from the verdict of this intensely acute observer, who had been the first to give Nietzsche's "Birth of Tragedy" a notoriety beyond the narrow circle of his friends; but that verdict is corroborated by the following aphorism from the second part of *Menschliches*: "*Unfaithfulness, as condition of mastership.*—It is no use: every master has only one pupil—and that one becomes untrue to him,—for he, too, is meant for mastership" (III. aph. 357).

And strikingly is Mons. Schuré's estimate confirmed by another anecdote of Frau Förster's. We all know that the festival of 1876 was in many ways a disappointment to the Bayreuth master, for the reasons stated in his "Retrospect" (p. 95 *infra*); but the wildest imagination could scarcely have conceived so droll a scene as this: "I remember our going to Wahnfried one morning, and finding the master just ready for a walk in the garden. I forget precisely what Wagner said, but suddenly my brother's eyes lit up—with an expression of the alertest expectation he hung upon the master's mouth—did he believe that Wagner was about to say: 'Oh friend, the whole festival is a sheer farce, it is nothing like we both had longed and dreamt of; my music, too, should have been quite different; I will return to simpleness and melody'? Did my brother yield to the false hope that Wagner would tell him something of the sort? However like it the beginning of his speech may have sounded, the continuation shewed at once the error. The happy light in my brother's eyes died out. No! Wagner was no longer young enough, to be able to take sides against himself." This is no mere fancy of Frau Förster's, for we find her brother writing to himself in 1878: "I will wait till Wagner acknowledges a work that is written *against* him." So that if Nietzsche really was a genius, among other of the symptoms one may fitly claim for him a want of modesty.

And what do his editors and biographer call that high-flown "Richard Wagner in Bayreuth"? A "farewell letter," if you please. One seems to have fallen plump into the land of topsy-turvydom; but in the autumn of 1886 Nietzsche himself remarks: "My pæan to Richard Wagner, for the occasion of his Bayreuth victory of 1876—Bayreuth represents the greatest victory ever won by artist,—a work that bears the strongest *look* of 'actuality,' was secretly a homage and an act of gratitude for a piece of my own past, for the fairest and alike the most perilous calm in my voyage—and practically a severance, a bidding of farewell" (III. 4), and in the autumn of 1888: "all the psychologically important passages are about myself alone,—without scruple one might place my name, or the word 'Zarathustra,' wherever the text gives the word Wagner. The whole picture of the *dithyrambic* artist is the picture of the *pre-existing* poet of the Zarathustra, drawn with abysmal depth and without touching the Wagnerian reality for one moment. Wagner himself had an idea of it; he did not recognise himself in the essay." These words may sound premonitory of that total eclipse which came over Nietzsche's reason a few months later; yet they are nothing but an echo of what he told his sister about his Schopenhauer-essay in 1875 (see *Das Leben F. N.'s*, II. 168).

Can anyone wonder, then, that Wagner long had felt uneasy as to the staunchness of his friend? Take this private confession of Nietzsche's own, written in the summer of 1878: "I have not the talent of being faithful, and, what is worse, not even the vanity to appear so" (XI. p. 131).

After Bayreuth the two met once again, for the last time. Nietzsche had obtained a year's leave of absence, on the score of ill health, and spent the first few months at Sorrento together with a proved old friend of Wagner's. There the master saw him several times; but the younger man had already commenced to write his "Menschliches," the work that was destined, almost intentionally, to part them for ever. I have given several extracts from this work in footnotes to the text of the present volume, as it is here that the profound antagonism of the two men's natures first comes to light: Wagner the creative artist who dies of a seizure of the heart, Nietzsche the reflective critic who a few years later passes to a living death through a malady of the brain. In this weird book the author begins his attack on everything that men had hitherto held holy; pity, love, friendship, genius, morality in its wider sense, religion in its every form,—all are made the targets of his scorn. It must have come as a thunder-clap to Richard Wagner. However strange he may have thought the behaviour of his friend for some time past, there had been nothing to prepare him for such a sudden transformation.

Originally the book was meant to be anonymous; but the publisher—curiously enough, the printer of the Bayreuther Blätter—objected to the loss of advertisement involved in such a course, and Nietzsche consented to his name appearing on the title-page. As his sister tells us, this necessitated the altering of several aphorisms, originally too personal, and the substitution of the term "the artist" for the name of Wagner wherever that name had formerly stood. In a letter written to Freiherr von Seydlitz in June 1878, just after the publication of *Menschliches*, Nietzsche remarks: "If Wagner knew everything that I have on my heart *against* his art and aims, he would consider me one of his bitterest foes—which I certainly am not." This did not prevent him from sending two copies of the book to Wahnfried with a sportive dedication in doggerel verse. Ten years later he tells us that he received at the same time a copy of the *Parsifal* textbook, sent by Wagner, with an inscription: "Hearty greetings and good wishes to his dear friend Friedrich Nietzsche, Richard Wagner, Oberkirchenrath" (the last word, "Upper-Church-Counsellor," is one of the master's playful sallies, for he never had anything to do with the Church). Nietzsche's memory must have played him false, however, when he talks of the "two books having crossed," for *Parsifal* was issued in December 1877, and it is improbable in the highest degree that Wagner should have delayed till the following May before transmitting a copy to an intimate friend with whom he had no cause for quarrel that he knew of; moreover Nietzsche unconsciously gives us the correct date of his receipt of *Parsifal*, when he says: "Did it not sound like the crossing of daggers? At anyrate we both felt it so: for both kept silence.—About this time appeared the first 'Bayreuther Blätter': I understood *for what* it was high time.—Incredible! Wagner had become pious." The first *Bayreuther Blätter* appeared in January 1878; Nietzsche's book not until May. So that Wagner's silence is easily explained: if his younger friend could not even acknowledge the receipt of his last great drama, and merely replied by sending him a book in utter opposition to every view they previously appeared to hold in common, and further could accompany it with jesting verses, the insult could only be met with what the young man's sister describes as "icy silence." By a singular breach of etiquette Frau Förster has revealed to us what was thought of *Menschliches* at Wahnfried,—

had it helped her case, she might have been pardoned in consideration of her deep and self-sacrificing affection for her brother; but the letter which she received some ten months later from Frau Wagner, in answer to her own epistolary attempt to patch up matters, simply shews in what a dignified manner the whole affair was treated by the master and his wife: not a word of personal offence is contained in this reply, but the deepest pity for the young man's not having had sufficient strength to withhold such evidence of his illness. One tiny passage I feel bound to quote: "I have read very little of this book, as that little told me that your brother would one day thank me for not having made a more thorough acquaintance with it. The author of 'Schopenhauer as Educator' scoffs at Christianity! And that in the tone which everyone adopts! But let us say no more about it: the author of this work I do not know, but your brother, who has given us such glorious things, I know and love; and that thought lives in me." Nor is it out of place to mention that in January 1880 Nietzsche writes to the friend with whom he had stayed at Sorrento in 1876-77, "I think of Wagner with lasting gratitude, for to him I owe one of the strongest stimuli to mental independence. Frau Wagner is the most sympathetic lady I have met in life.—But for all correspondence, and above all a renewal of friendship, I am quite powerless. It is too late." Strange, that Nietzsche still should feel himself the aggrieved party, when he had already written his second volume of *Menschliches*, containing far more unmistakable attacks on Wagner. But the "double nature" to which one of his editors alludes with approbation—a second case of Mr Hyde and Dr Jekyll—appears to make him constantly oblivious of the side of his personality opposed to that on which he happens to be standing at any given moment. And thus we find him saying at a later period (? 1888) that he wrote the conclusion of the first part of his Zarathustra "at the sacred hour when Richard Wagner died in Venice."

How did the master reply to *Menschliches, Allzumenschliches*? A reference to the accompanying index will place the reader in possession of all the more important hints, and he will find that only in one solitary instance is there anything beyond a combating of the tenets themselves; in that exception the author is indicated in a manner sufficiently plain to Nietzsche and his more immediate friends. The passage occurs on pages 73 to 74 of the present volume; to any outsider it must have seemed impersonal enough, in all conscience, for it distinctly assails a growing tendence of the day, and Nietzsche was by no means so celebrated at the time that the average man of education could have put his finger on the page and named him as the party meant. That the passage was inspired by Richard Wagner's glance at *Menschliches*, of course is not to be denied, especially as it contains the expression "all things human and inhuman" (a sufficiently discreet allusion to the title of the work), and as Nietzsche calls his first aphorism, "Chemistry of ideas and feelings." The attack upon "Philologists," however, had been commenced by Wagner six years earlier, in Nietzsche's favour; what the latter author did not like, was the turning of the tables upon himself and his limping materialism. His sister tells us that those pages "very much altered the tone in which her brother thought of Wagner," and that he was particularly annoyed at being accused of "spinning in a constant whirl, now flying from accepted views, then flying back in some confusion." But in July 1887 he himself confirms the master's telling criticism: "In *Menschliches* I first brought those hypotheses to light of day, clumsily, as I should be the last to conceal from myself, still un-free, still without a language of my own for these things of my own, and with many a relapse and vacillation" (VII. 291). Could Wagner's judgment be more fully endorsed? The only wonder is, that the master should have expressed himself with such great restraint and moderation, after so severe a blow as this open recusance of his most promising disciple.

And almost yearly throughout the remainder of his life was he met by a fresh stab, dealt either overtly or from under cover by the man to whom he had shewn such fatherly kindness, the man who, in those happy days at Tribschen, had twenty-three times been his guest. One can only hope that he read but few of these bitter phrases; at all events the allusions to Nietzsche become rarer and more distant, till in 1882 we have no more. Had Wagner lived but five or six years longer, it is even possible that his assailant's foulest thrust, the "Case of Wagner," might never have been delivered; not that any rapprochement was to be anticipated, but even in the self-centred heart of Nietzsche a chord of admiration would surely have been struck by the dignity of Wagner's silence.

As it is, a few months after the publication of that vile lampoon, we find him saying: "Here, where I am speaking of the recreations of my life, I lack the word to express my gratitude for that which formed my deepest and my heartiest solace. This, beyond all doubt, was the intimate communion with *Richard Wagner*. I would give little for the rest of my human relations; at no price would I cut out of my life the days of Tribschen, days of trust, of cheerfulness, of sublime inspirations,—of *deep* moments. I know not what others have gone through with Wagner: *our* heaven was never traversed by a cloud" (Life, II. 27).

Again I have been betrayed into an inordinately long discussion of the Wagner-Nietzsche question, far longer than I had intended. But the more one goes into this matter, the more is one convinced that Nietzsche was the only opponent within measurable distance of the master. To those who have merely read that hysterical "Case of Wagner" this will naturally appear a ridiculous assertion; to those who have not read beyond his *Menschliches* it will seem exaggerated: but, take the mass of Nietzsche's writings, and you cannot deny in him the makings of a genius. What value will be set on his work in future days, it is difficult to estimate, for even his editors regard it as alternately a "torso" and a "beginning." Those eight stout volumes published during his normal state of health, and those four volumes of practically "posthumous" sketches (with one or two more to follow?) might some day have been reduced to a coherent system, had his reason not finally broken down for good. But, as the works now stand, they are so bewildering in their almost utter chaos, their stringing-together of jewels and glass beads, without so much as an index to guide one, that one is obliged to largely qualify that "genius." I have given some instances of the author's so-called "double nature," and these supply such evidence of mental, if not moral instability, that I can only call his intermittent gift "a genius in shatters." Though I cannot pretend to have read *all* his works as yet, I have closely studied a very large section of them, and dipped into the remainder. From the year 1878 onwards, they may be summed up in almost the last words he ever wrote: "There is no soul" (VIII. 187).

Before closing this long-winded preface, I still have a few words to say about Richard Wagner's own ideals. *They* may be summed up thus: "There is a soul in all that lives." None but the most superficial critic could have written as follows: "Richard Wagner, apparently the most complete of victors, fell suddenly,* helpless and broken, before the Christian cross" (Nietzsche, Vol. III. Preface, written Sep. 1886). In no single respect is this statement true, except in that "Siegreichste" — "the most victorious." Even if it is permissible to connect the characters and subjects of an artist's artwork directly with his life and tenets, it can never be too strongly emphasised that the artwork necessarily deals with symbols, though it can never be a symbol in itself. In each of Richard Wagner's dramas, after *Rienzi*, the subject is taken from the legends of his people; in each he pierces through to the ideal behind the story's outward form, and all are thus at once dissimilar and akin. *Parsifal* is no exception to the rule, saving that it more closely knits the bonds of art and religion. The characters in *Parsifal*, and the scene in which they move, are ideal through and through: it is not the life of earth, nor can it ever have been meant to typify a possible life on earth, under present conditions. The root idea of the drama is "*Mitleid*"—compassion; "*Keuschheit*," chastity, is only incidental to the story, since a hero with such a mission as that of Parsifal could no more turn aside to paths of sensual pleasure than could a soldier in the sublime self-offering of battle. Charity, not chastity, is the keynote of this wondrous mystery-play; and those who find in it a purely monkish motive, may be asked how Amfortas came to be the *son* of good King Titurel.

* It should be stated that Friedrich Nietzsche descended from a long line of clerics—of almost purely Polish blood—and, though left fatherless at the age of barely five, his youth was marked by the profoundest piety; in fact, he was originally desirous of entering the Church himself. With his extraordinarily capricious memory, he here seems to have forgotten that in 1869 he wrote to a friend as follows: "Wagner has recently given me a manuscript 'On State and Religion,' written as a memorandum to the young King of Bavaria, of such a height and transcendentalism, of such nobility of thought and Schopenhauerian earnestness, that I only wish I were a king, to receive such admonitions."—W. A. E.

Is not Kundry herself admitted to the temple of the Grail at last, and that by Parsifal? And if she dies before the altar, is it not her only possible release, the wiping out of centuries of carking memory? Who would not feel that the introduction of a love-element into such a story would have been its vulgarising at once? Yet Gurnemanz sufficiently indicates, with one little touch, that the natural force of sex is not decried as sinful in itself, when he asks the youth: "How harmed he thee, the faithful swan? To seek his mate he flew aloft, with her to circle o'er the lake and hallow its waters to healing." No: the type of mind that can see in Parsifal an emasculated decadent, is twin to that which finds in *Tristan und Isolde* nothing but a low debauch. The master's latest treatment of the marriage question, in that Fragment he left unfinished at his death, is so entirely in accord with his views expressed in 1848 that no candid critic could possibly have found a "morbid asceticism" in his last ideal.

Again, is it true that Wagner in his latest years "fell helpless before the Christian cross?" If a religious drama was to be presented to any European nation, except the Turks, where else could the poet go for his religious symbols, but to the Christian gospels? How little of suddenness was displayed in this course, may be proved in a very few words. Turn back to Vol. IV. of the present series and on page 137 you will find Richard Wagner addressing a public meeting in 1848 as follows: "That will be the *fulfilment of Christ's pure teaching*, which enviously they hide from us behind parading dogmas." Go on to 1849, the period when Wagner was the nearest to Positivism: "The son of the Galilean carpenter, who preached the reign of universal human love—a love he could never have enjoined on men whose duty it should be to despise their fellows and themselves. . . . Thus would *Jesus* have shewn us that we all alike are men and brothers; while *Apollo* would have stamped this mighty bond of brotherhood with the seal of strength and beauty, and led mankind from doubt of its own worth to consciousness of its highest godlike might. Let us therefore erect the altar of the future, in Life as in the living Art, to the two sublimest teachers of mankind:—*Jesus, who suffered for all men; and Apollo, who raised them to their joyous dignity!*" (I. 38 and 65). Pass to 1850: "The enthralling power of the Christian myth consists in its portrayal of a *transfiguration through Death*" (II. 159). Then take this passage from a letter to August Roeckel, written in 1855: "How divine is the open confession of the nullity of this world, in the original idea of Christianity; and how superb are Buddha's teachings, which through our fellow-suffering make us one with all things living." In 1865 he extols the "time when the Spanish *auto* brought the sublimest mysteries of Christian Dogma upon the stage, and set them in dramatic parables before the Folk," and eulogises Goethe's model of religious instruction in the third part of *Wilhelm Meister* (IV. 112). In 1870 he writes: "'To-day shalt thou be with me in Paradise'—who has not heard these words of the Redeemer, when listening to the Pastoral Symphony?" (V. 92).

But beyond these earlier references to Jesus Christ himself, we have many, many a page upholding the true religion of Christianity. Omitting dates, I will merely quote a few of these passages in their chronologic order: "The *garb* of Religion is, so to speak, the *costume* of the Race by which it mutually recognises itself, and that at the first glance. . . . So long shall we have states and religions, till we have but *one* Religion and no longer any State. . . . Not through its practical importance for the State, i.e. its moral law, is Religion of such weight; for the root principles of all morality are to be found in every, even in the most imperfect, religion: but through its measureless value to the Individual, does the Christian religion prove its lofty mission, and that through its Dogma. . . . In this sacred allegory an attempt is made to transmit to worldly minds the mystery of the divine revelation . . . that sublime and strengthening solace which Religion alone can give. . . . It was the spirit of Christianity that rewoke to life the soul of Music. And Music lit the eye of the Italian painter, inspiring it to penetrate the veil of things and reach their soul, the Christian spirit, fast decaying in the Church. . . . The religion of the Holy Gospels, not consisting in the pomp and glamour of church-ceremonies, but in its serious promises of comfort to the human soul" (Vols. I. 65, II. 202, IV. 26, 27, 31, V. 121, 288).

It was natural that the Bayreuth master's occupation with his mystic drama should incline him to ponder the religious question even more absorbingly than at any previous epoch in his life. But I can see no alteration in his attitude toward the Christian religion itself. At no time had he rejected that religion, at no time did he give in his adhesion to any existing Church's interpretation thereof. Even in these latest essays, which have roused the odium atheologicum of bitter and coarsely aggressive materialists, there is only one expression (in "Hero-dom and Christendom," page 283) which at all approaches the lines of ecclesiastic dogma, and that is qualified by the cautionary note with which the paragraph begins. Mysticism, of a most profound nature, is certainly writ large over much of the matter in these articles; but the author repeatedly warns us against the attempt to take too literally any attempt to render into the language of our daily intercourse the things that lie beyond the world of Time and Space: only in the language of Tone can these deep mysteries be given an unambiguous tongue.

Should anyone ask me for my precise idea of the religious belief of Richard Wagner, I could only answer: "the same belief as that of every great creative mind." To such a genius the notion of a God who accepts the sacrifice of his own Son as an *expiation* for the sins of a guilty and backsliding world must needs be in itself repugnant. However much the unenlightened bigotry of their times may have made a Dante or a Milton frame their higher thoughts to fit into this system of a God of punishment and vengeance, in days when the advance of Bible-criticism has shaken the fabric of all established Churches to its very foundation the truthful spirit of earth's highest sons escapes from the cramping outward structure, to find the ideal Religion uprising from the Church's ruins. "Within the deepest, holiest inner chamber of man's heart" is its seat and temple, and there it lives a life inviolate, only to be divined from its high influence on man's actions. But when the genius comes to speak of it, what language shall he use? Shall he call it Music, or choose a name enhallowed by two thousand years of reverence? Though every fact in the canonic Gospels be proved a fancy gradually engrafted on the simple tale of the life of earth's divinest son, who called himself the Son of Man, that personality itself has come to represent the holiest instincts of men who feel that life is not a thing delimited by Force and Matter, who *know*—by organs of experience too delicate to cope as yet with such a clumsy battering-ram as Logic—that life is grander, broader, more ethereal, than this temporary segregation into warring units. And whatever form we may give to our individual belief, in a world where every fleeting joy is followed by returning horror—nay, scarce seems possible without an injury to others,—could there be a more inspiring thought than of that one Exemplar "beckoning to the highest pity, to imitation of this breaking of all self-seeking Will"?

WM. ASHTON ELLIS.

Christmas, 1897.

SPOHR'S "JESSONDA" AT LEIPZIG.

Über eine Opernaufführung in Leipzig.

This letter "On an operatic performance at Leipzig" appeared in the Musikalisches Wochenblatt, *January 1875, a musical weekly founded by E. W. Fritzsch, and of which he still is editor and publisher.*

TRANSLATOR'S NOTE.

Esteemed Herr Fritzsch!

FOR the opening of the new year of your "Musikalisches Wochenblatt" you desire a contribution from my pen? Please accept as such this letter, which really is merely meant to tell you that I have little or nothing more to say to readers of musical journals. You know my views upon the efficacy of this class of literature, and how little I find myself at home therewith. A publisher invited my co-operation for a musical paper started at the commencement of this dying year; declining, I openly declared to him those views, basing them, among other things, on the recent experiences my participation in your Wochenblatt had gained me: of that communication you obtained a fragmentary knowledge, which made you doubt the frankness of my interest in your paper. Your informant had omitted to tell you, of course, that I coupled that statement with a tribute to the energy and excellence of the intentions governing you in the conduct of your journal; by which I implied that nothing save the consciousness of such intentions could move me, under any circumstances, to take part in a musical paper. But there's the rub: once more I have convinced myself, at closest quarters, that such a journal can only keep afloat by taking count of the most conflicting interests; whereby the very best intentions of the publisher become so seriously crossed at last, that they can but almost seem discarded.

And then the question still remains: "who *reads* these musical papers? To *whom* is directed, and *who* is influenced by quite the best judgment delivered therein?" Suppose one says "the *musicians*," I fear, now that they all write for papers themselves, they also will imagine they know everything much better than the individual who to-day and here is passing sentence. I believe that every musician pooh-poohs a musical paper, when laid before him, unless it happens to be praising himself. Very well: it is the music-loving public, that studies such a paper? I rather think that's what is reckoned on; and it may be that here and there a good effect is wrought on this side. But certainly a public such as this will never read too thorough-going, let alone too philosophical a treatise, that drags its endless length through weekly number after number. Yet that is just what the unlucky publisher must have, if he means at once to fill his leading columns and maintain a serious, *i.e.* instructive tendence. You have seen that I could not prevail on myself to hand you over my longer essays for disarticulation in your journal. The "to be continued in our next" inevitably figures as a bird-scare to the reader who merely wants to peck, but has not strength to pluck the fruit. If one therefore must rule these more substantial essays out of place in such a weekly paper, the next question is: *whatever* can one find, to fix the reader's interest? Reviews, maybe, of newly-issued compositions? Except when it was very smartly written, I must confess that I myself have never yet been tempted to wade through a review of the kind: whether in jest or earnest, the writer knows his mind—for one must assume that he really has acquainted himself with the piece of music criticised; but what does the reader know about it all? And yet, so it seems, a musical paper must make a salient point of such reviews; reviews that (taken seriously) can interest no one but the composers of the new pieces themselves, for even their publishers look to nothing but the summing-up, if "good" or "bad." To the real public of music-lovers (if we are to accept that definition of the subscribers to a music-journal) such reading offers little prospect of enjoyment.

For my part I must admit that, even when glancing through the Wochenblatt you so kindly send me, I commonly have only breathed again at sight of a letter from your excellent contributor *W. Tappert* of Berlin. Then my heart cheers up. For there I find the only proper treatment for certain questions so highly symptomatic of our modern Culture, certain interests of our now so marvellously ramifying "musical" public. None of them should one in truth take seriously, even though the thought goes near at times to make one's heart break. Were I living, like Herr Tappert, in a great capital of "Germania," and had I his peculiar wit, it is conceivable that I too might oftener send a contribution to your Wochenblatt. From my little poked-away Bayreuth the thing is hard to compass. However, as I should like to give some substance to this letter, I will use the experiences of a recent one-day's trip to "Paris minor"—that Leipzig which already somewhat prides itself on stir and movement—for an attempt to recommend myself to your readers as reporter. Perhaps I may thus succeed in convincing them of the rightness of a feeling which has come over me, that I missed my true vocation when I took to opera-composing, and not to criticising. Especially for a theatrical reporter I had every qualification—many more, at least, than the best-known critics of our great political papers; above all, much practical experience of the matter, with the attendant capability of saying how one might do things better, when one had done them badly or incorrectly. And how swiftly might I thus have won an influence that nothing could impair! In Vienna, for instance, if I could not bear a certain composer I should have made the performance of his new opera a sheer impossibility, simply by setting everyone in dread of me, from the singers and conductors to the highest Intendance itself: * for, brave though our soldiers be upon the field of battle, at home all go in mortal terror of the "Press." To raise myself to such a lofty perch, alas! I have neglected: what boots it, if now I try to somewhat retrieve my missed vocation in a modest Musikalisches Wochenblatt? Eh! could I reach the "Neue

* Alluding to Hanslick's tactics on the occasion of the abortive rehearsals of *Tristan und Isolde*, 1862-63.—Tr.

freie Presse," or the "National-Zeitung," things soon would wear another look! So for to-day I will just content myself with a few remarks on the performance of Spohr's "*Jessonda*" which I heard the other day in Leipzig, without pretending to aught beyond.

Who attends a stage-performance, especially of an opera, so rarely as myself, is certain to be more or less overtaken by a feeling highly favourable to the occurrence. In particular the sound of the orchestra always exerts a truly magical effect on the man who has passed his time in such great retirement. This experience was mine at hearing the overture to "Jessonda." Not that everything here was as it should be: the passages for the wood-wind were taken a shade too tamely; on the other hand the horn's first solo was blown too loud, and with a perceptible taint of affectation—in which I recognised the failing common to all our cornists since the invention of the ventil-horn. But what could such slight demurs avail, against the puissance of the orchestral event that here enveloped me? That these demurs could only feebly raise their heads, to me was witness of the salience of the whole impression. This frame of mind resulted in an inclination toward unreserved indulgence, to let my happy mood be ruffled by no matter what. And in such good humour I could set down all the lapses of the further representation to the inevitable consequences of our having formed so singularly inchoate an art-genre as the German "Opera." He who has not arrived at a true estimate of this latter—despite his utmost warmth of veneration for our great masters of music—is in no position to rightly judge those consequences in the performance, and therefore approaches their criticism from a false stand-point. In the treatment of the so-called "numbers" of an opera with absolutely no regard to what is passing on the stage, a practice of Spohr as well as others, there is everything to make a regisseur indifferent in advance —to say nothing of the performer, particularly in his capacity of *singer*, who thus is kept in one perpetual fluster. So that I cannot altogether blame the regisseur who has to march a numerous chorus through the wings during an orchestral postlude of the most thoughtless brevity, prior to the first change of scene, for paying less and less attention to harmonising the 'stage-business' with the orchestra as his work proceeds.

And this may make him leave the Portuguese army for a longish while drawn up before the footlights, staring blankly at the audience with no mind for all the bustle of a camp, at the beginning of the second act; for he thinks that the composer's only care and object is to get his "chorus" well and soundly sung. Nor can one really say much against it, since the composer's flagrant disregard of the scenic action might easily have lured the regisseur to those absurd vagaries which frequently crop up at theatres where an ambitious stage-manager is trying to make his mark. And in fact this opera depends for all its strong effects on nothing but the composer's happy combinations: a proof whereof was given us by the grand choral scene in the third act, which took place within a covered temple instead of in an open court exposed to all the winds of heaven, and, variously bungled in the acting, was rescued only by the splendid singing of a powerful choir.

Thus our "Opera" would never really have left the Oratorio style, had we not made haste to stud it with pleasing or effective pieces for the principal persons in the drama. And if an opera is to succeed at all, these vocal pieces remain the chief consideration, especially in the performance. Where lyric dalliance comes so aptly as in certain moments of the second act, there the composer treads his happiest field; as in the charming flower-duet for the two women, and even the love-duet of the young Brahmin with his sweetheart—for albeit the latter shades toward affectation, the public always welcomes it with marked delight. But the fact of his feeling bound to end up every vocal number with a flash, a burst of lyric brilliance, often lowers him to positive ridicule. What once for all does not reside in the capacity, nay, in the very nature of the German, namely *élégance*, he thinks he cannot do without; and his having to make shift with a sort of Meissen-brewed champagne, if he means to keep true to his fatherland, must leave him tasteless in this singular attempt.

Thus the greatest failings of our German opera-composers appear to spring from one root-fault, the *want of self-reliance.* But whence have they ever had the chance of gaining such a confidence? From encouragement by our royal courts, perhaps—at which, whenever Art and Music form the topic, the first thought flies to foreigners, black-bearded for choice, and at any rate such as speak their German with a foreign accent? Or is it the attitude of our theatre-goers, that haply might inspire our masters with that self-reliance? Who ever could suppose it, after glancing at the operatic repertoires set year by year before a German audience? One might imagine the whole collection immediately dictated by our royal chancelleries.

One curse of every German, which even the noble Weber could not flee from, Spohr still less could escape; having as violin-virtuoso matured a pleasing genre in the "Polacca," together with a certain elegance of passage-writing, he hoped to turn them to good account in Opera too. As a fact, in "Jessonda" almost everyone sings "*à la Polacca*"; and though the High Priest of the Brahmins abstains, his pupil rushes to this world-redeeming motive at his first falling-away from the Indian belief—which strikes one as almost too familiar for the postlude to his aria at his spirited exit in the second act, especially when the young Brahmin disports, as at Leipzig, a blonde moustache and whiskers.—But just consider what is asked of our singers, with these runs and fioriture mostly taken from the close of arias in Spohr's book of studies for the violin. No Rubini, no Pasta or Catalani, could ever have been equal to singing these passages, though the departed Konzertmeister David might certainly have reeled them off as child's-play.

If the last-named eccentricity forms an insuperable obstacle to a sound style of vocalisation, the composer's want of self-reliance lays the singer still more perilous snares in the curious incorrectness of the declamation. Knowing the so-called higher genre of Opera only from works of the French or Italian Muse—to be candid, solely in translation—the German tone-poet takes the foreign incidence of accent, namely on the last syllable, for a musical law; and, with his rooted mistrust of himself, he treats his mother-tongue accordingly (should "Fatherland" occur, for instance). It may matter very little that the text is thus maltreated in the so-called melody of Aria—for example

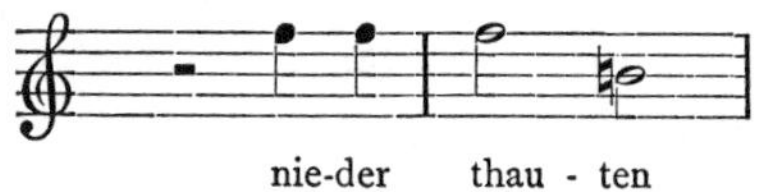

which at once is followed by a correct

for here one might say: "If only you'll sing prettily, and with a nice purely-musical accent, we'll pass over all the rest." But when it comes to "Recitative," for no other reason than the supposed dramatic hopelessness of the German language, one gets a sort of operatic dialect of an unintelligibleness often quite appalling. This slavery to an un-German accent, which brings such instances to light as

or

is the more regrettable with Spohr, particularly in his "Jessonda," as this very opera shews how earnestly he strove to shape the recitative of even "Opera" to bring out all the meaning of the German words—that "recitative," however, which is so utterly un-German that with us it will always remain an unmanageable outpost.

However, I merely meant this fugitive sketch of the faults in the German genre of Opera as premise to an encouraging conclusion as to the good qualities of our singers and musicians. Upon renewed acquaintance, I could not shut my eyes to the unusual difficulties with which our German operists have to contend; and it is most promising to find them able nevertheless to produce such fine effects as to make one forget all those drawbacks. A figure such as that of the Portuguese General, Tristan d'Acunha, though treated somewhat too tamely by the composer, can deeply interest us when represented by an artist of the talent of Herr Gura. This time there was no room for carping: the whole impersonation was pure and noble. The performer's first appearance exercised a charm: when, summoned by Nadori, he descends the hill to the women with the question, "Who is it, doomed to such a death?" to me he was an embodiment of tragic dignity and most touching simplicity. How difficult, nay, impossible it is, to replace the distinction of so virile an artistic temperament by even the most studied display of single personal advantages—such as an agreeable exterior, good lungs and throat, and so forth—one promptly discovers in the surroundings of one of these "hewn from the rock." Here everything strikes home, and even the most unsingable of Spohr's "violin-passages" no longer harms the rendering, for the singer chains us from beginning to end, and thus diverts our notice from the weak externals of his task. And here accordingly we see the influence of that rare event in Opera, a higher artistic propriety: his comrade stays sympathetically at his side when he recounts his griefs, whereas in a similar situation poor Jessonda finds herself abandoned by her confidante—to whom the tale is obviously a weariness—and the more eagerly must vent her heart-aches on the audience from the footlights, reminding us that we are at the "Opera" after all.

But let this side-glance be my last fault-finding. Enough

if one can testify that the excellent impressions of such an evening, as I lately passed in the Leipzig theatre, effaced the less propitious. For so good a result the *power of Music* must certainly be held chiefly responsible, even when one cannot deny that the dramatic interest—however much it is often clogged by the librettist's sugary "poetic diction" —has its own large share therein. But in this particular work of Spohr's, in which his whole onesidedness is almost raised to the rank of a natural law (at anyrate of *his* nature), the preponderant share must be adjudged to the music. Its execution was conducted by Kapellmeister Schmidt with marked intelligence and reverential love: merely his Tempo was spoilt here and there by a touch of timidity, to be explained, again, by that lack of self-confidence which is innate in all German musicians. None trusts himself to say straight out: "So is it." No: without the authority of a great example, and harassed by the bickerings of ignorant reporters, all sway uncertain to and fro. So, with that portion of self-confidence which I have made my own, I would advise the present Leipzig Kapellmeister to take in future all the tempi in 6/8 beat allotted to the Bayaderes, for instance, considerably faster than he dared to do (presumably because of the signature "Allegretto"); the Ballet-master might give a corresponding fire to the dances, steps and gestures of the Indian Hierodules: and we then should recognise these tiny choruses for Spohr's most truly masterly inspirations, even as dramatist.

But enough for to-day.—

With the best of greetings,

Yours sincerely

RICHARD WAGNER.

Bayreuth, 28 Dec. 1874.

Bayreuth.

Bayreuther Blätter.

*   *
*

Under this heading are assembled those publications of the master's that bear upon the plans connected with his settlement in Bayreuth, together with his shorter "Introductions" from the "Bayreuther Blätter." Then follow the larger essays of his latest years, which likewise appeared in the same journal with solitary exception of the letter from Venice dated December 1882.

(Note by Baron Hans von Wolzogen, editor of vol. x. of the *Gesammelte Schriften.*)

I.

HOUGH at the close of last year's performances of my Bühnenfestspiel at Bayreuth the satisfactory impression produced on the great majority of the audience afforded me the utmost encouragement to repeat and carry out the work begun, on the other hand it could not escape me that, to keep intact the original character of my undertaking, I virtually should have to start all over again.

After the later course of the performances had happily disproved the deterrent reports first circulated by a powerful section of the press, their outward success became so pronounced that a speculative entrepreneur could have drawn substantial profit from their frequent and immediate repetition. What hindered such a repetition was not only the impossibility of detaining the executant artists at Bayreuth any longer, but also my strenuous conviction that upon this road, of offering our labours to a merely paying public, we should completely abandon the tendence originally promised to my patrons.

It is this same consideration that makes me shrink today from publicly announcing a repetition of the festival for the present year and offering entrance-cards for sale, although my business friends are of opinion that, with the great reduction now possible in the price of seats, such tickets would easily and quickly be disposed of in the most distant quarters.

To explain this reluctance I have but to point to the words of my first "Appeal to the Friends of my art." After stating the character of my enterprise, for the means of attaining my goal I addressed myself to none but friends of my art and such as might feel glad to further the tendence of my undertaking. Now, though I really had the satisfaction of finding that it was solely such well-wishers who provided me with the means of taking my enterprise in hand and carrying it through its earlier stages, yet circumstances intervened that compelled me in the end to turn to the curiosity of the general public with an offer of tickets for sale. Thus both my work and the artists who devoted their powers to its execution, in the most unselfish spirit, were placed in a false position as injurious to the one as to the other. Hence arose the misapprehension, that I wanted to force my work and its style of performance down the throats of the regular opera-public; whereas my only aim, distinctly stated, had been to present the gift to none but willing helpers.

I therefore feel bound to strictly return to my original intention, as I could not possibly consent to leave the genuine furtherers of my undertaking in the most embarrassing position toward those whom nothing but the desire to harm my work and its influence has ranged beside them. Nor am I less bound to do this in the interest of my artists, whom I led to expect that not only their labours, but their whole relation to their public, would set them in a sphere of artistic intercourse above the abuses of our customary operatic performances. As yet we are only in the beginnings of a new style; on every hand we have defects to remedy, to plane down imperfections such as necessarily appear in so young and withal so uncommonly complex an enterprise. These exercises—full of import for German theatric art, as I hope—ought not to be pursued before those who watch them with a hostile non-intelligence; no, we must be assured that we are in the company of men who feel alike and wish to form by mutual interaction the only effectual *High-school of Dramatic-musical portrayal*; a school which many have attempted to found in different ways, but never with success.

My tendence in this regard was understood from the beginning by those who, in response to my first appeal, at once proceeded to form societies (*Vereine*) for its furtherance. Not including the richest section of the public in their membership, these Vereins were unable to push their material support of the enterprise to the length of attaining our final goal—little as that support was to be underrated in itself; yet by the plainly-uttered spirit of their union they supplied the moral basis of the whole undertaking. To these hitherto-active Vereins I therefore turn to-day, begging them to issue to more distant friends of my art the invitation to form a

Patronat=Verein

FOR THE SUPPORT AND MAINTENANCE OF THE STAGE-FESTIVALS AT BAYREUTH.

In the name I give to this Verein I denote the whole field desired for its activity. Unlike the earlier assistance of my patrons, it will no longer embrace the first foundations of the undertaking, the building of a Festspielhaus and providing it with scenic necessaries, but simply the yearly repetition, continuance and extension of performances, already detailed by me elsewhere. According to a plan to be decided later, for each of the three performances* in every year this Verein would take a thousand seats at a hundred marks [£5] apiece, and each such seat would be made over to none but a member duly enrolled in the Verein in compliance with its statutes. But, as it has always been my aim to allot a considerable number of free places to the needy, especially to young people eager to improve their minds, and on the other hand the choice of worthy candidates has always been attended with great difficulties, I should think we here might find a fit and proper point of union with the highest State-authorities themselves.

In my very earliest announcements I indicated the sympathy of the Imperial authorities as the reward I awaited and claimed to win when once I had succeeded in placing the special character of my artistic tendence, and

* Complete performances of the *Ring*, that is to say, each performance lasting four nights.—Tr.

of the undertaking thereon founded, in a clear light through the first performances of my work. Now if I dare hope that far-seeing men of the German nation will follow the lead of Frenchmen, English and Americans, who have already expressed in plain and definite terms their appreciation of the significance of my labours, I then indeed should sue for that reward, and accordingly would gladly commission the proposed Allgemeiner Patronat-Verein to ask the Reichstag for a substantial contribution to the yearly Bühnenfestspiels. To be of any service, this endowment would need to amount to a hundred thousand marks [£5,000], in return for which sum the Reich would receive a thousand seats for free distribution among those deemed worthy of such a distinction. Through this one measure, moreover, the idea of a nationalisation of the whole undertaking would be realised in the most expedient fashion, and to its great renown ; and thus for the first time would a theatric institute receive the stamp of national importance even in respect of its administration. For the highest State-authorities would hereby gain an interest in the maintenance of the original character—sufficiently defined by me—of this institution that so completely differs from all other standing theàtres, since it would be their earnest concern to see that its inner management was kept entirely free from speculation on monetary profit, and devoted solely to the culture of the prescribed artistic tendence.—

It would lead too far, to here advance proposals for this future administration; nor is it necessary, as everything relating thereto will easily and quickly be arranged by men whose only interest lies in the thing itself, and not in any outward profit. Therefore I earnestly wish the first step to be speedily taken, perhaps through a meeting of delegates from each Verein; and to that end have I to-day addressed the honoured Presidents of all existing Wagner-Vereins.

Bayreuth, 1. January 1877.

2.

[PROPOSED BAYREUTH "SCHOOL."]

PROSPECTUS PUBLISHED WITH THE STATUTES OF THE PATRONAT-VEREIN.

I HEREBY declare myself ready, in course of the requisite number of years, and with the support of the necessary assistant teachers, to conduct such practices and exercises as I deem indispensable not only to prepare a company for performing my own dramatico-musical works, but in general to enable singers, bandsmen and conductors, to rightly and intelligently render kindred works of a truly German style.

These practices, three at least of which I propose to personally attend in every week, shall commence with January 1 of next year, 1878; and I invite such singers and musicians in general to take part therein, as either have completed their curriculum at the existing Music-schools, or stand on the same level of musical technique with the former. The shortest term for which participants must pledge themselves, will be to remain in Bayreuth from the first of January to the thirtieth of September of one year of practice.

1878

Under the guidance of a special singing-master, all good dramatic works of distinctively German masters will be studied and performed by singers, male and female, according to my own instructions; and as we assume that the voice is already formed and finished, there will be no lessons in that department, but exclusively in proper mental conception and the higher mode of rendering. In these lessons such musicians will already assist as desire either to improve their general musical culture, or to qualify themselves for conducting dramatic performances. For this purpose a mastery of the pianoforte is indispensable, as our exercises will at first be accompanied solely on that instrument. Beyond their attendance at the vocal practices, however, experienced pianists shall also study the great instrumental works of our German masters, particularly Beethoven's—from pianoforte arrangements, to begin with—under my guidance for their proper understanding in respect of tempo and expression, as preliminary to the conducting of orchestral performances themselves.

It will depend on the responses to my invitation whether in the third quarter of the year, i.e. from July 1 to September 30, we are able to form a complete orchestra from players who have likewise passed our standing Music-schools, not only to play through our classical Instrumental-music under my direction, but also to accompany the singers' practice in the rendering of dramatic music-pieces—which at like time would mature the players in the higher operatic style of accompaniment. Should the assembled number of young musicians not prove sufficient, or not comprise the requisite variety of specialists, the gaps might be filled by members of a Royal Kapelle on holiday at the time, and in course of the three summer months we thus should obtain a large enough band to already partly convert the practices into public performances. In any event during the second quarter, i.e. from April 1 to June 30, practices in string-quartet-playing shall take place, and the proper rendering for our classical Quartets be thereby established.

Under my guidance, all the aforesaid separate branches of practice shall be united by lectures in which their culture-historical and æsthetic tendence, insofar as it aims at a German style not fostered hitherto, or not successfully, will be discussed with a view to mutual enlightenment.

The second year of training

1879

(again from January 1 to September 30) shall be devoted to similar studies, which now, however, will be applied to my own dramatic works and their particular mode of rendering; whilst the practices and performances with orchestra, in the summer quarter, will already embrace extensive sections of my earlier operas.

The third year

1880

(again commencing with the first of January) shall culminate in the summer quarter with complete stage-performances of some of my earlier works (if possible, the *Fliegender Holländer*, *Tannhäuser* and *Lohengrin*); to which, and similarly prepared, in the fourth year

1881

would be added *Tristan und Isolde* and the *Meistersinger*. Then the fifth year

1882

will bring the *Ring des Nibelungen* to light in similar fashion. In the sixth year

1883

the whole series of my dramatic works shall finally be completed with the first performance of *Parsifal*.—

(It is scarcely to be expected that all the singers and musicians who enter on the first of January 1878 will be able to attend the practice and performances of the Bayreuth school down to the close of the sixth year; but in any case there would probably remain a nucleus of eligible candidates equipped for the final representations, and these would form the source of constant renovation of the school, in which, moreover, they might be retained as teachers and exemplars.)

Bayreuth, 15. September 1877.

3.

INTRODUCTION TO THE FIRST NUMBER OF THE BAYREUTHER BLÄTTER.

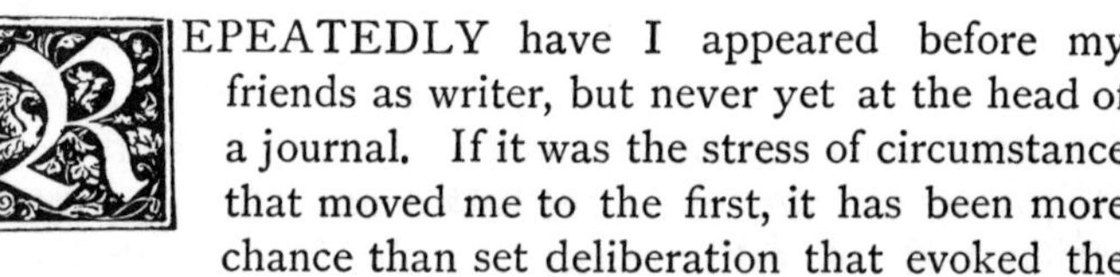

REPEATEDLY have I appeared before my friends as writer, but never yet at the head of a journal. If it was the stress of circumstance that moved me to the first, it has been more chance than set deliberation that evoked the last resolve: through its execution I hope for the present maintenance and strengthening of the bond which holds the friends of my art together for the furtherance of its practical tendences.

I may pass over the final inducement to publish these "Bayreuther Blätter," as already well-known to the Vereins in question; but with reference to my prospectus of the fifteenth September last I have to state that, of all the extensive plans there sketched, the issue of these Blätter has alone proved instantly feasible.

The miracles of our day take place on other fields than that of German Art and its furtherance by the mighty. And a miracle of the most unheard-of kind would it have been, had my scheme for the formation of a thoroughly efficient fellowship of musico-dramatic artists, to practise and conserve an art-style entirely native to us Germans, at once been comprehended in all quarters, or at least in the right quarter, and its execution suitably helped on. Who knows the arduous toil with which I brought about what I have reached already, knows also that I am accustomed to do without miracles of German State-culture; I have learnt to cheerfully content myself with the warm interest of friends however powerless, and so I gladly leave it to a Ministry of National Culture to affiliate branches of the wonderful Berlin High-school of Music in the chief provincial cities of the North-German leading Monarchy. This, in truth, is the sole conspicuous outcome of the publication of my plan. On the other hand it is gratifying to see that the number of adherents to my tenets is increasing, especially in the smaller towns, and that these friends—although with nothing at command but their own slender purses—have banded themselves in a wide-spread union; to which I propose to confine my future works and dealings.

If these Leaves (*Blätter*) were originally to be the channel for communications from the School to the outlying members of the Verein, they certainly must now subserve an end more abstract. Thus we all shall fare as I have always fared myself: whereas my only ambition has been to secure quite concrete art-performances, for a length of time I have had to try and explain myself with the pen of the theorist. True, I had guarded against calling the object of my prospectus by the name of "School,"—that name was simply given it in the circulars of our Administrative Council for sake of brevity and common parlance.* No, I very providently had spoken of mere "exercises and practices under my guidance." For it had come home to me that whoever speaks in modern Germany of a "School" for dramatico-musical art, does not know what he is saying, whilst he who goes the length of founding, equipping, directing such a school, and inviting pupils to be taught there, does not know what he is doing. I challenge all directors of so-called "High-schools"—schools, that is, for teaching something more than instrumental technique, or harmony and counterpoint—to say from whom, then, they and their appointed teachers learnt that "higher" thing which entitles them to give their institute so grand a label? Where is the school that taught themselves? Haply at our theatres and concerts, those privileged establishments

* This seems to account for the brackets appearing at the end of the "Prospectus" on page 21 *antea*.—Tr.

for the ruin and maltreatment of our singers, and in particular of our bandsmen? Whence have these gentlemen obtained so much as the proper tempo of a single classical piece they perform? Who shewed it to them? Tradition, perhaps? But we have not one tradition for such works. Who taught them the rendering of Mozart and Beethoven, whose works have grown up wild among us, and certainly without the tending of their authors? Why, only eighteen years after Weber's death, and at the very place where for many years he himself had led their performance, I found the tempi of his operas so falsified that nothing but the faithful memory of the master's widow, then still living, could assist my feeling hereanent!—I, too, have been to no school for the purpose: but I reaped a negative lesson as to the proper rendering for our great works of music from my deep and growing disgust at the performances I heard of our great music, whether at High-school concerts or on the military parade. On the strength of these lessons, however, it in nowise occurred to me to found a "School," but just to direct certain "exercises and practices" whereby I hoped my young friends and myself would arrive at an agreement as to the right tempo and proper rendering of our great music, and rear on that agreement a general understanding.

My friends will see that I was aiming at a thoroughly practical intercourse with those who were to derive their instruction from that intercourse itself. Now admittedly these "Blätter," in which we must take our refuge for the present, cannot help us to instruction in that sense. It therefore only remains for us to mutually instruct ourselves upon the causes of those hindrances to a noble cultivation of the German artistic faculty on the field which we have entered, and the exertions it will need to triumph over them. The execution of my Bayreuth Bühnenfestspiels has shewn, on my side, that I had in eye the fostering of this faculty through a living Example. For the nonce I must content myself with merely having thereby given a serious stimulus to many an individual. To strengthen the effects of that stimulus, to wit the impressions, thoughts and hopes aroused, we now must seek in combination.

Wherefore these "Blätter" are meant as a mere vehicle of correspondence within the Verein itself. The friends immediately allied with me for that purpose will never address themselves to representatives of public art-opinion who stand outside the Verein, or even assume the air of talking to them. What those gentry represent, we know: if they let fall a word of truth from time to time, we may be sure it is based on an error. And if ever we take count thereof, it will not be to correct them, but to teach ourselves; in which latter sense they may often be most profitable to us.

In return, our little sheet will seem quite despicable in the eyes of those great papers. Let us hope they will pay no heed to it at all; and if they call it a nook-and-corner tract, in their sense that will be an inappropriate title, since our nooks extend all over Germany. Nevertheless we might gladly accept the anticipated nickname, and for sake of a good omen it brings to my mind.

In Germany it is always the "nook," and not the large capital, that has been in truth productive. What should we ever have got, had we waited for the reflux from our great Market-places, Promenades and Ring-streets; what but the putrid leavings of a national production that once had thither flowed? A good spirit watched over our great poets and thinkers, when it banned them from these larger towns of Germany. Here, where servility and crudeness tear the morsel of amusement from each other's mouth, can nothing be brought forth, but merely chewed again. And our *German* capitals, at that? The blazoners of our national shame, to our own disgust and horror! How must a Frenchman feel, an Englishman, ay, even a Turk, when he traverses a German parliamentary city and everywhere finds just *himself*, in vilest copy, but not one trace of *German* originality? And then this broad-cast good-for-nothingness exploited for the benefit of holders of the National Debt by an "all-powerful" daily Press—at which the highest Ministers sit trembling in their Cabinets—as if to see whether the "German," after all, is worth powder and shot as Moltke taught us!—

As far as we are concerned, anyone in these capitals who doesn't seek himself a quiet "nook"—in which, unheeded and unheeding, to puzzle out the answers to the riddle "What the German is?"—may be made a Privy Councillor, or what not, and despatched by the Herr Kulturminister to arrange the musical affairs of other centres upon occasion.

Of this we petty-town folk know just nothing. At anyrate we lack both large and lesser opera-houses; we have neither a well nor a badly conducted orchestra, at most a regimental band whose renderings shew us how Herr Upper-Court-Kapellmeister at the royal seat is minded as to tempo and that sort of thing; and our home affairs are represented by one morning paper, a "Tageblatt" that for us comes out almost too often. But we feel quite cosy in our nook, and still have our Originals. Also, as we get no bite of public art, we neither have a vitiated taste.—However, as, taken alone, we don't count for much in the greater Fatherland, we cherish the good old German custom of periodic *federal gatherings*; and behold! when from all our "nooks" we come together as athletes, riflemen or singers, of a sudden you have the genuine "German" as he is, the stuff from which such splendid things have been made at times already.

From these "nooks" of the German Fatherland have I, too, received the strongest and most cheering encouragement to my work, whereas the great business-towns and capitals have done little but poke fun at it. And to me this seems fair evidence of the goodness of my cause, as to which I see more plainly every day that only on a soil entirely remote from the traffic of our greater world and its public directors, will it ever prosper. What none of these powers either will or can help forward, might well be accomplished by the union of such forces as, powerless when taken singly, combined can bring to life a thing of whose nobility and excellence the fewest have as yet an inkling.

From those outside I therefore only ask for disregard. Nothing more. If they're annoyed by performances of my works in their great cities, let them rest assured it is none of my seeking.—

So let us stop at these modest Blätter until our power increases. I promise them my lifelong co-operation. Only, my friends will readily understand that, after speaking to them in nine printed volumes, I have little new to say; on the contrary, it would please me much if these friends themselves explained to one another what the thing is all about, and how it may be carried farther, especially by novel applications. As I probably shall thus be very often cited in the third person, it will ipso facto be somewhat delicate to frequently intrude myself in the first.

And thus I shall be indulged with the leisure to devote myself in peace to the completion of the music for my "Parsifal," which I engage, in such kindly circumstances, to at all events have ready for a first performance in the summer of 1880. That performance shall take place under similar conditions to those attending the first of the "Ring des Nibelungen"—only, this time quite beyond mistake *among ourselves*!

4.

A WORD OF INTRODUCTION TO HANS VON WOLZOGEN'S "DECAY AND RESCUE OF THE GERMAN TONGUE."

[Bayreuther Blätter, February 1879.]

HAVE induced the excellent friend who undertakes the editing of these Blätter to place the accompanying work before the reading-circle of our Patronat-Verein in single instalments, and with the shortest possible intervals, prior to its publication as an independent volume. What the fortune of a book from the pen of myself or my friends may be upon our public mart of literature, we are unable to judge precisely; of my most important treatises I know that they have mostly been skimmed by none but those commissioned to demolish them. On the members of our Verein, however, I would impress the need of taking seriously the object that unites us. To those who merely meant their entry into the Verein as a means of securing admission to the first performance of a new opera of mine, it certainly may seem hard to be asked to attentively follow my friends' strict expositions of the tendence which we keep in view with that awaited performance also. But our Patrons must have gathered from the founding of these Blätter, that I lay great stress on this attention. And in that regard I have to regret my present failure to attract musicians of earnest mind to our assistance, since not only the variety of our requisite discussions, but also the character thereof, would have gained by their co-operation. The Germans, however, appear to have an extraordinary amount to do, though the un-Germans always find time enough to smear their sheets with critical smudges. In the meantime those of my friends who feel more called to devote their talents to the wider culture-tendence of my efforts, are left in almost sole possession of the field. Not that I think this a misfortune, since I hitherto have rather had to view as such the judgment of my art and tenets almost exclusively by impotent musicians. When the literate took up arms at last, we could but deem it a good symptom; for now we had to engage in the open with the most dangerous assailants—as these know better what is at stake, than those broken-down musicians—and the question accordingly passed over to a realm where it must be handled in all seriousness. Upon this realm, in my belief, no step so sure and steadily progressive has yet been taken, as that of my friend with the accompanying larger treatise. May all, who look for more from me than an extra-opera-performance, agree with my opinion of the weightiness of this important work; for this wish it was, that made me urge my friend to print his treatise in these Blätter.

5.

ANNOUNCEMENT TO THE MEMBERS OF THE PATRONAT-VEREIN.

BELIEVE it will be no wholly unexpected tidings to those members of our Verein who have followed my reports on our situation, if to-day I announce to them that the first performance of "Parsifal" cannot take place in 1880. Yet I hold myself bound to make this explicit statement, for sake both of avoiding all misunderstandings and of giving those members who merely joined the Verein in anticipation of the performance projected for next year, and not from sympathy with our general tendence, the opportunity of retiring with full claim to the reimbursement of their contributions.

It must remain for the growth and reinforcement of our Verein itself, on the other hand, to enable me to fix the date of that performance, and therewith to announce the provision for a periodic series of Stage-festivals.

Bayreuth, 15. July 1879.

6.

INTRODUCTION TO THE YEAR 1880.

ITH our entry on another year I really ought to feel somewhat diffident of appearing before my friends. Among them will be many who might lay on me the blame for the delaying of a new stage-festival at Bayreuth, though very few have openly avowed their disillusion by quitting our Verein. But in any case the earnestness of our association has gained through the sifting brought about by that compulsory postponement. As to the sentiments of those who have lately joined us—and they are by no means few—we need no longer be in doubt. And since I thus may take it that I am addressing none but the like-minded, I may hold myself released from the embarrassment of going into lengthy explanations. If we are agreed to have no Bühnenfestspiel before the periodic repetition of such feasts has been ensured us, we are fortunate in having nothing for the present but to take our higher aims in eye; and to become quite clear about them, may perhaps need no less time than it will cost to scrape our means together.

Nothing, in fact, seems farther from our public situation of the day, than the founding of an artistic institution whose use, nay, whose whole meaning is understanded of the veriest minority. Indeed I believe I have done my best to state both things distinctly: but who as yet has heeded? An influential member of the Reichstag assured me that neither he nor any of his colleagues had the faintest notion of what I want. And yet, to further my ideas I can only think of such as know absolutely nothing of our Art, but devote themselves to politics, trade or business; for here a ray may sometimes strike an open mind, whereas among those interested in our present Art I fancy I might seek such mind in vain. There reigns the obstinate belief that Art is but a métier, its object to feed its practitioner; the highest-placed Court-theatre Intendant never gets beyond that, and consequently it does not occur to the State to mix itself in things that rank with the regulation of Commerce. There one swears by Fra Diavolo's "Long live art; above all, the lady-artists," and sends for Patti.

Let us admit our Art to be our very greatest enemy, and that we really should fare much better if we looked to our Politicians and Culture-protectors in general, undeterred by the prospect of treading some toilsome by-ways to reach them. Indeed I fear these paths will lead us very far afield, and cost a deal of time. A plethora of milliards in the German Reich is no more to be thought of; even for new-won battles we should now have no more funds at hand, and how much less for culture-matters! seeing we no longer are able to pay sufficient schoolmasters, notwithstanding that their urgent need for saving the Folk from revolutionary thoughts has lately been discovered. Where frozen labourers are found upon the street, there really should be no question of even the Art that waxes fat in our midst upon its honoraria; and how much less of that we have in mind, which brings us no returns, but only outlay. Yet, 'spite of hunger, misery and want, many pictures still are painted, and books innumerable printed; so that it seems there is no dearth of fuel, but merely its employment in the wrong place, on parlour-walls and study-tables. That "something is rotten in the state of Denmark," we have on high authority; nevertheless I find the locale too narrowly taken. From the rotten stuff we throw to them, our German pigs get notable trichinæ—which points, again, to a scurvy state among ourselves: for safety, our public will soon have to take to the soldier's pease-pudding. Our peasant, pledged land and plough to the Jews, is said to never arrive at wholesome food or a decent appearance till he enters the military service; perhaps 'twould be better for us all, with goods and chattels, wife and child, art and science, and everything else one can think of, to join the army also; at least we thus should rescue something from the Jews, to whom alas! our hops and malt have passed already.

All things considered, the time would seem to me ill-judged, were my friends to ask anything of the German "Reich" just now for the Bayreuth idea. The only question, is whether the auspicious moment will ever come. True, there are many who view the present calamities as merely transitory, while others deny them point-blank; for hunger and misery, they say, we shall always have with us, but to keep a keen scent for good trade notwithstanding is proof of a force inexhaustible, a force one should swear by and never allow to be cried down as baseness (*Niederträchtigkeit*).

The Book-trade, already adduced, seems to wish to attest this: so beautifully, so nattily, on such fine paper and with such splendid copper-plates, have the Germans never printed books before; and every public is catered for, even the little Jew getting his Christmas-box with hopeful verses from the Talmud, and Nihilists of every stripe their philologic cauls at six marks each: only the hungering and frozen are left in the cold. I, too, was approached with the request to provide a piano-arrangement of "Parsifal" for my friends' Christmas-table. I declined: may my friends not take it ill of me! But before I give my last work away, I must have learnt again to hope—which at present is impossible. Not that I beseech anyone to manufacture hope for me, as some perhaps might think to effect by the discovery of an art-of-the-future-minded "Peabody." One day we hear of such a human-benefactor's vast bequests: of the benefactions we hear no further. If a new American Crœsus, or a Mesopotamian Crassus, to-day were to settle his millions upon us, we may be sure they'd be placed under lock by the Reich, and Ballet would shortly be danced on my grave.

Yet another Hope might quicken once more in me, if only I could see it stirring in the breasts of others. It comes not from without. Men of science persuade us that Copernicus reduced the ancient Church-belief to ruins with his planetary system, since it robbed God Almighty of his heavenly seat. The Church however, as all may see, has not felt materially embarrassed by that discovery: for it, and all believers, God dwelleth still in Heaven, or—as Schiller sings—"above the starry tent." The god within the human breast, of whose transcendent being our great Mystics were so certain sure, that god who needs no heavenly-home demonstrable by science, has given the parsons more ado. For us Germans had he become our inmost own; but our Professors have done him many a harm: they cut up dogs, to shew him in the spinal marrow—where it is to be presumed they at most will light on the Devil, who even may pack them neck and scruff. Yet this approachless god of ours had begotten much within us, and when at last he had to vanish, he left us—in eternal memory of him—*Music.* He taught us, too, us poor Cimmerians, to build, to paint and poetise: but the Devil has turned it all to printing, and now gives it us at Christmas for our book-desks.

Our Music he shall not thus deal with; for still it is the living god within our bosom. Let us guard it therefore, and ward off all profaning hands. For us it shall become no "literature"; in it resides our final hope of life itself.

There is something special in our German Music, ay, something divine. It makes its acolytes all martyrs, and instructs by them the heathen. What else is Music to all other culture-nations, since the decaying of the Church, than an accompaniment to dance or vocal virtuosity? We alone know "Music" as *herself*, and to us she gives the power of all regeneration and new-birth; but only while we hold her holy. Were we to lose the sense of genuineness in this one art, we had lost our last possession. May it therefore not mislead our friends, if precisely on this field, of Music, we shew a front implacable to whatsoe'er we rate as spurious. Indeed it wakes in us no little pain, to see the downfall of our musical affairs so utterly unheeded; for so our last religion melts away in jugglery. Let our painters and poets run riot as they please; at least they don't disturb one, if one neither looks nor reads: but music—who can shut his ears to it, when it pierces through the thickest walls? And where and when, with us, is music not made? Announce the end of the world, and a grand Extra-concert will be arranged for the event! Against complaints of the neighbours of physiological laboratories, that they could not endure the dreadful howling of the dogs there tortured, it was advanced by vivisectors that still less possibly could one hold out in the neighbourhood of a Music-Conservatorium. At Stuttgart over six-hundred pianoforte-mistresses are said to be instructed every day: corollary, six-thousand hours of exercises in private houses. And then the Concert-establishments, the Musical Academies and Oratorio-unions, the soirées and matinées of Chamber-music! Who composes for all these music-making conventicles, and—*how* can they ever be composed for? We know quite well: not one true word does their music say. And we, who have to hear it, put out thereby the last light the German God had left in us to find our way back to him!—

Once, at a banquet in my honour at Leipzig, I gave my kind hosts the advice to strengthen their good resolutions above all by *abstinence*. I re-echo that counsel to-day. Only in answer to a noble need, can the Arcane reveal itself; nothing can evoke the beauteous vision, save the force of our desire therefor. Upon us Germans our great Music has bestowed the power of ennobling far and wide; but that power must be potent, to incend the flame by whose pure light we at last shall haply find full many an exit from the misery that surrounds us everywhere to-day.

Christmas 1879.

7.

TO THE HONOURED PATRONS OF THE STAGE-FESTIVALS AT BAYREUTH.

WHAT has induced me to announce a renewal of Bühnenfestspiels by the production of "Parsifal" in the summer of 1882, is not so much the state of the Patronate funds, as a consideration of the endless delay to which that renewal would be exposed if I made it, and more particularly the yearly repetition of our festivals, depend upon the fulness of those funds. Alike to prove my gratitude to my friends for their sympathy, in most cases their self-sacrifice, and to ensure myself, while yet alive, the possibility of obtaining completely correct performances of all my works with the needful distinctness of style and lastingness of influence, I have decided to give out my latest work for representation in the Stage-festival-house at Bayreuth, but there exclusively, and to admit thereto the general public. After the prior rights of existing members of the Patronat-Verein shall have been met beyond all doubt, the performances will be repeated in a strictly public sense during one whole month—August in all probability—and for that purpose be previously advertised both far and wide; whereby it is reckoned that the extraordinary receipts will not only entirely cover the cost of this first year's performances, but also provide the means for resuming our festival in the following year—in which, as for the future in general, at Bayreuth alone is "Parsifal" to be performed. Upon the further results of the festivals restricted for the present to this one work, must depend the gaining of the means to gradually bring forward all my works; and it finally would remain for a faithful Patronate of these Bühnenfestspiels to preserve to the friends of my art the true spirit of performance of my works, in the sense of their author, beyond my lifetime.

Bayreuth, 1. December 1880.

8.

INTRODUCTION TO COUNT GOBINEAU'S "ETHNOLOGICAL RÉSUMÉ OF THE PRESENT ASPECT OF THE WORLD."

[Bayreuther Blätter, May-June 1881.]

HAT will be the destiny of the "Bayreuther Blätter" after its immediate function—that of reporting on the work of the Patronat-Verein—has been fulfilled, must be contingent upon the measure of interest that can now already be awakened in its readers by our excursions into realms of culture and civilisation which at first might seem remote, but in our opinion lie too pressingly near us.

If I am correctly informed, my thoughts on "Religion and Art" have found no unfavourable reception with our readers. As we take our stand upon the field of Art, and only from that base do we attempt to find a right and reason for exploring the remotest regions of the world, our friends might certainly deem it fittest, and even most agreeable, if we always placed Art or one of its special problems in the foreground. Only, it has been borne in upon me that, just as in the proposed Bühnenfestspiels, and the house expressly planned and built therefor at Bayreuth, I had to gain myself a basis for the right performance of my artistic works, so for Art itself, for its proper standing in the world, a new soil must first be won; a soil that cannot be supplied, in the first place, by Art itself, but by the world—that selfsame world to whose familiar understanding it is to be offered. For this we had to take our general state of culture, our Civilisation, and try how it might look reflected in our floating ideal of a noble art: but the mirror stayed dark and featureless, or gave us back a grinning parody of our ideal. So we will lay aside the mirror, for our next day's march, look eye to eye upon the carking world, and tell ourselves without disguise or terror what we think of it.

When Saint Francis, after long and serious illness, was led again before the wondrous landscape of Assisi and asked how it now pleased him, he answered, turning from the ecstasy of inner vision of the world to look once more upon its semblance: "Not more than erewhile." We asked Count Gobineau, returned from weary, knowledge-laden wanderings among far distant lands and peoples, what he thought of the present aspect of the world; to-day we give his answer to our readers. He, too, had peered into an Inner: he proved the blood in modern manhood's veins, and found it tainted past all healing. What his insight shewed him, will be a view distasteful to our learned men of Progress. Who knows Count Gobineau's great work "On the Disparity of the Races of Man," will probably have convinced himself that here are none of those mistakes so common to the everyday inquirer into the daily progress of mankind. We, on the contrary, can but be grateful to that work of one of the shrewdest of ethnologists for an explanation why our truly lofty minds stand lonelier every day, and—perhaps in consequence—grow ever rarer; so that we can imagine the greatest artists and poets surrounded by a world to which they have naught to say.

However, as we found in Schopenhauer's very demonstrations of the badness of the world the guide to an inquiry into the possibility of its redemption, there perhaps is hope that even in the chaos of impotence and unwisdom which our new friend lays bare to us we may find—if once we thrust into it fearlessly—a clue that leads to higher outlooks. Perchance that clue would not be visible, but only audible—a sigh of deepest pity, haply, such as once we heard from the Cross on Golgotha, and now goes up from our own soul.

My friends know what I deduce from that audible sigh, and divine the paths it opens to my mental vision. But only on the road whereon such dauntless minds conduct us, as that of the author of the following essay, can we hope to see the dawning of those paths.

This briefer work, undoubtedly, is merely meant to give a general survey of the present condition of the world, taken rather from a political standpoint; to those well-acquainted with the issue of the researches contained in its author's masterpiece, already mentioned, it may seem little more than the familiar table-talk of the profoundly-versed and wide-experienced Statesman, in answer to the equally intimate question, what he really thinks will be the end of our world-complications. It nevertheless should arouse in our friends that horror we so much need to shake us from our optimistic lethargy, and make us earnestly look round us for the only access to those paths I spoke of.

Modern.

The article "Modern" originally appeared in the Bayreuther Blätter *for March 1878.*

TRANSLATOR'S NOTE.

N a pamphlet lately sent to me an "important Jewish voice" is cited, its words being given as follows :—

"The modern world must gain the victory, since it wields incomparably better weapons than the old world of orthodoxy. The power of the pen has become the world-power, without which one can hold one's ground on no domain; and of that power you orthodox are almost wholly bare. Your men of learning write finely, intellectually, it's true, but simply for their fellows; whereas the Popular is the shibboleth of our time. Modern journalism and romance have been captured entire by the free-thinking Jew-and-Christian world. I say, the free-thinking Jewish world—for it is the fact that German Judaism now works so forcibly, so giant-like and so untiredly at the new culture and science, that the greater part of Christendom is led by the spirit of modern Judaism either consciously or unconsciously. To-day, for example, there is scarcely a newspaper or magazine that is not directly or indirectly conducted by Jews."—

Too true!—A thing like that I had never read before, and thought our Jewish fellow-citizens were none too pleased to hear such matters talked of. But now that we are met with such plain-speaking, we perhaps may insert an equally candid word ourselves without the instant fear of being variously maltreated as ridiculous and yet most hateful persecutors of the Jews, and tumultuously hissed upon occasion. Perchance we may even be allowed to make clear a few fundamental terms to our Culture-purveyors—whose world-power we don't for a moment question; certain terms they may not employ in quite the proper sense, and upon whose explanation, if they really mean honestly by us, their "gigantic exertions" might have a good result for all.

To begin with "the modern world."—If this does not simply mean the world of to-day, the time in which we live—the "now-time," as it is so euphoniously styled in modern German—our latest culture-mongers must be thinking of a world such as never existed before: a "modern" world, unknown to the world at any previous epoch—: an entirely novel world in fact, which has nothing at all to do with the worlds preceding it, and therefore shapes itself by its own judgment to its good pleasure. In truth this world must now appear a wholly new, unprecedented world to the Jews, who—as a national body—still stood remote from all our cultural efforts just half a century ago; this world on which they entered so suddenly, and have appropriated with such increasing force. Correctly speaking, they should consider themselves the only novelty in this old world: avowal of that, however, they seem only too keen to avoid, and to want to make themselves believe that this old world of ours has suddenly become brand-new through their mere entry on it. To us this seems an error, which they really ought to diligently rectify,—always assuming that they mean honourably by us, and truly wish to help us in our decay, merely used and aggravated by them hitherto. Let us assume this unconditionally.—

Taken strictly, then, our world was new to the Jews; and all they undertook, to set them straight therein, consisted in the appropriation of our ancient heritage. This applies before all to our language—for it would be rude to refer to our money. Never yet has it happened to me, to hear Jews employing their pristine tongue among themselves; on the contrary, it has been a perpetual surprise to me to find in every land of Europe that the Jews understood German, though alas! they mostly spoke it in a jargon manufactured by themselves. I fancy this crude and illegitimate acquaintance with the German tongue—which some inexplicable destiny must have brought to them—may have been a peculiar obstacle to their proper understanding and true adoption of the German world upon their legitimation therein. The French Protestants who settled in Germany after being driven from their home, in their descendants have become completely German; nay, Chamisso, who came to Germany as a boy speaking nothing but French, grew up to a master of German speech and thought. It is astonishing, how difficult this appears to be to the Jews. One might believe they went too hastily to work in the adoption of the wholly-alien, betrayed by just that unripe knowledge of our speech, their jargon. It belongs to another inquiry, to clear up the character of that falsification of speech which we owe to the commingling of the "modern" in our cultural evolution, particularly under the form of Jewish journalism; for to-day's theme we have merely to point to the many trials our language long had suffered, and how the brightest instincts of our great poets and sages had only just succeeded in restoring it to its productive individuality, when—in conjunction with the remarkable process of linguistic and literary development above denoted—it occurred to the flippancy of a consciously unproductive set of Epigones to cast adrift the irksome earnestness of their forerunners, and proclaim themselves as "Moderns."

Awaiting the original creations of our new Jewish fellow-citizens, we must protest that even the "Modern" is not their own invention. They found it as a weed upon the field of German literature. I myself beheld the early flowering of the plant. At that time it called itself "Young Germany." Its cultivators began with a war against all literary "Orthodoxy," by which was meant the belief in our great poets and sages of the previous century; attacked the so-called "Romanticism" that followed these (not to be confounded with the "journalism *and* romance"—!—of the "important Jewish voice" adduced above); went to Paris, studied Scribe and E. Sue, rendered them into a slipshod-showy German, and ended in part as

Theatre-directors, in part as journalists for the popular fireside.

That was a good commencement, and on such a groundwork, if only well supported by the power of the purse, with little trouble and no further ingenuity the "Modern" might be trimmed into a "modern world," to be victoriously set against an "old world of orthodoxy."

But to explain what this "modern" really means, is not so easy as the Moderns imagine; unless they will admit that it stands for a very shady thing, most perilous to us Germans in particular. That we will not suppose, however, as we are assuming that our Jewish fellow-citizens mean well by us. On the same assumption, are we then to conclude that they have no idea of what they say, and merely drivel? We deem it useless here to trace the history of the concept "Modern," a term originally allotted to the plastic arts in Italy to distinguish them from the Antique; enough, that we have learnt the influence of "Mode" in development of the French nation's spirit. The Frenchman can call himself "modern" with a peculiar pride, for he *makes* the Mode, and thereby rules the whole world's exterior. Should the Jews push their "gigantic exertions in common with liberal Christendom" to the length of likewise making a Mode for us, then—may the god of their fathers reward them for conferring such a boon on us poor German slaves of French fashions! Meanwhile the outlook is altogether different: for, spite of all their power, they have no approach to Originality, especially in the application of that force they vaunt as irresistible, the "power of the quill." With foreign plumes one may *decorate* oneself, as much as with the exquisite names under which our new Jewish fellow-citizens now present themselves no less to our astonishment than our delight, whilst we poor old burgher and peasant families have to content us with a paltry "Smith" or "Miller," "Weaver," "Wainwright" etc., for all futurity.* Foreign names, however, do not much matter; but our feathers must have

* "Schmidt," "Müller," "Weber," "Wagner."—

grown from our own skin if we do not merely want to deck ourselves, but to write from our heart with them, and so to write as thereby to gain the victory over a whole world—which had not occurred to any Papageno before. But this old world—or rather, this German world has still its originals, whose feathers yet grow without aid from cantharides; and our "important voice" itself admits that our learned men write "finely and intellectually," though it is to be feared that they soon will unlearn all their little fine writing, under the perpetual contagion of Jewish journalism; already they speak and hold silence "self-talkingly,"* just like that modern "pen-power." "Liberal Judaism" has nevertheless a "giant's work" before it, ere all the original parts of its German co-citizens shall have been entirely ruined, ere the plumes that have grown on our skin shall write nothing but plays on un-understood words, falsely rendered "*bons mots*" and the like, or even ere all our musicians acquire the strange art of composing without inspiration.

It is possible the Jews' originality will then reveal itself upon the field of German intellectual life to us as well, namely when no man understands his own words more. Among the lower classes, our peasants for instance, the care of giant-working Liberal Judaism has already brought things almost so far that the erewhile most intelligent can no longer utter a sensible word, "self-talkingly," and thinks he understands the purest nonsense.

Candidly, it would be difficult to anticipate much help for ourselves from the modern Jew-world's victory. I have become acquainted with earnest and gifted individuals of Jewish descent who, in the endeavour to draw closer to their German fellow-citizens, have really devoted much labour to thoroughly understanding us Germans, our speech and history; but these have turned entirely away from the modern world-conquerings of their former co-religionists, nay, have even made quite serious friends with myself, for example. These few are thus excepted

* "Selbstredend" for "self-evidently."—Tr.

from the "Moderns," with whom the journalist and essayist alone find full acclamation.

What reality may lurk behind that "orthodoxy" which the "important voice" expects to vanquish under convoy of the "Moderns," is not so easy to discover: I suspect that this word as well, so plumped upon our extant world of mind, is somewhat dimly understood, and used at random. If applied to Judaic orthodoxy, one perhaps might take it to mean the teachings of the Talmud, departure from which might not seem inadvisable to our Jewish fellow-citizens; for, as much as we know thereof, observance of those teachings must make a hearty companionship with us uncommonly hard to them. But it would not profoundly concern the German Folk, which liberal Judaism wants to help; and that sort of thing, well, the Jews must arrange with themselves. Christian orthodoxy, on the other hand, can really be no business of the liberal Jews,—provided their excess of Liberalism has not had them baptised in an hour of weakness. So they probably mean more the orthodoxy of the German Spirit in general,—a kind of right-belief in our stock of German science, art and philosophy. But this right-belief, again, is hard of comprehension, and certainly not easy to define. Some folk believe, while others doubt; even without the Jews a deal is criticised, disputed, and, broadly speaking, nothing right produced. The German, too, has his love and joy: he rejoices at the harm of others, and "loves to blacken the shining." We are not perfect. Let us therefore treat this as a fateful theme, which we had better leave untouched to-day; the same with "Popularity," which the "important voice" upholds as Shibboleth of our time. Indeed I pass this by with the greater pleasure, as "Shibboleth" inspires me with terror: for upon closer investigation of the meaning of this word I have learnt that, of no particular importance in itself, it was employed by the ancient Jews in a certain battle as means of detecting the tribesmen of a race they proposed, as usual, to root quite out; who pronounced the "Sch" without a hiss, as a soft "S," was slaughtered. A decidedly fatal "*mot d'ordre*" in the fight for Popularity, especially with us Germans, to whom the lack of Semitic sibilants might be most disastrous if it ever came to an actual battle delivered by the Liberal-modern Jews.

Even for a minuter illustration of the "modern," these few remarks may prove sufficient. For the possible enlivenment of any member of our Patronat-Verein who reads these lines, I will therefore close them with a facetious rhyme that once occurred to me. It ran:

"In prudence let the old go moulder; *
superior persons all are modern."

* "Modern," as a true German verb, means "to rot."—Tr.

PUBLIC AND POPULARITY.

Publikum und Popularität.

The three chapters of Publikum und Popularität *originally appeared in the* Bayreuther Blätter *for April, June and August, 1878, respectively.*

TRANSLATOR'S NOTE.

I.

> "The bad is not the worst, for seldom can it deceive;
> the middling is far worse, so many it good believe."

So says an Indian Proverb.

Now who are the "Public," to which both the Bad and the Middling are offered? Whence does it gain its power of discrimination, and especially the seemingly so arduous recognition of the Middling, since the Good does not offer itself to it at all? For the token of the Good is this: it stands on its own ground (*für sich selbst da ist*); and the public, reared on the bad and mediocre, must raise itself before it can approach it.

Everything, except the good, has its Public. Never do we find an exploiter of the mediocre referring to his confederates, but always to the "public," as those by whom he must shape his course. An instance. Not long ago a younger friend of mine begged the now departed publisher of the "Gartenlaube" to insert a serious correction of a defamatory article upon myself, my work and purpose, which had found the customary space in that agreeable paper. The intensely popular publisher declined, as he had to "consider his public." That was the public of the "Gartenlaube": no small one, either; for I lately heard that this highly respectable (*solide*) folk-sheet rejoices in an enormous number of customers. However, there plainly exists another public, at the least no smaller than that bond of readers, namely the immeasurably varied public of the theatres: I will merely say, of Germany. And here we have a curious fact. The Theatre-directors attend to the needs of this public in much the same fashion as the immortal publisher of the Gartenlaube, for instance, consulted those of his; with few exceptions, they cannot abide me, just like the editors and reporters of our great political papers: but they find their profit in giving their public my operas, and when the journalists tax them with it, they excuse themselves by their needful deference to this public of theirs. Now, what relation bears the public of the "Gartenlaube" to this other? Which is the genuine article? This or that?

In any case here reigns a great confusion. One might have supposed that such a fortuitous aggregate, as the readers of a newspaper, had no true right to be called a Public, for by nothing does it prove exertion of initiative, still less of judgment; no, its character is that passiveness which discreetly shirks the pains of thinking or judging for itself, and the more doggedly as many years of wear impress upon this sloth the seal of firm conviction. It is otherwise with the public of the Theatre: undeniably this takes initiative, and quite directly speaks its likes and dislikes, often to the amazement of those most interested. It can be grossly duped; and so far as the journals have an influence, especially on the Directors, the bad—but not so much the middling, strange to say—can drag an audience's favour through the deepest mire. But it also knows to regain its feet after every fall, and this inevitably happens when something good is offered it. Once give it that, and chicane has lost all power over it. About two years back a well-to-do burgher of a minor town applied to one of my friends for a patronate-seat at the Bayreuth Bühnenfestspiels: upon learning from the "Gartenlaube" that my affair was swindling and extortion, he withdrew that application. Finally he yielded to curiosity, and attended a performance of the "Ring des Nibelungen"; with the result that he informed my friend he should return to Bayreuth for every representation of the work in future. Probably he concluded that for once in a way the Gartenlaube had asked too much of its public, namely that it should remain without impression in presence of the enacted artwork.

That would be going a little too far, with the Theatre-public! To it, one sees, an appeal is possible: if it has not yet learnt to judge, it still receives direct impressions, and that through sight and hearing, as also through emotion. What makes an actual judgment hard to it, is that its sensations can never be quite pure, since at the best it is only offered the middling, and with the claim to rank as the good.

I began by saying that the good never offered itself to the public, and I have appeared to contradict myself by presuming that it really was offered to it in a given case, the case of my Bayreuth Bühnenfestspiels.

Upon this I should like to make myself intelligible. Without pretending to set up a general principle valid for all epochs of culture, I simply take in eye our public art-conditions of the day, when I assert that it is impossible for anything to be truly good if it is reckoned in advance for presentation to the public and this intended presentation rules the author in his sketch and composition of an artwork. On the other hand, that works whose genesis and composition lie entirely remote from this intention must be offered to "the public" notwithstanding, is a dæmonic fate deep-seated in the inner obligation to conceive such works, a fate which dooms the work to be surrendered in some sort by its creator to the world. Ask the author whether he regards his work as still belonging to him, when it is lost upon those paths where the mediocre alone is met, and that the mediocre which poses for the good. But the case undealt-with by our Indian proverb is that of the good appearing publicly in none save the dress of the middling, and being offered in this disfigurement to the same verdict as the mediocre, because in this world of ours the good can as little come to adequate appearance in its own pure form, as perfect justice.

We are still speaking of the public of our theatres. Before it are set the works of our great poets and composers: they certainly belong to the rare, indeed the unique good, that we possess; but the mere fact of our possessing them, and treating them as our property, for us has cast them into the common stock of the mediocre. Beside what other products are they placed before the public? The very circumstance of their being given us on the selfsame stage and by the same performers who feel at home in those products, as also that we end by taking this dishonouring conjunction and commingling as a thing of course, quite plainly proves that people think this Good can be made intelligible to us only when dropped to the level of the mediocre. But the Middling is the broad foundation, and to it all forces are trained and trimmed; so that it most naturally is rendered by our actors and singers both better and more correctly than the Good.

This it was necessary to first establish, for our inquiry, and I think the premise's correctness will not be much disputed: namely, that only the Mediocre is given well at our theatres, i.e. in keeping with its character, but the Good badly, because in character of the mediocre. Who pierces through this veil and sees the Good in its true purity, can, strictly speaking, be no longer numbered with the theatre-public of to-day; though it is highly characteristic of a *theatre* public, that such exceptions are met with here alone: whereas a mere reading-public, especially of a newspaper, is forever barred from that glimpse of the truly good.—

What then is the character of the Mediocre?

By this term, I should say, we commonly signify that which brings us no new and unknown thing, but the known-already in a pleasing and insinuating form. In a good sense, it would be the product of Talent—if we agree with Schopenhauer that Talent hits a mark we all can see, but cannot lightly reach; whilst Genius, the genius of "the Good," attains a goal we others do not even see.

Hence Virtuosity proper belongs to Talent, and the musical virtuoso affords the clearest illustration of the preceding definition. The works of our great composers we have always with us; but he alone can perform them rightly, and in the master's spirit, who has the talent. To let his virtuosity sparkle solely for itself, the musician often trumps up pieces of his own: these belong to the class of the mediocre ; whereas their virtuosity cannot in itself be strictly ranged in such a class, for we must candidly confess that a middling virtuoso is of no class at all.—A virtuosity very near of kin to that denoted, accordingly the exercise of Talent proper, we find most pronounced in the literary profession among the French. As instrument they possess a language that seems purposely built for it, whose highest law is to express oneself cleverly, wittily, and in every circumstance neatly and clearly. It is impossible for a French author to gain acceptance, if his work does not before all else comply with these requirements of his native tongue. Perhaps the very excess of attention he thus has to devote to his expression, to his style regarded in and for itself, makes it difficult for a French writer to have novelty of thought, to recognise a goal which others don't yet see ; and for the simple reason, that he would be unable to find for these wholly new ideas the happy phrase that at once would strike all readers. This may account for the French having such unsurpassable virtuosi to shew in their literature, whilst the intrinsic value of their works —with the great exceptions of earlier epochs—seldom rises above the mediocre.

Now, nothing more perverse can be imagined, than the adoption by German writers of that attribute which makes the French such brilliant virtuosi on the ground of speech. The attempt to treat the German language as an instrument of virtuosity could only occur to those to whom the German tongue is truly alien, and who therefore twist it to improper uses. None of our great poets and sages can be rated as virtuosi of speech : every one of them was in the same position as Luther, who had to ransack every German dialect for his translation of the Bible, to find the word and turn to popularly express that New he had discovered in the sacred books' original text. For what distinguishes the German spirit from that of every other culture-folk is this, that its creative sons had first seen something ne'er yet uttered, before they fell a-writing,—which for them was but a necessary consequence of the prior inspiration. Thus each of our great poets and thinkers had to form his language for himself; an obligation to which the inventive Greeks themselves do not appear to have been submitted, since they had at command a language always spoken by the living mouth, and therefore pliant to each thought or feeling, but not an element corrupted by bad pensters. In a poem from Italy how Goethe bewailed his being doomed by birth to wield the German tongue, in which he must first invent for himself what the Italians and French, for instance, found ready to their hand. That under such hardships none but truly original minds have risen to production among ourselves, should teach us what we are, and at any rate that there is something peculiar about us Germans. But that knowledge will also teach us, that if virtuosity in any branch of art is the evidence of talent, this Talent is denied in toto to the Germans, at least in the branch of Literature: who toils to acquire a virtuosity in this, will stay a bungler; if, following the musical virtuoso who composes pieces of his own, he trumps up poetical sketches for setting off his fancied virtuosity, however, they will not even belong to the category of the Mediocre, but simply of the Bad, the wholly null.

But this Bad, since null, is the element of all our "modern"— so-called belletristic — literature. The compilers of our numerous Histories of Literature seem to be thinking of this when they air their strangely ill-assorted theories, as for instance that we nowadays do no good work since Goethe and Schiller once led us from the path —to guide us back to which, must be the calling of our feuilletonist street-arabs. Who plies this sturdy trade till his sixtieth year, with great ignorance but due shamelessness, obtains a pension from the Minister of Culture. No wonder the really good, the work of genius, is uncommonly hateful to these men of printed German intellect, for it so very much upsets them; and how easy they find it to provide themselves with partners in that hate: the whole reading public, nay—the whole journal-ridden nation itself, stands stoutly by their side.

Eh! Through our rulers' most incredible misconceptions of the German character, and the resulting stubborn mistakes and full-blown blunders, it had been made so excessively easy for us to be Liberal. What the proper meaning of Liberalism might be, we could calmly leave to its preachers and agents to discover and work out. Before all else we cried for Freedom of the Press, and whoever had once been locked up by the Censor became forthwith a martyr, or at the least a man of truth whose judgment might be followed anywhere. If he brought the returns from his journal to an income of half a million thalers for himself [£75,000], the martyr was further admired as a very clever man of business. And this still goes on despite the fact that, after their decreeing us liberty of the press and universal suffrage from pure love of the thing, the foes of Liberalism are no longer so easily to be assailed. But in valorous fight, i.e. in the attack of something or other denounced as dangerous, resides the power of the journalist, the charm he exerts on his public. So the word goes forth: "We've got the power; 400,000 subscribers stand at our back, and look towards us: what shall we be mauling next?" Soon comes the whole army of writers and reviewers to assistance: all are "liberal" and hate the uncommon, particularly what goes its own way without worry about them. The rarer such a prey, with the heartier accord all rush upon it when it shews itself for once. And the public looks on, always from behind, having at least the enjoyment of mischief, combined with the satisfaction of standing up for the People's Rights; for even in artistic matters, of which it knows nothing at all, it is always the world-famed head reviewers of the largest and most approved of Liberal papers who reassure its conscience that its hooting of their victim is quite in place. On the contrary, the only worthy use to which to put so astoundingly amassed a journal-power never occurs to its controllers: namely, to drag to light some unknown or misjudged great man, and bring his cause to general recognition. Beyond the proper heart for this, they above all lack the needful mind and understanding, and that in every province. While these Liberal newspapers were clamouring for freedom of the press, they let the national-economist Friedrich List * go unheeded to the ground with all his great and pregnant plans for the German people's welfare, sagely leaving it to posterity to erect a monument to this man who certainly did not need *Freedom*, but *uprightness of the Press* for execution of his plans,—a monument the pillar of its shame. Where would great Schopenhauer have remained, that only German free-man of his time, had an English reviewer † not unearthed him for us. Why! even to-day the German nation knows no better of him than what one railway-passenger may gather from his neighbour, namely that Schopenhauer's teaching is to shoot oneself dead.—Such are the flowers of education one picks from the cosy Gartenlaube on a balmy summer-evening.

But this all has yet another side. In the latter part of our inquiry we have lit exclusively upon the leaders of the public, and left the public's self beyond our ken. Those gentry are not so thoroughly responsible for the harm they work, as may appear to the strict surveyor of their actions: after all, they do what they are able, both in the moral and the intellectual sense. Their name is legion: our littérateurs are as the sands upon the shore, and each desires to live. They might turn their hands to something more useful and cheering, 'tis true. But it has become so easy, and therefore so attractive, to dawdle in the paths of litera-

* A notable opponent of Adam Smith's political economy, and ardent advocate of a German Zollverein and national system of transport; born in 1789, he shot himself dead in 1846.—Tr.

† In the *Westminster Review* of April 1853, i.e. just seven years before Schopenhauer's death. The writer of the article (said to be Oxenford) thus describes the position: "All over Germany were professorlings dotted about, receiving their snug salaries, and, without a spark of genius in their composition, retailing the words of some great master of philosophic art, and complimenting each other, as each brought out his trifling modification of a system which had been slightly modified from some previous modification, and yet could not Schopenhauer get a word of notice— not so much as a little abuse." —Tr.

ture and journalism, especially since it pays so well. Who helps them to indulge in this aggressive literary idling, that costs so little learning and yet so speedily rewards?

Obviously this is the Public itself, to which in turn they have made it a delightful habit to give way to sloth and shallow pleasures, to warm it at a fire of straw, to yield to the German's peculiar bent to gloat over others' misfortunes and doat on flattery of himself. The favour of this public I should not trust myself to court: whoever liefer *reads* than *hears*, *sees* and *experiences* for himself—be it in the railway-carriage, the café or the Gartenlaube—is not to be reached by any amount of writing or printing from *our* side. Ten editions are swallowed there of a libel on one whose own writing they don't so much as take into their hand. And when all is said, this has its reason, deep-seated in the metaphysical.

What other public I have in mind, and what auspicious consequences might be awaited from it for the future of our hapless public Art and Culture, I have already hinted; my views hereon I now propose to make plainer—or in the modern virtuoso-language, to set clear (*klarzustellen*)—in a second article, to follow.

II.

If I place at the head of this article "*eritis sicut deus scientes bonum et malum*," and follow it up with "*vox populi vox dei*," I shall have fairly well defined the route I now propose to take in our inquiry, needing nothing further than the disagreeable company of "*mundus vult decipi.*"—

What is *good*, and what is *evil*? And who decides the point?—*Criticism*? We thus might call the exercise of true capacity to judge; only, the best of criticism can be no more than a subsequent collation of the qualities of a work with the effect it produced on those before whom it was set. The best criticism, such as that of Aristotle, would accordingly be rather an attempt—unfruitful by its very nature—to afford guidance for future production; provided it did not betray itself a mere pastime of the Understanding in analysis and explanation of a judgment already arrived-at on quite another path.

If after assigning this meaning to it, we bid goodbye to Criticism in the same way as we already have been obliged to treat the Reading-public for whom it is intended, our main inquiry narrows down to that living assemblage before whom the artwork is directly placed.

We will begin by confessing that it would be hard to unreservedly ascribe to a modern audience those important qualities we necessarily should fain, or must, adjudge to that "*vox populi.*" True, that in it come out the evil attributes of every crowd; here indolence by side of licence, coarseness matched with affectation, but above all unreceptiveness and insensibility to impressions of profounder kind, are met with to the full: though we must admit that, as with every multitude, one also meets those elements of sympathetic self-abandonment without whose aid no Good has ever passed into the world. Where would have stopped the action of the Gospels, had not the crowd, the "*populus*," included in itself those elements?

The real evil is, that the German audience of to-day is

composed of such very miscellaneous factors. So soon as a new work creates a stir, curiosity drives everybody to the theatre, which even in the ordinary run is regarded as the place of meeting for all who crave distraction. At the theatre whoever would prefer a highly entertaining and instructive spectacle to the mostly bad performances, let him turn his back upon the stage and view the public,—an operation to which the inner structure of our theatres so lends itself, that in many seats, if one does not wish to rick one's neck, it almost seems compulsory. In such a survey we soon shall find that a large proportion of the audience has fallen on the theatre to-night in error and from false supposition. What brought them here may certainly be gauged as nothing but the quest of entertainment, and that in the case of every comer; only, the strange diversity of receptiveness, in kind as in degree, is plainer to the physiognomical observer of a theatre-public than anywhere else—even than at church, since there hypocrisy conceals what here dares figure unabashed. Nor are the various grades of society and education, to which the spectators belong, by any means an index to the individual's receptiveness: in the dearest, as the cheapest seats, one meets the same phenomenon of interest and apathy packed side by side. At one of the excellent first performances of "Tristan" in Munich I observed a vigorous dame of middle age in the last extremity of boredom during the third act, while the cheeks of her husband, a grey-beard superior officer, were streaming with tears of the deepest emotion. Again, at a performance of the "Walküre" at Bayreuth an elderly gentleman much-prized by me, and of the friendliest disposition in life, complained of the intolerable length of the scene between Wotan and Brünnhilde in the second act; on the contrary his wife, who sat beside him, an estimable and domesticated matron, informed him that her only regret would be that anyone should rid her of the profound emotion in which this heathen god's bewailing of his fate had held her chained.—Such instances shew plainly that the natural receptiveness toward direct impressions from theatric representations and the poetic aims behind them is just as infinitely varied as the temperament itself, quite apart from any question of degrees of culture. The first lady would have been charmed by a changeful sparkling ballet, the second gentleman by a clever and exciting drama of intrigue, to which their partners might have stayed indifferent.—What is one to do, to give the heterogeneous throng the sop for each? The Theatre-director of the Prologue to *Faust* seems willing to suggest a means.

The French, however, have better understood the point already, at least for their Parisian public. For every genre they cultivate a special theatre; this theatre is frequented by those to whom that genre appeals: and thus it comes that, apart from all intrinsic worth of their productions, the French invariably turn out good work, namely homogeneous stage-performances presented to a homogeneous audience.

How stands it with ourselves?

In the larger of our German cities, where, consequent upon the abandonment of the theatres to speculation, so-called Genre and Folk theatres have arisen beside the houses maintained by the Courts, the Parisian model may have been somewhat more nearly approached. Not to disparage the doings of these theatres—though we scarcely can rate them very high, if only for reason of their offering hardly any original products, but mostly mere "localised" foreign wares—we will gladly assume that, in answer to their differentiation of genre, there will also take place in the greater public a sifting of those elements whose crude admixture has distressed us in its puzzling physiognomy. It seems, however, that the *Opera-houses*, if only for the attraction of their scenic and musical pomp, will always be exposed to the danger of setting their work before a public deeply cloven in itself, and widely unlike in its receptive powers. We perceive that each reporter can give his own colour to the favour or disfavour shewn by so utterly dissimilar a public: in fact an absolutely correct judgment in this regard might be harder to arrive at here than anywhere else.

That the character of the doings at these Opera-houses itself is mostly blamable for the confusions hence arising, is undeniable. For here one misses all attempt at developing a Style, whereby at least the artistic taste of the public might acquire a little certainty, a refinement of its sense of *Form* enabling it to so far control the psychologic accident of its impressions that they shall not depend on nothing but the temperament. To the French their good theatres have made it easier to cultivate their sense of Form, and that most advantageously. Whoever, coming straight from Germany, has witnessed a Parisian audience's spontaneous seizure of a delicate nuance on the part of the actor or musician, and in general of any manifestation of a fitting sense of form, will have been sincerely surprised. The Parisians had been told that I condemn and banish Melody: long years ago, when I gave them the Tannhäuser-march at a concert, after the sixteenth bar of the first cantabile the audience interrupted the piece with a positive storm of applause. Something akin to this sense I have also found in the Vienna public: here it was palpable that everybody was following the development of an intricate melodic thought with keen attention, for, arrived at the phrase's close, they broke into the liveliest demonstrations of delight. Nowhere else in Germany have I happened on the like; from little but summary explosions of enthusiasm have I been able to gather that, taken in the mass, I have found a general susceptibility.

The one means of ensuring ourselves the verdict of the public, namely a calculation of its sense of Form, nay, of its artistic taste in general, has to be discarded by him who offers his products to the German Theatre-public of nowadays. It is truly dispiriting to have to remark that even our best-educated do not really know the difference between a good and a bad performance, or detect the details that have here succeeded, there miserably failed. Were I, for instance, intent on bare appearance, I might almost rejoice at this sad experience; compelled to hand the pieces of my "Ring des Nibelungen" to the theatres for further representation, I might find a curious comfort in the thought that the pains I took with the Bayreuth festival-performances of my work, to bring it to portrayal as correctly and authoritatively as possible in every respect, are there not missed at all, on the contrary that gross exaggerations of subtle scenic hints (e.g. the so-called Fire-magic—*Feuerzauber*) are deemed far more effective than as carried out by my directions.

Therefore he who must turn to the German public, can count on nothing save its widely varying susceptibility to emotional, rather than artistic, impressions; and, however its judgment may be warped by raging journalism, this public is still to be regarded as a purely naïve receiver, which one has only to seize by its true element of soul, to completely rid it of that read-up prejudice.

But how is a man to proceed, who feels bound to appeal to this naïve receptivity, when experience tells him that it is the very thing the majority of playwrights also count on and exploit in favour of the Bad? With them prevails the maxim "*mundus vult decipi*," which my great friend Franz Liszt once playfully turned into "*mundus vult Schundus.*" * Whoso abjures that maxim, having neither an interest nor a pleasure in duping the public, would therefore probably do better—for so long as he is granted the leisure to belong entirely to himself—to leave the public altogether out of view; the less he thinks of this, and devotes himself entirely to his work, as from the depths of his own soul will there arise for him an Ideal Public: and though this too will not know much of art and art-forms, the more will he himself grow versed in Art and its true Form, that form which shuns remark and whose employment he merely needs for clearly and distinctly conveying his multiform inner vision to the toil-less sensibility of breathing souls outside him.

Thus is born, as I before have said, what alone we can

* "*Schund*" = "garbage."—Tr.

term the *Good in art.* 'Tis exactly like the *Morally good*; for this, as well, can spring from no intention, no concern. On the contrary, we might define the *Bad* as the sheer aim-to-please both summoning up the picture and governing its execution. As we have had to accord our public no developed sense of artistic form, and hardly anything beyond a highly varying receptivity, aroused by the very desire of entertainment, so we must recognise the work that merely aims at exploiting this desire as certainly bare of any value in itself, and closely approaching the category of the morally-bad in so far as it makes for profit from the most questionable attributes of the crowd. Here comes into full play the rule of life: "the world desires to be deceived, and we'll deceive it."

Nevertheless I should not term the coarseness betrayed in application of this maxim the absolutely Bad, as yet; here the naïvety of the world-child—which, half awoken, half benumbed to the general illusion about the true meaning of life, now gets through life as best it can—may at times arrive at an expression that brings a slumbering talent to our view. If the meaning of a worthy *popularity* is scarcely to be fixed with certainty, having regard to the deplorably unclear relation of Art to our modern Publicity, we can only credit those who make it their business to entertain the public in the sense just mooted with a *modern* popularity. I believe, in fact, that most of our "popular" play-writers and opera-composers have consciously made for nothing but to dupe the world for sake of wheedling it: that it has been possible to do this with talent, eh! with sparks of genius, should only incite us to a still closer consideration of the character of the Public, for a serious recognition of the latter would surely lead to a far more lenient verdict on those engaged in serving it, than the intrinsic value of their labours permits us to pronounce. This problem I believe I have already plainly indicated, when I concluded my *Remembrance of Rossini* (in the eighth volume of my Gesammelte Schriften *) with the remark

* Volume IV. of the present series.—Tr.

that the small intrinsic value of his works was not chargeable to his natural gift, but simply to his public (only think of the Vienna Congress!). And to-day a valuation of this same Rossini will plainly shew us what is the really *Bad* in art. It is impossible to class Rossini with the bad, and out of the question to rank him with the mediocre composers; but as we decidedly cannot associate him with our German art-heroes, our Mozart or Beethoven, we here are left with a scarcely definable equation, perhaps the same as our Indian proverb so cleverly expresses in the negative when it calls bad, not the *Bad*, but the *Middling*. For there still remains the most repulsive sight of all, namely the attempt to trick alike the public and the judgment of true artists, much as if light and faulty wares were offered as of full weight and solid. But in this sight—which I have tried to sufficiently characterise in various earlier writings—our whole present world of Public Art beholds its face with a contentment all the smugger as our whole official judgment-seat, Universities, High Schools and Ministries at the head, continually award to it the meed of full solidity.

Reserving for a later article the description of this *public* which takes an academic pleasure in that only *Bad*, I should like to give my theme a comforting provisional close to-day by an attempt to unearth the true "*vox populi*," in contrast to that academic-posing public.

I have denoted the workshop of the truly *Good* in art; it lay remote from the Public proper. Here the art of creation remained a secret, perchance a mystery to the creator himself. The finished work affrights the artist's seeming fellows: is it all awry and new, or trite and old? The point is argued. It seems as if the thing were a miscarriage. At last it steps before the public,—ay, our Theatre-public: at first this finds itself at sea; here something appears too long, there a little lingering could be wished. Disquiet, worry, agitation. The work is repeated: it improves on acquaintance; the unwonted grows familiar, as a thing intelligible from of old. The vote is cast: the "verdict of God" is pronounced, and the reporter—goes on reviling. I believe that on no domain of art can one hear to-day a more distinct "*vox dei.*"

The wish to withdraw this infinitely weighty, this only redeeming process from the sway of Chance, and let it take place undisturbed, inspired the author of these lines with the plan for the stage-festivals at Bayreuth. In its first attempt at execution his friends, alas! were denied that undisturbedness above all aimed at. Once more the motleyest gathering trooped together, and we after all experienced little beyond another "Opera-performance." So the problematic "*vox populi*" must be appealed to once again. The "Ring of the Nibelung" is exchanged at Court and City theatres for hard cash, and another new experience has to be made on the puzzling ground.—

To devote a closing word to the "Popularity" in my superscription, though I propose to treat it somewhat more exhaustively later, I now will give an inkling of the interesting problem to be discussed, by a further reference to the fate aforesaid of my Bühnenfestspiel. Many of my well-wishers are of opinion it is providential that this work of mine should be forced to go the round of the world, for it is thereby ensured that popularity which must necessarily be denied it with its solitary performances in our Bayreuth Festival-playhouse. Now, to myself, grave errors seem to lie at back of this opinion. What our theatres have lately made the property of their subscribers and occasional visitors, cannot rank in my eyes as having become popular, i.e. a possession of the Folk, by that act of appropriation. Only the highest purity in the commerce of an artwork with its public, can form the needful basis of a noble Popularity. Rating the *vox populi* very high, I cannot recognise the "popular" of nowadays as product of the "*deus*" of that "*vox.*" What have the sixty editions of the "Trompeter von Säckingen" to tell me? What the 400,000 subscribers of the Gartenlaube?—

But more of this another time.

III.

After reviewing the public of newspaper-readers and that of theatre-goers, our outlook on the *populus* and the popularity which it confers is at present somewhat gloomy. I am afraid it will become still gloomier if we now direct our gaze towards the *academic* public. "When the People speaks, I hold my tongue," I have made one of my Meistersingers say; and we may take it that a like proud maxim is the first principle of all Cathedra-ism, let the dais be set in the schoolroom or in the college-hall. Yet Academism starts with this advantage, that its physiognomy is popular in itself: only open the capital "Fliegende Blätter," and even the peasant in the railway-carriage at once will recognise the "professor," so often made harmless fun of in the witty cuts of Munich artists; and when this type is supplemented by the certainly no less popular *student*, with the child's-cap perched on one side of his head, in jack-boots, and driving a beer-swelled paunch before him, we have alike the teacher and the pupil of "*Science*" who haughtily look down upon us artists, poets and musicians, as the belated offspring of an obsolete mode of viewing the world.

But although the exterior of the wardens of this Science is popular in the people's eyes, they unfortunately have not the smallest influence on the Folk itself, and cleave exclusively to the Ministers of German States. True, that the latter are for the most part mere jurists, and have learnt little more at the university than what a prospective English statesman picks up in his career of advocate; but the less they know of "science" proper, the more intent are they on dowering and increasing the university-forces of the land; for the foreigner, you see, is never tired of telling us that, although we otherwise are not of much account, at least our universities are splendid. Our Princes in particular, further famed abroad for an admirable military drill, are always glad to hear talk of their universities, and outvie each other in their "advancement"; a King of Saxony, for instance, could lately get no peace till the number of students at Leipzig had overtaken that of the Berlin University. How proud the cherishers of German "science" well may feel, with such marks of favour showered on them from the highest quarters!

That this zeal from above is directed exclusively to the satisfaction of a by all means worthy vanity, I should not like to say. Their intense anxiety about the discipline of those departments which may be employed for turning out servants of the State, proves that our rulers have also a practical aim in their nursing of Gymnasia and Universities. Not long ago we were furnished with most instructive information on this point by a pamphlet of the Göttingen professor P. de Lagarde, giving us a tolerable insight into the objects of State-ministers and their special views on what may be made good use of in the various sciences. Our Governments' great solicitude to secure exceptional powers of endurance, we may judge from the draconic regulations now coming to our knowledge as regards the daily hours of study, particularly in the Gymnasia. If, concerned about the health of his son, a father inquires of a Gymnasium-director whether the scheme of lessons, usurping all the day, could not leave at least an hour or two at liberty in the afternoon, were it only for the exercises that still must be prepared at home, he is told that the Herr Minister will never hear of such a thing, that the State requires tough workers, and the young blood must begin betimes to harden his sitting-hide upon the school-bench, to accustom it to feeling no inconvenience from whole days spent in later life upon the office-stool. Spectacles seem to have been expressly invented for this system of instruction; and the reason why people in earlier times had clearer heads, must plainly be that they also saw more clearly with their eyes and had no need of glasses.—On the other hand, with true State-pædagogic instinct, the university-years seem to be abandoned to the letting-off of adolescent steam. The future Civil Servant in particular, with a completely free hand in the disposal of his time, has no terror save the bugbear of the final State-examination; and even that he manages to scrape through by getting up the catch recipes of Jurisprudence at the eleventh hour. The happy years between he devotes to his evolution as "student." There "form" * is studied; the "mill" †, the "colours of one's corps," adorn his rhetorical imagery down to his days of parliamentary service, ay, even to the post of Chancellor; the "beer-salamander" ‡ assumes the office of that care and trouble which once "blew Falstaff up and made him fat before his time." § Then comes the "cram" ("*Büffelei*"), the examination, at last the appointment, and —the "philistine ‖" is hatched, needing nothing but the due servility and leathern rump to help him to the dizziest pinnacles of State-control in time; from whence, again, the School below is ruled and strictly watched lest haply any should fare better than Herr Minister himself once fared. —These are the men who in their State-bureaus, their Chambers of Deputies and Reich's-parliaments, would have to give their decision on public art-establishments and plans for their improvement, for instance, were one so short-sighted as to commend the same to furtherance by the State. As theatre-goers, they affect the genre of "Einen Jux will er sich machen."

* "Comment"—student's slang for "accepted custom."—Tr.

† "Mensur'—"student's duel."—Tr.

‡ According to Flügel, "a mode of drinking in honour of a person, etc., on festive occasions, when all persons present, at certain commands given, have to rub their beer-glasses on the table, repeating the word *Salamander* (probably a mere ludicrous corruption of '*all' an'nander*,' i.e. *reibt alle Gläser an einander*!) then to drink off a certain quantity, and lastly to set down the glasses simultaneously with a smart rap."—Tr.

§ From *Henry IV.*, First Part, Act II., scene iv., "when I was about thy years, Hal, I was not an eagle's talon in the waist; I could have crept into any alderman's thumb-ring: a plague of sighing and grief! it blows a man up like a bladder."—Tr.

‖ In students' slang the "*Philister*" is the "townsman," as against the "gownsman." For further remarks on German student-life, see Vol. IV., pp. 47-48.—Tr.

So much for the *utilitarian* round of our Academic officialdom. Close by, however, there runs another, with claims to quite an ideal use, from whose correct accomplishment the academician promises the healing of all the world: here reign pure *Science* and its eternal *Progress*. Both are committed to the "Philosophic faculty," in which Philology and Natural Science are included. Indeed that "progress" on which our governments expend so much, is furnished almost solely by the various sections of Natural Science; and here, if we mistake not, stands Chemistry at top. True that this latter stretches forth a popularly-useful arm into practical life, as one may see by the constant progress in the science of adulteration; but its labours not immediately addressed to public use have also made it the real delight and benefactor of the other philosophic branches, whereas Zoo- or Biology is at times so disagreeable as to much upset the branches more particularly allied with State-theology—though the resulting oscillations of these latter may at anyrate assume the air of moving life and progress. On Philosophy proper, however, the accumulating discoveries of Physics, above all of that same Chemistry, react as veritable charms, from which even poor Philology may draw her ample share of profit. For in this last department there is absolutely nothing new to drag to light, save when the archæologic excavator chances on a buried tablet, of Latin antiquity in particular, enabling some break-neck philologist to amend certain hitherto-accepted modes of spelling; an undreamt "progress" which assists the great professor to astounding fame. From Physical Science, however, especially when they foregather on the field of Æsthetics, both philologists and philosophists obtain peculiar encouragement, nay obligation, to an as yet illimitable progress in the art of criticising all things human and inhuman.* It seems, to wit, that from that science's

* Alluding to F. Nietzsche's "*Menschliches, Allzumenschliches*"—"Human, All-too-human"—first published in May 1878; the two immediately succeeding sentences, and the last of this paragraph, are peculiarly applicable to the "case of" Nietzsche.—Tr.

experiments they derive profound authority for an altogether special skepsis that sends them spinning in a constant whirl, now flying from accepted views, then flying back again in some confusion—which ensures them their appointed share in the general everlasting Progress. The less the notice paid these scientific saturnalia, the more boldly and relentlessly are noblest victims slain and sacrificed on the altar of Skepsis. Every German professor is bound to at one time have written a book that makes him famous: now it is not given to everyone to discover a positive novelty; to arouse the needful stir one therefore has recourse to branding a predecessor's views as fundamentally false; and the more considerable, and for the most part misunderstood the author now derided, the greater the effect. In lesser cases such a thing may become amusing, for instance when one Æsthete forbids the creation of types, and the next re-grants that privilege to poets. 'Tis graver where all Greatness in general, and the so highly objectionable "genius" in particular, is dubbed pernicious, nay, the entire idea of *Genius* cast overboard as a radical error.

This is the outcome of the newest scientific *method*, which dubs itself in general the "historical school." If the true historian had been growing more cautious every year, and relying on nothing but well-authenticated documents, such as had to be diligently sifted out from the most diverse of archives; and if he believed that thereby alone could he establish an historic fact, there was little to be said against the practice, albeit many a sublimity wherewith tradition thitherto had kindled our enthusiasm must be cast into the waste-paper-basket, often to the sincere regret of the historical researcher himself. Poor History was thus reduced to such a pitch of dulness that one found oneself moved to enliven it with all kinds of piquant frivolities, as in the newest portraitures of Nero and Tiberius, where cleverness has already gone somewhat too far. But the dauntless judge of all things human and divine, the latest product of the Historical school of applied philosophy, will never touch an archive not first subjected to the tests of Chemistry or

Physics in general. Here all necessity for a metaphysical explanation of those phenomena in the life of the universe which remain a little unintelligible to purely physical apprehension is rejected with the bitterest scorn. So far as I can understand the doctrines of its pundits, the upright, cautious *Darwin*, who pretended to little more than an hypothesis, would seem to have given the most decisive impetus to the reckless claims of that *historical* school by the results of his researches in the province of biology. To me it also seems that this has chiefly come about through great misunderstandings, and especially through much superficiality of judgment in the all-too-hasty application of the lights there won to the region of Philosophy. The gravest defects I deem the banishment from the new world-system of the term *spontaneous*, of *spontaneity* itself, with a peculiarly overbearing zeal and at least a thought too early. For we now are told that, as no change has ever taken place without sufficient ground, so the most astonishing phenomena—of which the work of "genius" forms the most important instance—result from various causes, very many and not quite ascertained as yet, 'tis true, but which we shall find it uncommonly easy to get at when Chemistry has once laid hold on Logic. Meanwhile however, the chain of logical deductions not stretching quite so far as an explanation of the work of Genius, inferior nature-forces generally regarded as faults of temperament, such as impetuosity of will, one-sided energy and stubbornness, are called in to keep the thing as much as possible upon the realm of Physics.

As the progress of the Natural Sciences thus involves the exposure of every mystery of Being as mere imaginary secrets after all, the sole concern must henceforth be *the act of knowing*; but intuitive knowledge appears to be entirely excluded, since it might lead to metaphysical vagaries, namely to the cognisance of relations which are rightly withheld from abstract scientific comprehension until such time as Logic shall have settled them upon the evidence of Chemistry.

Though we have only superficially described the issue of the newer, so-called "historical" method of Science (as is unavoidable by men outside the esoteric pale), I believe we are justified in concluding that the purely comprehending Subject, enthroned on the cathedra, is left with sole right to existence. A worthy close to the world-tragedy! How this solitary Comprehender may feel in his exclusive grandeur, it is not easy to conceive; we only hope that, arrived at end of his career, he may not have to repeat the cries of *Faust* at the beginning of Goethe's tragedy. In any case, we fear, not many can share with him his joy of knowing; and to us it seems that the State, so careful else of the common benefit, may be spending too much money on this unit's private happiness, should the latter even prove a fact. That common benefit indeed must be in sorry case, were it only since we find it difficult to regard this unadulterated Comprehender as a man among men. His course is from before the lectern to behind it; a wider scope for learning life, than this change of seat allows, is not at his command. The beholding of the things he thinks, is mostly denied him from youth up, and his contact with the so-called actuality of Being is a fumbling without feeling. Assuredly were there no universities or professorships, in whose support our pedant-proud State is so studiously lavish, not a soul would really notice him. With his colleagues and the other "culture-philistines"* he may form a public of his own, joined here and there by bookworm princelets and princesses for academic junketings; to Art—which the Goliath of Knowledge more and more regards as a mere rudiment from an earlier stage of human reason, not unlike the os coccyx we still retain from the animal tail—he only pays attention when it offers archæologic prospects of his launching some Historical thesis: thus he prizes Mendelssohn's

* "Bildungsphilistern," a word which Nietzsche claims to have coined; see the second chapter of his first *Unzeitgemässe Betrachtung* (a slash at David Strauss), where he devotes ten pages to a definition of the obvious meaning.—Tr.

Antigone and pictures about which he may read without seeing them: but influence on art he only exerts when obliged to be present at the founding of Academies, High-schools and the like; and then he does his righteous best to stop all productivity arising, since it easily might lead to a relapse into the Inspiration swoon of exploded civilisations. The very last thing to occur to him, would be to address the *people*, which for its part never troubles its head with scholars; so that it certainly is hard to say upon what path the Folk is ever to arrive at a little comprehension. And yet 'twere no unworthy task, to earnestly work out this latter problem. For the Folk gets its learning on a diametrically opposite path to that of the historic-scientific Comprehender, i.e. in his sense it learns nothing. Though it does not reason (*erkennt*), still it knows (*kennt*): it knows its great men, and loves the Genius those others hate; and finally, to them an abomination, it honours the Divine. To act upon the Folk, then, of all the academic faculties there would remain but that of *Theology*. Let us examine that, to see if the State's extravagant outlay on higher educational establishments can afford a single hope of beneficial influence on the Folk itself.—

Christianity still endures; its oldest churchly institutions stand even with a firmness that makes desperate cowards of many toilers for State-culture. That a heartfelt, truly blest relation to Christ's precepts exists among the generality of present Christians, is certainly not so easy to aver. The educated doubts, the common man despairs. Science makes God the Creator more impossible each day; but from the beginning of the Church the God revealed to us by Jesus has been converted by the Theologians from a most sublime reality into an ever less intelligible problem. That the God of our Saviour should have been identified with the tribal god of Israel, is one of the most terrible confusions in all world-history; it has avenged itself in every age, and avenges itself to-day by the more and more outspoken atheism of the coarsest, as the finest minds. We have lived to see the Christian God condemned to empty churches, while ever more imposing temples are reared among us to Jehova. And it almost seems right that Jehova at last should quite suppress the God so monstrously mistakenly derived from him. If Jesus is proclaimed Jehova's son, then every Jewish rabbi can triumphantly confute all Christian theology, as has happened indeed in every age. What a melancholy, what a discreditable plight, is that of our whole Theology, maintained to give our doctors of the church and popular preachers little else than the guidance to an insincere interpretation of the truths contained in our priceless Gospels! To what is the preacher bound fast in the pulpit, but to compromises between the utmost contradictions, whose subtleties must necessarily confound our very faith itself and make us ask: Who now knows Jesus?—Historical criticism, perchance? It casts in its lot with Judaism, and, just like every Jew, it wonders that the bells on Sunday morn should still be ringing for a Jew once crucified two thousand years ago.* How often and minutely have the Gospels been critically searched, their origin and compilation exposed beyond a doubt; so that one might have thought the very evidence of the spuriousness and irrelevance of their contradictory matter would at last have opened the eyes of Criticism to the lofty figure of the Redeemer and his work. But the God whom Jesus revealed to us; the God no god, no sage or hero of the world, had known before; the God who, amid Pharisees, Scribes and sacrificial Priests, made himself known to poor Galilean shepherds and fishermen with such soul-compelling power and simplicity that whoso once had recognised him, beheld the world and all its goods as null; this God who never more can be revealed, since this first

* Nietzsche begins his 113th aphorism of "*Menschliches, Allzumenschliches*" with these very words:—"On a Sunday morning, when we hear the old bells booming, we ask ourselves: Is it possible that this should be for a Jew, crucified two thousand years ago, who said he was the son of God? The proof of such an assertion is wanting."—In the next paragraph the reference to "free minds" applies again to Nietzsche, who gave himself (apparently himself alone) that title, and dedicated his work just named to the memory of Voltaire.—Tr.

time was He revealed to us for ever:—this God the critic always views with fresh distrust, because he feels obliged to take Him for the maker of the Jewish world, Jehova!

We may console ourselves that after all there are two varieties of the critical mind, two methods of the science of comprehension. The great critic *Voltaire*, that idol of all "free minds," judged the Maid of Orleans on testimony of the historical documents of his day, and accordingly felt justified in the view set forth in his filthy poem on the "Pucelle." Before *Schiller* there lay no other documents: but whether it was another, presumably a faulty mode of criticism, or that Inspiration so decried by our free-spirits, that led him to recognise in this maid of France "humanity's all-noble type,"—not only did his poetic canonisation of the heroine bestow upon the Folk an infinitely touching and e'er-loved work, but it also anticipated Historical criticism, hobbling after, which a lucky find has at last put in possession of the rightful documents for judging a marvellous phenomenon. This Jeanne d'Arc was virgin, and necessarily, because in her all natural instinct, miraculously reversed, had become the heroic bent to save her country. Behold the infant Christ on the arms of the Sistine Madonna. What our Schiller was given to recognise in the wondrous freer of her fatherland, had here been shewn to Raphael in the theologically defaced and travestied Redeemer of the world. See there the babe, with eyes that stream on you the sunrays of determinate and sorely-lacked redemption; and far beyond you, to the world itself; and farther still, beyond all worlds yet known: then ask yourselves if this "*means*" or "*is*"?—

Is it so utterly impossible to Theology, to take the great step that would grant to Science its irrefutable truths through surrender of Jehova, and to the Christian world its pure God revealed in Jesus the only?

A hard question, and undoubtedly a still harder demand. Yet both might take a more menacing form if the problems still soluble upon the basis of a noble Science should one day be propounded by the Folk itself, and solved in its wonted fashion. As I already have hinted, the doubting and the despairing sections of mankind may finally combine in the so trivial confession of Atheism. We are already witnessing it. Nothing else seems expressed in this confession, as yet, than great dissatisfaction. Whither that may lead, however, is food for reflection. The politician handles a capital in which a large part of the nation has no share. Never, since the abolition of slavery, has the world been more conspicuously divided into those who own and those who do not. Perhaps it was imprudent to admit the unpropertied to a voice in legislation intended solely for possessors. The consequent entanglements have not been slow to arise; to face them, it might reward wise statesmen to give the non-possessors at least an interest in the maintenance of Property. Much shews that such an act of wisdom is improbable, whereas repression is deemed easier and more swiftly efficacious. Indisputably the instinct of preservation is stronger than one commonly supposes: the Roman Empire maintained itself in a state of dissolution for half a thousand years. The period of two-thousand years, which great historic civilisations have hitherto covered in their evolution from barbarism back to barbarism, would carry ourselves to somewhere about the middle of the next millennium. Can one imagine the state of barbarism at which we shall have arrived, if our social system continues for another six-hundred years or so in the footsteps of the declining Roman world-dominion? I believe that the Saviour's second advent, expected by the earliest Christians in their lifetime, and later cherished as a mystic dogma, might have a meaning for that future date, and perchance amid occurrences not totally unlike those sketched in the Apocalypse. For, in the conceivable event of a relapse of our whole Culture into barbarism, we may take one thing for granted: namely, that our Historical science, our criticism and chemistry of knowledge would also have come to end; whilst it may be hoped, on the contrary, that Theology would by then have come to a final agreement with the Gospels, and the free understanding of Revelation be opened to us without Jehovaistic subtleties—for which event the Saviour promised us his coming back.

And this would inaugurate a genuine popularisation of the deepest Knowledge. In this or that way to prepare the ground for cure of ills inevitable in the evolution of the human race—much as Schiller's conception of the Maid of Orleans foreran its confirmation by historical documents—might fitly be the mission of a true Art appealing to the Folk itself, to the Folk in its noblest, and at present its ideal sense. Again, to even now prepare the ground for such an Art, sublimely *popular*, and at all times so to prepare it that the links of oldest and of noblest art shall never wholly sunder, our instant efforts may not seem altogether futile. In any case, to such works of art alone can we ascribe ennobling Popularity; and none save this dreamt-of Popularity can react on the creations of the present, uplifting them above the commonness of what is known to-day as popular favour.

THE PUBLIC IN TIME AND SPACE.

Das Publikum in Zeit und Raum.

The following article originally appeared in the Bayreuther Blätter *for October 1878.*

TRANSLATOR'S NOTE.

HIS title may serve to introduce a general survey of those relations and connections in which we find the artistically and poetically productive individual placed towards the social community assigned to him as representant of the human race for the time being, and which we to-day may call the Public. Among them we at once remark a pair of opposites: either public and artist fit each other, or they absolutely do not. In the latter case the Historic-scientific critic will always lay the blame upon the artist, and pronounce him unfit for anything; for it thinks it has proofs that no pre-eminent individual can ever be aught save the product of his spacial and temporal surroundings, of his day in fact, that historic period of the human race's evolution into which he happens to be thrown. The correctness of such an assertion seems undeniable; merely it fails to explain why, the more considerable that individual, in the greater contradiction has he stood with his time. And this cannot be so lightly disposed of. To cite the sublimest of all examples, the cotemporary world most certainly did not comport itself toward Jesus Christ as though it had nursed him at its breast and delighted in acknowledging him its fittest product. Plainly, Time and Space prepare us great perplexities. If it indeed is impossible to conceive a more fitting place and time for Christ's appearance, than Galilee and the years of his mission; and if it is obvious that a German university of the "now-time," for instance, would have offered our Redeemer no particular facilitation: on the other hand we may recall the cry of Schopenhauer at Giordano Bruno's fate, that stupid monks of the blessed Renaissance era should have brought to the stake in fair Italy a man who on the Ganges, at the selfsame date, would have been honoured as wise and holy.

Without going into the trials and sufferings of great

minds in every age and country, too plainly visible, and consequently without touching on their deeper cause, we here will only note that their relation to their surroundings has always been of tragic nature; and the human race will have to recognise this, if it is ever to come to knowledge of itself. True religion may already have enabled it to do so; whence the eternal eagerness of the generality to rid itself of such belief.

For us, our first concern must be to trace the tragedy of that relation to the individual's subjection to the rules of time and place; whereby we may find those two factors assuming so strong a semblance of reality as almost to upset the "Criticism of Pure Reason,"* which ascribes to Time and Space no existence but in our brain. In truth it is this pair of tyrants that give great minds the look of sheer anomalies, nay, solecisms, at which the generality may jeer with a certain right, as if to please the Time and Space it serves.

If in a review of the course of history we go by nothing but its ruling laws of gravity, that pressure and counter-pressure which bring forth shapes akin to those the surface of the earth presents, the wellnigh sudden outcrop of over-topping mental heights must often make us ask upon what plan these minds were moulded. And then we are bound to presuppose a law quite other, concealed from eyes historical, ordaining the mysterious sequence of a spiritual life whose acts are guided by denial of the world and all its history. For we observe that the very points at which these minds make contact with their era and surroundings, become the starting-points of errors and embarrassments in their own utterance: so that it is just the influences of Time, which involve them in a fate so tragical that precisely where the work of intellectual giants appears intelligible to their era, it proves of no account for the higher mental life; and only a later generation, arrived at knowledge through the very lead that remained unintelligible to the contemporaneous world, can seize the import of their

* Kant's.—Tr.

revelations. Thus the seasonable, in the works of a great spirit, would also be the questionable.

Instances will make this clear. *Plato's* surrounding world was eminently political; entirely apart therefrom did he conceive his theory of Ideas, which has only been properly appreciated and scientifically matured in quite recent times:* applied to the spirit of his day and world, however, he bent this theory into a political system of such amazing monstrosity that it caused the greatest stir, indeed, but at like time the gravest confusion as to the real substance of his major doctrine. On the Ganges he would never have fallen into this particular error about the nature of the State; in Sicily, in fact, it served him badly. What his epoch and surrounding did for the manifestation of this rare spirit was therefore not exactly to his advantage; so that it would be absurd to view his genuine teaching, the theory of Ideas, as a product of his time and world.

A second case is that of *Dante*. In so far as his great poem was a product of his time, to us it seems almost repulsive; but it was simply through the realism wherewith it painted the superstitious fancies of the Middle Ages, that it roused the notice of the cotemporary world. Emancipated from the fancies of that world, and yet attracted by the matchless power of their portrayal, we feel a wellnigh painful wrench at having to overcome it before the lofty spirit of the poet can freely act upon us as a world-judge of the purest ideality,—an effect as to which it is most uncertain that even posterity has always rightly grasped it. Wherefore Dante appears to us a giant condemned by the influences of his time to awe-compelling solitude.

To call to mind one further instance, let us take great *Calderon*, whom we assuredly should judge quite wrongly if we regarded him as product of the Jesuit tenets prevailing in the Catholicism of his day. Yet it is manifest that, although the master's profundity of insight leaves the Jesuit world-view far behind, that view so strongly influ-

* By Schopenhauer.—Tr.

ences the outward texture of his works that we have first to overcome this impression, to clearly seize the majesty of his ideas. An expression as pure as the ideas themselves was impossible to the poet who had to set his dramas before a public that could only be led to their deeper import by use of the Jesuitic precepts in which it had been brought up.

Admitting that the great Greek Tragedians were so fortunate in their surroundings that the latter rather helped to create, than hindered their works, we can only call it an exceptional phenomenon, and one which to many a recent critic already appears a fable. For our eyes this harmonious conjunction has fallen just as much into the rut of things condemned by Space and Time to insufficiency, as every other product of the creative human mind. Precisely as we have had to allow for the conditions of time and place with Plato, Dante and Calderon, we need them to complete a picture of Attic Tragedy, which even at its prime had quite a different effect at Syracuse to that it had at Athens. And here we touch the crux of our inquiry. For we now perceive that the same temporal surrounding which was injurious to a great spirit's manifestation, on the other hand supplied the sole conditions for the physical presentment of its product; so that, removed from its time and surroundings, that product is robbed of the weightiest part of its effect. This is proved distinctly by the attempts at resurrection of these selfsame Attic tragedies upon our modern boards. If we are obliged to get time and place, with their manners and particularly their State and Religion, explained to us by scholars who often know nothing at all of the subject, we may be sure we have forever lost the clue to something that once came to light in another age and country. There the poetic aim of great minds appears to have been fully realised through the time and place of their life being so attuned as almost palpably to conjure up that aim itself.

But the nearer we approach affairs within our own experience, especially in the province of Art, the smaller grows the prospect of harmonious relations even distantly akin. The fact of the great Renaissance painters having to treat such ghastly subjects as tortured martyrs, and the like, has already been deplored by Goethe; into the character of their patrons and bespeakers we have no need to inquire, nor into the reason why great poets starved at times. Though this happened to great Cervantes, yet his work found widespread popularity at once; and it is the latter point we must deal with, seeing that we here are discussing the detrimental influences of time and place upon the form and fashion of the artwork itself.

In this respect we notice that, the more seasonably a producer trimmed his work, the better did he fare. Till this day it never occurs to a Frenchman to draft a play for which theatre, public and performers, are not on hand already. A perfect study in successful adaptation to circumstances is offered by the genesis of all Italian operas, Rossini's in particular. With every new edition of his novels our Gutzkow announces revisions in step with the latest events of the age.—Now take the obverse, the fate of such works and authors as have not caught the trick of time and place. The front rank must be given to works of dramatic art, and especially those set to music; since the mutability of musical taste emphatically decides their fate, whereas the recited drama does not own so penetrant a method of expression as to violently affect an altered taste. In Mozart's operas we may plainly see that the quality which lifted them above their age, also doomed them to live beyond their age, when the living conditions that governed their conception and execution are no more. From this singular fate all other works of the Italian school of Opera were saved; not one has outlived the time to which alone it belonged, and whence it sprang. With the "Nozze di Figaro" and "Don Giovanni" 'twas otherwise: it is impossible to regard these works as destined merely for the wants of a few Italian Opera seasons; the seal of immortality was stamped upon them. Immortality!—A fatal boon! To what torments of being is the departed soul of such a masterwork exposed, when dragged to earth again by a modern theatrical medium for the pleasure of a later generation! If we attend a performance of "Figaro" or "Don Juan" to-day, would we not rather nurse the tender memory that it once had lived with full strong life, than see it hustled through an existence wholly strange to it, as one resuscitated for maltreatment?

In these works of Mozart's the elements of the flowering-time of Italian musical taste combine with the spacial conditions of the Italian Opera-house to form a very definite entity, in which the spirit of the close of the eighteenth century is charmingly and beautifully expressed. Outside these conditions, and transplanted to our present time and milieu, the eternal part of these creations undergoes a disfigurement which we seek in vain to cloak by fresh disguise and adaptations of its outward form. How could it ever occur to us to wish to alter anything in "Don Giovanni" for instance—a course deemed requisite by almost every enthusiast for this glorious work at one time or another—if the figure it cut upon our boards did not actually pain us? Almost every operatic regisseur has at some time attempted to trim "Don Juan" to the day; whereas every intelligent person should reflect that not this work must be altered to fit our times, but ourselves to the times of "Don Juan," if we are to arrive at harmony with Mozart's creation. To mark the futility of all attempts at reviving this particular work, I do not even touch on our altogether inappropriate means of performance; I pass over the disastrous effect on the German public of German translations of the Italian text, as also the impossibility of replacing the so-called "recitativo parlando"; and I will assume that we had succeeded in training a troupe of Italians for a perfectly correct performance of "Don Giovanni": looking from the stage to the audience, we should only find ourselves in the wrong place—a shock we are spared by our utter inability to imagine such an ideal performance at the present day.

Still more plainly does all this shew forth in the fate of

the "Magic Flute." The circumstances in which this work came to light were this time of poor and petty sort; here it was no question of writing for a firstrate Italian troupe of singers the finest thing that could anywhere be set before them, but of descending from the sphere of a highly developed and richly tended art-genre to the level of a showplace for Viennese buffoons where music had hitherto been of the very humblest. That Mozart's creation so immeasurably exceeded the demands addressed to him that here no *individual*, but a whole *genus* of the most surprising novelty seemed born, we must take as the reason why this work stands solitary and assignable to no age whatsoever. Here the eternal and meet for every age and people (I need but point to the dialogue between *Tamino* and the *Speaker*) is so indissolubly bound up with the absolutely trivial tendence of a piece expressly reckoned by the playwright for the vulgar plaudits of a Viennese suburban theatre, that it requires the aid of an historical commentary to understand and approve the whole in its accidental dress. Analysis of the various factors of this work affords us speaking proof of the aforesaid tragic fate of the creative spirit condemned to a given time and place for the conditions of its activity. To save himself from bankruptcy, the manager of a Viennese suburban theatre commissions the greatest musician of his day to help him out with a spectacular piece designed to hit the taste of its habitual public; to the text supplied Mozart sets music of eternal beauty. But this beauty is inextricably embedded in the work of that director, and—waiving all affectation—it remains truly intelligible to none but that suburban audience of Vienna for whose ephemeral taste it was intended. If we would rightly judge and perfectly enjoy the "Zauberflöte," we must get one of the spiritualistic wizards of to-day to transport us to the Theater an der Wien in the year of its first production. Or do you think a modern performance at the Berlin Court-theatre would have the same effect?

Verily the ideality of Time and Space is sorely tried by such considerations, and we finally should have to regard them as the densest of realities, compared with the ideality of the artwork proper, did we not detect beneath their abstract forms the concrete Public and its attributes. The diversity of the public of the selfsame time and nation I tried to indicate in my previous articles; in the present I have sought to prove a like diversity in time and place, yet will leave untouched the tendencies peculiar to each age and nation, if only from fear of losing myself in fanciful assumptions—as to the artistic tendences of the newest German Reich, for instance, which I probably should rate too high were I misled by personal considerations into measuring them by the action of the Director-in-chief of the four North-German Court-theatres.* Nor, having taken our theme on its broadest lines, should I care to let it dwindle into a question of mere local differences, though I myself have experienced a remarkable instance of their determinant weight, in the fate of my *Tannhäuser* in Paris; whistled out of the Grand Opéra (for good reasons!), in the opinion of qualified judges at a house less ruled by its stock public my modest evening-star might perchance have still been twinkling in the French metropolis beside the sun of Gounod's "Faust."

More serious aspects of the public varying in time and space were those that crowded to my mind when seeking to account for the fate of *Liszt's* music; and as it was these that furnished the real incentive to my present inquiry, I think best to close it with a discussion of them. This time it was a fresh hearing of Liszt's *Dante* Symphony that revived the problem, what place in our art-world should be allotted to a creation as brilliant as it is masterly. Shortly before I had been busy reading the *Divine Comedy*, and again had revolved all the difficulties in judging this work which I have mentioned above; to me that tone-poem of Liszt's now appeared the creative act of a redeeming genius, freeing Dante's unspeakably pregnant intention from the

* Berlin, Hanover, Cassel and Wiesbaden. Not till 1881 was the *Ring des Nibelungen* performed in the German metropolis, and then in the little Victoria-theatre by Neumann's travelling company, conducted by Anton Seidl, the Intendant of the Berlin Court-theatre (von Hülsen) having declined to permit a performance at his own establishment saving under the bâton of his own incompetent conductors.—Tr.

inferno of his superstitions by the purifying fire of musical ideality, and setting it in the paradise of sure and blissful feeling. Here the soul of Dante's poem is shewn in purest radiance. Such redeeming service even *Michael Angelo* could not render to his great poetic master; only after Bach and Beethoven had taught our music to wield the brush and chisel of the mighty Florentine, could Dante's true redemption be achieved.

This work has remained as good as unknown to our age and its public. One of the most astounding deeds of music, not even the dullest admiration has as yet been accorded it. In an earlier letter upon Liszt * I tried to state the outer grounds of the German musician's abominable ill-will toward Liszt's appearance as creative composer: they need not detain us to-day; who knows the German Concert-world with its heroes from General to Corporal, knows also with what a mutual insurance-company for the talentless he here has to do. No, we will merely take this work of Liszt's and its fellows to shew by their very character their unseasonableness in the time and space of the inert present. Plainly these conceptions of Liszt's are too potent for a public that lets *Faust* be conjured up for it at the Opera by the sickly Gounod, in the Concert-room by the turgid Schumann.† Not that we would blame the public: it has a right to be what it is, especially as under the lead of its present guides it cannot be otherwise. We simply ask how conceptions like Liszt's could arise amid such circumstances of time and place. Assuredly in something each great mind is influenced by those conditions of time and place; nay, we have seen them even confuse the greatest. In the present case I at last have traced these active influences to the remarkable advance of leading minds in France during the two decads enclosing the year 1830. Parisian society at that time offered such definite and characteristic instigations to its

* Gesammelte Schriften und Dichtungen, vol. v.—R. WAGNER.—Vol. III. of the present series.—Tr.

† During a performance of the Dante Symphony in Leipzig, at a drastic passage in the first movement a piteous cry was heard from the audience: "Ei! Herr Jesus!"—R. WAGNER.

statesmen, scholars, writers, poets, painters, sculptors and musicians, that a lively fancy might easily imagine it condensed into an audience before whom a Faust- or Dante-Symphony might be set without fear of paltry misconstructions. In Liszt's courage to pen these compositions I believe I detect as determining cause the incitations of that time and local centre, nay, even their special character—and highly do I rate them, though it needed a genius such as Liszt's, superior to all time and space, to win a work eternal from those promptings, however badly it may fare just now at Leipzig or Berlin.—

To take a last look back upon the picture afforded us by the Public astir in Time and Space, we might compare it with a river, as to which we must decide whether we will swim against or with its stream. Who swims with it, may imagine he belongs to constant progress; 'tis so easy to be borne along, and he never notes that he is being swallowed in the ocean of vulgarity. To swim against the stream, must seem ridiculous to those not driven by an irresistible force to the immense exertions that it costs. Yet we cannot stem the rushing stream of life, save by steering toward the river's source. We shall have our fears of perishing; but in our times of direst stress we are rescued by a leap to daylight: the waves obey our call, and wondering the flood stands still a moment, as when for once a mighty spirit speaks unawaited to the world. Again the dauntless swimmer dives below; not life, but life's true fount, is what he thrusts for. Who, once that source attained, could wish to plunge again into the stream? From sunny heights he gazes down upon the distant world-sea with its monsters all destroying one another. What there destroys itself, shall we blame him if he now disowns it?

But what will the "public" say?—I fancy the play is over, and folk are taking leave.—

A RETROSPECT

OF THE

STAGE-FESTIVALS OF 1876.

Ein Rückblick

auf die

Bühnenfestspiele des Jahres 1876.

The following article appeared in the Bayreuther Blätter *of December 1878.*

TRANSLATOR'S NOTE.

ERHAPS I am not wrong in assuming that it will not be unwelcome to friends of the idea which found shape in the Bayreuth Bühnenfestspiels to receive a more detailed account of my personal opinion of the actual first performances that took place a little over two years back. Shortly after those performances I had occasion to address a few remarks to their existing patrons, inviting them to crown an undertaking they had already helped so far, by covering the resultant deficit. What I could only briefly express on such a cheerless errand, I now feel called to state at somewhat greater length; nor with the glad memory of that deep artistic satisfaction which I was privileged to reap shall I shrink from mingling references to the outward failure of my pains.

If seriously I ask myself, *who* enabled me to erect on the hill by Bayreuth a great stage-edifice equipped according to my wishes, a building which it must remain impossible to the whole modern theatric world to copy; as also, how in it there gathered round me the best of musical-dramatic forces, to voluntarily attempt a new, unparalleledly hard and onerous artistic task, and solve it to their own amazement—in the front rank I can only place those executant artists themselves; for it was the knowledge of their readiness to co-operate, that supplied the leverage for the efforts of the extremely few lay friends of my idea to collect the requisite material means.

Well do I remember that day in 1872 when the foundation-stone of the Bühnenfestspielhaus was laid: the chief singers from the Berlin Opera had willingly assembled, to take the scant solo-passages in the choruses of the "Ninth" Symphony; the choicest vocal unions from many a town, the finest instrumentalists of our largest orchestras, had eagerly embraced my simple friendly invitation to join in the execution of a work I wished to see regarded as the foundation-stone of my own artistic structure. Who passed that day of happy hours, must have borne away a feeling that the achievement of my further enterprise had become an object of widely-ramifying artistic and national interests. As to the artists' interest I was not mistaken: to the last moment it stayed true to me, and closely interwoven with my undertaking. In the assumption that I had also roused a national interest, however, I most certainly was at fault. And this is the point from which my actual Retrospect must start, with no idea of blame or accusation, but simply of recording an experience and fathoming its character.

The dazzling outward accompaniments of the stage-festivals at last achieved in those sunny days of the summer of 1876 might well create unusual stir on all sides. Most true it seemed, that never had an artist so been honoured; for although one had heard of such a man being called to emperors and princes, nobody could remember their ever having come to him. Many indeed might think it nothing else than sheer ambition, that fired me with the idea of my undertaking, since it surely should have contented my purely artistic needs to see my works performed in every town with lasting applause. Certainly I appeared to have been prompted by something quite outside the artist's sphere; and this theory I found expressed in the congratulations of most of my distinguished guests upon the dogged courage with which I had brought to port an enterprise in whose achievement no one had believed, and least of all their highnesses themselves. I could but perceive that it was more their wonder at the accomplished fact, than any heed of the idea inspiring all my undertaking, that had drawn on me the notice of the highest regions. Accordingly my illustrious guests might also view that greatly enviable mark of condescension as terminating their concern. After their greetings no illusion on this point could possibly occur to me, and my only astonishment was that so high an honour should ever have been conferred upon my Bühnenfestspiels.

Nor did this long remain a riddle to me, when I reflected on the mainspring to whose ceaseless activity alone I owed the material consummation of my undertaking. It was the noble devotee of my artistic ideal whose name* I divulged to my friends when I dedicated to her my pamphlet on the "Festival-playhouse at Bayreuth." Candidly I confess that without the canvass carried on with never-flagging energy by this lady of high social rank and universal estimation it would have been useless to think of obtaining the means of defraying the most elementary costs, of pursuing the enterprise at all. Untired as invulnerable, she exposed herself to sneers at her zeal, nay, to open insults from our so nicely-mannered journalism. Though folk had no faith in the mirage that inspired her, her inspiration itself it was impossible to withstand; one gave one's offering, to oblige an honoured lady. For myself, though deeply touched at this discovery, I could but feel ashamed to owe eventual success, less to belief in my work or an actual stir in the mental life of the supposedly re-awoken nation, than to the irresistible solicitations of an influential patroness. It previously had been my dearest wish to see my Festivals presented to the nation by a German Prince as a royal gift, and in my exalted protector and kingly benefactor I had found the very prince to give it full effect; but the mere report roused such a storm of opposition, that it became my duty to at least ward off the vilest insults from a princely head by voluntarily withdrawing from all attempt to carry out the project. My next proud thought was an appeal to the haply re-awoken German Spirit in those spheres to which its cultivation would necessarily seem a point of honour. I made no delay in courting the interest of the Imperial Chancellor for the pursuance of my work.

It does not ill beseem the German nature, to cherish grand illusions. Had Herr Doctor Busch by then thought fit, however, to publish the Versailles table-talk of our

* Baroness M. von Schleinitz; see Vol. V. p. 320.—Tr.

Reich's re-former, not for a moment should I have yielded to the illusion of being able to rouse those spheres to sympathy with my idea. The despatch of my brochure on "German Art and German Policy" having met no recognition, undeterred I continued my suit with a very earnestly couched request to honour at least the last two pages of my pamphlet on the "Festival-Playhouse at Bayreuth" with a perusal. The absence of all reply had to teach me that my plea for notice in the highest regions of the State was held presumptuous; in which, as I likewise saw, they maintained their never-missed accordance with the greater Press. But my indefatigable benefactress had contrived to waken, and keep awake, a benevolent interest on the part of the honoured head of our Reich. At a time of serious obstacles to the undertaking's progress I was advised to respectfully approach the Kaiser with a view to substantial assistance, though I did not decide on this step till I heard that a certain fund for the furtherance of national interests was placed at the sole and personal disposal of the suzerain. It was assured me that the Kaiser at once had granted my petition, and commanded the Imperial Exchequer accordingly; but, on the remonstrance of the President of that office for the time being, the affair had been dropped. I then was told that the Chancellor himself had known nothing at all of the matter, Herr Delbrück having kept it entirely in his own hands: nor was it any wonder that the latter should have dissuaded the Kaiser, since he was purely a man of finance and troubled himself about nothing else. Herr Falk on the other hand, of whom I thought as a possible advocate, was purely a jurist and knew of nothing else. The Exchequer directed me to the Reichstag; I replied to this advice, however, that I had meant to appeal to the grace of the Kaiser and the insight of the Reichskanzler, not to the fads of Messieurs the Deputies. Later, when the deficit had to be met, people again suggested a motion in the Reichstag, and wished the affair entrusted to the party of Progress, whose fall was always the lightest. I soon had enough of Reich and Kanzel.

Far more cheering were the efforts of those true friends of my undertaking who had founded unions in the most diverse towns of Germany, and even abroad, for the gathering of contributions. Gladly would I have called these Vereins my only truly moral supports, had an unavoidable evil not shewn itself. Owing in particular to the initial necessity of considerable building operations, our costs were too heavy to be met by the none too wealthy friends of my art themselves; I was obliged to maintain an unusual price for the Patronate-vouchers, with the result that smaller sums were clubbed together for their purchase, and each Verein distributed them among its members by ballot. As the collectors' prime aim was to enrol as large as possible a number of contributors, it was inevitable that there should be those among the latter to whom the idea of the undertaking was of no account whatever, and who could only be attracted by the prospect of a lottery-prize, to be turned into profit by sale to third parties. The evil consequences were only too evident: the seats for our festival were publicly hawked, and vended just like those for a metropolitan operatic performance. For a very large part we again had to do with a mere Opera-public, with reporters and all the other ingredients; so that all our arrangements, such as the performers' and author's refusal to make the habitual response to the so-styled "call," had lost all meaning. Once more we were criticised and pulled to pieces, exactly as if we were working for pay. But when the deficit came, and I thought right to beg my Patrons to cover the loss on an undertaking which I strictly had made over to them, I found that it really had had no patrons, but simply spectators on very dear seats. Apart from a landowner in Austrian Silesia, who most honourably regarded his patronacy as involving a higher duty, it again was only my few devoted, but now depleted personal friends, that answered my appeal. And seriously, what else could be expected, seeing that the most substantial donations had before been those obtained by my one and tireless benefactress from the Sultan and the Khedive of Egypt? Under the load of debt that weighed on me, and not upon my Patrons, I should have been altogether crushed at last, had I not once more received an aid which at the commencement of this undertaking it had been my proud desire to dispense with, but without whose active intervention a large part of even the preliminaries could never have been taken in hand; an aid from one who,* mindful of the old unworthy storm, desired that it should stay anonymous.

Such were the "Bühnenfestspiels of 1876." Who would ask me to repeat them?

Unfortunately I have had to begin by ruthlessly setting forth the outer side of the completed undertaking: for this outward state of things must be held responsible for at least the largest part of whatever did not quite succeed in the artistic execution.

"I *never* believed you would bring it about"—said the Kaiser to me. And by whom was this unbelief not shared? This it was, that caused so much unfinishedness; for in truth the loyal self-devoting artists who finally performed my work, inspired with the needful will, alone preserved their faith. Beyond these immediate executants, however, from the very first there stood by my side a man without whose ready aid I could never so much as have made a commencement. Our first concern was to build a theatre, for which the earlier Munich plans of Semper could strictly be used no farther than as they embodied my own suggestions; next, this theatre had to be provided with a stage of the most perfect adaptability to the most complex scenic movements; and finally the scenery had to be given so truly artistic a stamp, that for once we should be rid of all the fripperies of Opera and Ballet. My negotiations

* King Ludwig II. of Bavaria.—Tr.

about all this were conducted with *Karl Brandt* of Darmstadt, to whom my attention had been drawn by a characteristic incident to which I have referred elsewhere; after close examination of all the peculiarities of the project, we speedily decided that every arrangement should be taken over by this model of energy, insight and inventiveness, and thenceforth he became my mainstay in the whole realisation of my plan. It was he who recommended to me the excellent architect *Otto Brückwald*, of Leipzig, with whom he arrived at so successful an agreement upon every detail of the Bühnenfestspielhaus that this building, the only surviving witness to the soundness of my enterprise, now stands a marvel in the eyes of every expert.—The choice of a scene-painter was a matter of great anxiety until we found in the gifted Professor *Joseph Hoffmann* of Vienna the brilliant designer of those sketches after which the rising Brothers *Brückner* of Coburg, now leaping into prominence, at last prepared our decorations for the Ring des Nibelungen. Though no fault has been found with our building as yet by any intelligent person, single details in the mounting of our Festspiels have certainly roused adverse comment, especially from unintelligent wiseacres. Where individual defects resided, no one knew better than ourselves; but we also knew their origin. If the whole German Reich with its highest heads did not believe the thing would come to pass, down to the last moment, 'twas little wonder that this unbelief seized many an agent in its execution, particularly as every one of them had to suffer under the material difficulty of that insufficiency of funds which gnawed like a worm at all our labours. Despite the truly heroic efforts of our Administration (*Verwaltungsrath*), whose energy and self-sacrifice were beyond all praise, even the internal equipment of the theatre suffered many a halt, ending in a curious misunderstanding which caused my own best friends to charge me with preposterous exaggerations. By midday of the first representation of Rheingold the arrangements for illuminating the auditorium were really only so far advanced that the gas could at least be lit, though a careful regulation of the various fittings had been quite impossible. The result was, that the exact degree for lowering the lights could not be calculated, and against our will the auditorium became completely dark when we had merely meant to strongly shade it. This contretemps could not be remedied until the later repetitions of the whole festspiel: but all the reports referred to this first performance, and, after witnessing the second and third, it occurred to no one to defend us against the absurdest charges which an ungenerous criticism of those earliest days had brought upon us. We were just as unfortunate with the staging of the lindworm: this was set down as a simple buffoonery, because no one took the trouble to reflect that we had been obliged to make shift with an incomplete construction. The truth is that, German mechanicians not having had sufficient practice in that class of things, we had ordered it at great cost from a famous English maker of movable figures of beasts and giants; but, presumably owing to the general disbelief in the performances taking place at the time appointed, he delayed in sending us the separate sections of his work; so that we had to decide at the last moment upon bringing on the monster without its neck—which still lies undiscovered at one of the stations between London and Bayreuth—and the fastening of the head directly to the bulky carcase was at anyrate a great disfigurement.—Beyond these and similar troubles, no one had more cause than ourselves to deplore the unfinished state of some of the scenery. The linden-tree, whose leaves now shame us with their lifelike waving at those theatres which lately have taken the pains to mount "Siegfried," had to be hastily patched up on the spot, for our second act—and for the same reason, that eternal procrastination; whilst the closing scene of "Götterdämmerung" had to go without a proper treatment of its hinder settings for every representation.

Only a few of our spectators seem to have been so impressed by the unrivalled mass of scenery unrolled before them in endless variety during four whole days, that those relatively insignificant blemishes escaped their notice. In the name of these few I again and solemnly thank aloud the excellent collaborators in my work, above all that friend whom the cares and worries of those days almost broke down, but whose incredible energy most gloriously achieved the task begun—*Karl Brandt.*

And ever more friendly and more heartfelt will my thanks become, when I turn to memories of the only true enablers of my work, its dramatic performers and the bandsmen who so splendidly made firm the ideal ground to bear them.

Surely so single an eye to the whole, so complete an abandonment to the task in hand, has never dwelt in an artistic company. If the love of mischief ruled a large proportion of the audience at the first performances, nothing but the joy of succeeding could reward ourselves for all the cares and troubles which at times assailed our hopes of full success. And though this feeling moved us all, were it only for the pleasure of his comrades I must mention *Albert Niemann* as the fountain of enthusiasm in our bond. All would have felt impaired, had his co-operation been in doubt. Ready for each emergency, besides the rôle of *Siegmund* in the "Walküre" he offered to take over that of *Siegfried* in the "Götterdämmerung," leaving the less practised exponent of that rôle to confine himself to the youthful Siegfried of the preceding part. My predilection for a certain dramatic realism made me fear a break in the illusion, were the selfsame hero entrusted to two different interpreters on two successive nights; I declined Niemann's offer with thanks, and had sincerely to regret it; for apart from the difference in the artistic rank of the impersonators themselves, which was only to be expected, after the great exertions of the previous day the singer of Siegfried had not sufficient energy remaining for the hero of the final tragedy.—In general, also, we had great difficulties to overcome in the casting of the numerous principal characters in the work. Many a firstrate singer had I to leave unbidden, since I desired none but tall and imposing figures for my Gods, Giants and Heroes; so that it really was a stroke of luck, when it became possible to fully meet requirements in this respect as well. To everyone's surprise, even the two Nibelungen were a success in point of stature: "Mime" in particular enjoyed uncommon popularity, though I am astonished to this day that *Karl Hill's* performance as "Alberich" was rated far below its eminent worth. This latter experience only confirmed my opinion of our public's customary judgment, that at the best of times it more depends on ethical than upon artistic impressions: that Hill so completely fulfilled my urgent instructions to avoid those softer, sympathetic accents so natural to him, and give us nothing but headlong malice, greed and rage, even where he merely has to whisper as a scarce-seen ghost; that this uncommonly gifted artist hereby afforded us a character-portrait of such high perfection as has nowhere yet been met on the domain of Drama, —all this, I say, was overlooked in the repugnance of an audience of children to the wicked ogre of a fairy-tale. For my part I declare that I consider the ghostly, dreamlike dialogue between *Alberich* and *Hagen* at the commencement of the second act of the "Götterdämmerung" one of the most perfect things in our whole performance, and I regard it as a special providence that at the eleventh hour, after the withdrawal of the singer set down for the rôle of *Hagen*, I was able to obtain so capital a performer as the admirable basso *Gustav Siehr* of Wiesbaden. This artist, of whom I had never heard before, brought afresh to my knowledge the uncommon gifts there are to find among us Germans, and how easily they may be led to the most consummate exploits, if only rightly led. Siehr learnt the extraordinarily difficult part of "Hagen" in barely two weeks, and adapted himself so completely to this character in voice, enunciation, gesture, movement, gait and bearing, that he raised its acting to a masterpiece.

But if I would name a man in whose pre-eminent qualities I recognise a quite peculiar type of what the German can do on the realm of idealistic art through his inborn nature, and by his unmatched diligence and tender sense of honour, I point to the impersonator of my "Wotan," *Franz Betz.* Who more than myself had quailed at the thought of presenting in its entirety to a theatre-audience the enormously lengthy, almost monologic scene for "Wotan" in the second act of "Die Walküre"? I doubt if the greatest actor in the world would have approached a bare recital of this scene without legitimate alarm; and, though I here attested Music's power of summoning the remotest past to vivid life, the very difficulty of mastering this novel use of the musical element formed a wellnigh terrifying task; yet Betz so perfectly fulfilled it, that I may call his performance the grandest thing achieved as yet on all the field of musical dramatics. Imagine a French or Italian singer set this task, and how quickly he would have declined it as impossible. Here the Rendering—i.e. the management of voice, tone, and through these of speech itself—had to be nothing short of new-discovered, and practised with all the resources of a fertile brain. An arduous twelvemonth's preparation made my singer master of a style which he himself had first to invent for the occasion. Whichever of us witnessed the "Wanderer's" night-scenes in the second and third acts of "Siegfried" without being profoundly stirred by a thing scarce dreamt, but now become a terrible reality, we commend him to "Sir Bertram" in "Robert the Devil": to us he should never have come, and certainly no one invited him to Bayreuth.—

The master-masons of our playhouse honoured me with the gift of a large memorial tablet of black marble, which they wished to adorn the entrance to the theatre, and begged me to compose an inscription for it. I chose the form of an ordinary playbill, announcing the dates of first performance of the Bühnenfestspiel and the titles of its various pieces, with the names of the characters and their exponents; entirely in the mode of such advertisements I also named the constructors and managers of the stage-apparatus, with the conductor of the orchestra, my proved effector of impossibilities and pledge of all responsibilities, *Hans Richter*: but there was no more room on the tablet to inscribe, as I would so gladly have done, the names of all the countless helpers in my work, such as the excellent singers of the "Men," and in particular the all-fulfilling members of the band. These unnamed ones unfortunately felt sore-aggrieved: no reasonable explanation could mend the matter; to lay the storm, I had to leave the offending tablet out of sight for all the festival.—Well, I am almost afraid of falling into the same predicament to-day, if in my Retrospect I do not thank by name each one of my so valued artists. Yet I will rely on their having retained as deep an impression as myself of that last farewell upon the open stage in presence of the public, at the close of the representations; and I now will take a similar farewell of them, in thought, again. They, all of them, are the only ones who truly sped my work, the only ones to whom I look throughout the future in my not yet quite extinguished hope of a vital prospering of our Art.

That my omission of any further names will not be taken as a mark of disesteem or thanklessness by the female partners in our festival, I know for certain; for they, my admirable lady-singers—who stormed ahead of all in noble strife, like true Valkyries—never failed me in their deepest sympathy, their heartiest concern for the adventure, sincerest joy at its success. Yet I will point to two uttermost poles, between which rolled our whole performance like a mystic web of destiny encompassing a world. At the beginning, in the placid stream, the lovely "Daughters of the Rhine:" who ever saw or heard aught sweeter? At the end "Brünnhilde," tossed upon the ocean of her woe: who can remember being ever fired to warmer tragic pity, than by her?*—In all prevailed a fine enthusiastic will, begetting an artistic discipline not lightly to be matched—even by the Berlin General-Intendant,

* The "Rhine-daughters" were played by Frl. Lilli and Marie Lehmann and Frl. Lammert, "Brünnhilde" by Materna.—Tr.

who only missed among us a superior authority, without which, you know, really nothing can be done. An eye of wider range of vision might have also missed another element: a very talented singer, whom my tuition in several rôles of my operas had helped to great renown some years ago, declined to assist at our festival; writing from the Berlin Court-theatre she said, "one grows so *bad* here."

With us a magic charm made each one *good*.

And the profound conviction derived from this experience is my fairest guerdon of those days. How it may be preserved to me, to all of us, may constitute the question we next must put ourselves.

SHALL WE HOPE?

Wollen wir hoffen?
(1879.)

The following article originally appeared in the Bayreuther Blätter *for May 1879.*

TRANSLATOR'S NOTE.

HENEVER I have sat down of late to write an article for our Blätter the thought has always recurred to me, how much I already had written, printed and published, on the only thing I could have to say once more. And were I to suppose that many nevertheless would welcome a new communication from me, I still should have to fear the necessity of posing as a literary virtuoso to meet their expectations; which would involve me in the peculiar difficulty of having again and again to vary the same old theme, since I could not possibly decide on the expedient of our elegant inkpots (*Vielschreiber*) and write of things I know nothing about. I therefore could only address myself anew to persons thoroughly acquainted not only with my artistic works, but also with my former writings. Of such I might expect, however, that in future they will speak instead of me—so long at least as speaking and writing are still deemed necessary; though a most salutary end might be put to it all, if there happened to our Verein what a critic once proposed with a comedy of Iffland's, saying that it could be played no farther if one threw a purse of five-hundred thalers upon the stage in the first act. To have its due effect in our case, that purse must certainly be somewhat better lined; let us say, with the subsidies of the Prussian Court-theatre for bad operas, perhaps eked out by the amount of the Viennese Court-opera's deficit for Ballet and Italian singers. Such a remarkable occurrence might reduce our speaking and writing to a most praiseworthy minimum, to be devoted for the present to the preparation and support of the only true explainer, the deed itself.

But even if that unawaited interruption did arrive, the line lately taken by our discussions might lead, as I now am convinced, to most resultful ends beside the deed.

How easily even deeds may remain ineffectual, we have learnt from the fate of the Bayreuth Bühnenfestspiels: their sole result, so far as I can see at present, has been the incitement of many an individual to go behind the deed to its tendences. This needed a very earnest study of my writings, and it seems that these friends now think it of importance to urge others to repair a great and damaging omission in that regard.

I am quite of their opinion. In fact I never expect that other deed, the counterpart of ours, to come to pass before the thoughts which I associate with the "Artwork of the Future" have been marked, digested, and understood in their full extent.

Since those thoughts first occurred to me, and I worked them out to a broad connexion, neither life nor the concessions it has wrung from me have been able to woo me from knowledge of the rightness of my views anent the terrible defects in the relation of Art to this Life itself. To be sure, the various straits into which I fell as artist made me try, however toilsomely, to strike the rightful path on by-ways. Thus in the completion and production of the "Meistersinger"—which I at first desired to bring about in Nuremberg itself—I was governed by the idea of offering the German public a picture of its own true nature, so botched for it before; and I nursed the hope of winning from the nobler, stouter class of German burghers a hearty counter-greeting. A capital performance at the Munich Royal Court-theatre found the warmest reception; but, strange to say, it was a handful of *French* visitors who recognised the national element in my work, and greeted it as such with keen approval: nothing betrayed a like impression on that section of the Munich public here taken specially in eye. My hopes of Nuremberg, on the other hand, were disappointed out and out. True, the Director of the theatre in that town approached me with a view to acquiring the "new opera": at the same time I heard that a monument to Hans Sachs was mooted there, and I proposed to the Director that my sole honorarium should take the form of a contribution of the receipts from the first performance to the costs of erecting that statue; whereupon this gentleman did not so much as answer me. So my work took the usual tour round the other theatres: it was difficult to execute, seldom done fairly well, laid among the "operas," hissed by the Jews, and tolerated by the German public as a curiosity to be received with shakings of the head. Opposite the statue of Hans Sachs in Nuremberg there rose a sumptuous synagogue of purest Oriental style.

These were my experiences of the German burgher-world. As regards the German aristocracy, which I had addressed in my "German Art and German Policy," a former head of the Bavarian Government and very well-disposed towards me, Prince Klodwig Hohenlohe, declared to me that he would not find ten of his class to entertain my ideas: whether he made a trial with nine, or eight and a half, I am unaware. In any case an old Brahminic curse, condemning the leader of an exceptionally sinful life to rebirth as a hunter — the Brahmins' greatest horror — appears to weigh as yet on these heroic houses of Germania.

May the kindly reader pardon this digression, which I merely meant as a fairly easy illustration of that quest on by-ways alluded to above. Though these paths were those of wandering and illusion, again and again have they proved the justice of my previous estimate of Art's relation to our Life. So, un-misled by any divagation, I return to my ideas conceived just thirty years ago, and openly avow that later life-experiences have been unable to tone down aught in their expression.

This frank confession perhaps will frighten my friends of the Patronatverein. If the thoughts set down in my art-writings are to be henceforth carried out with no circumlocution, it would almost seem that I want to overthrow the whole state of things existing. But valued friends now fortunately come to my assistance, and review in our "Blätter" those dangerous essays with equal knowledge and good will. They will find it easy to dispel mistakes about me which once deceived police-officials and hurt Court-theatre Intendants; but, for sake of the art we want, it is just as essential to nurse no more illusions about the terrifying aspect of our outer and inner social life. And this last I hold the more needful, as today we have set ourselves the question: "*Shall we hope?*"

If we mean to take this question in deadly earnest, we surely must first ascertain *from whom* there might be aught to hope. We ourselves are the needy, and look around us for the helper. Nor am I the first who has declared our *State* incapable of speeding Art; rather does our great Schiller seem to me the first to have recognised and described our State-machinery as *barbaric* and utterly inimical to Art. An excellent friend,* who has recently undertaken the review of my writings for these "Blätter," with much discernment has cited the said utterances of Schiller's as prelude to his own work; please imagine them repeated as introduction to my following remarks.

Where and of whom shall we hope?

* C. F. Glasenapp in the *Bayreuther Blätter* for March 1879. The passages quoted by Glasenapp are taken from Schiller's "Letters on the Æsthetic Education of Man." Among them appear the following:—"We see, not merely individuals, but whole classes of men unfolding only *one side* of their faculties, whilst the rest are scarcely faintly outlined, like stunted plants. What single modern could step forth to battle with the single Athenian, man to man, for the prize of Manhood? The *solidarity* in our nature, which Art has destroyed, we must restore by means of a higher art. Can one expect this effect from the State? That is not possible: for the State, as at present constituted, has caused the evil. . . . So jealous is the State of the sole possession of its servants, that it would rather share its man with a *Venus Cytherea* than a *Venus Urania*. . . . All improvement in things political must start from the ennoblement of character—but how can the character grow noble under the influence of a barbaric State-system? To this end one must seek an instrument which the State does not supply. This instrument is Art, these fountains well from her immortal works. Every attempt at an alteration of the *State* will be *untimely*, and the hope based thereon *chimeric*, until the severance in the *inner* man is healed, and his nature completely developed to be itself the artist. . . . All other forms of communication *divide* Society. . . . the artistic alone unites Society, because it touches the Common-to-all." The parallelisms with Richard Wagner's "revolutionary" writings are too obvious to need pointing out.—Tr.

As their first and weightiest exercise the Jesuits set the pupils who enter their school the task of imagining with all their might and main the pains of eternal damnation, and expedite it by the most ingenious devices. A Paris workman, on the contrary, after my threatening him with Hell because he had broken his word, replied: "*O monsieur, l'enfer est sur la terre.*" Our great Schopenhauer was of the same opinion, and found our world of life quite strikingly depicted in Dante's "*Inferno.*" In truth a man of insight might deem that our religious teachers would do better to first make plain our world and life with Christian pity to their scholars, and thus awake the youthful heart to love of the redeemer from this world, instead of making —as the Jesuits—the fear of a devil-hangman the fount of all true virtue.

For an answer to the question whether we shall *hope*, in *my* sense, I certainly need my reader's inclination to follow me through the mazes of our present life with no too sanguine optimism: for him who here finds everything in order, *Art* does not exist, simply because he has no need of it. What higher guidance should he need, who founds his judgment of the things of this world on the comfortable theory of Constant Human Progress? Do or omit what he will, he is sure of always marching forward: if he sees high endeavours left resultless, in his eyes they were unserviceable to "constant progress"; for instance, if folk prefer to take their "Nibelungenring" in comfort at the theatre in their place of business, instead of facing the somewhat tiresome visit to Bayreuth, it is regarded as a sign of progress, since one no longer has to undertake a pilgrimage to something extraordinary, but the extraordinary is turned into the usual and brought to one's own door.

An eye for the Great is gladly dispensed with by the Progress-believer; the only question is whether he has replaced it by a proper eye for the Small. It is much to be feared that he no longer even rightly sees the smallest, since his loss of every ideal gauge deprives him of all power of Judgment. How correctly the Greeks beheld the smallest, because they first had rightly judged the great! But the theory of Constant Progress takes refuge in the "infinitely broader horizon" of the modern world, as compared with the narrow field of vision of the old. Admirably has the poet *Leopardi* recognised this very widening of man's horizon as the cause of mankind's loss of power to rightly apprehend the Great. To us, who stand at the centre of this infinitely extended horizon, the grandeurs that sprang from the narrower vision of the antique world are of far more crushing greatness, when once they suddenly confront us from the bowels of the earth, than ever they were to that world which saw them rise unnumbered. With justice Schiller asks what modern unit would measure himself against the Athenian, man to man, for the prize of manhood?—But the ancient world had also *religion.* Who derides antique religiousness, let him read in Plutarch's writings how this classically cultured philosopher of the later, ill-reputed era of the Romo-Grecian world expresses himself on heresy and unbelief, and he will admit that we scarce could get its equal from our theologians of the Church, to say nothing of anything better. Our world, on the contrary, is irreligious. How should a Highest dwell in us, when we no longer are capable of honouring, of even recognising the Great? And if perchance we recognise it, we are taught by our barbarous civilisation to hate and persecute it, for it stands in the way of general progress. But the Highest—what should this world have to traffic with that? How can it be asked to venerate the sorrows of the Saviour? 'Twould be as though one did not think it perfect! For sake of decency (and the widened horizon) one has patched up a sort of divine worship sufficient for the day: but what "educated" person gladly goes to church?—Before all, "Away with the Great!"—

If the Great is disliked in our so-called wider field of vision, the Small grows more and more unknowable, as I have mentioned already, since smaller day by day; as our constantly-progressive Science shews by splitting up the atoms till she can see nothing at all, which she imagines to be lighting on the Great; so that it is precisely she who feeds the silliest superstition, through the philosophisms in her train. If our Science, the idol of the modern world, could yield our State-machinery but so much healthy human reason as to find a means against the starving of fellow-citizens out of work, for example, we might end by taking her as good exchange for a church-religion sunk to impotence. But she can do nothing. And the State with its "social order" stands stock-still in the "widened circle" like a lost child, its only care to prevent its being stirred. For that it pulls itself together, makes laws and swells its armies: valour is drilled and disciplined, to guard injustice against ill consequences should need arise. When *Agesilaos*, at the time of the confined horizon, was asked which he held higher, valour or justice, he replied that he who was always just had no need at all of valour. Methinks one may call such an answer *great*: which of our lords of hosts will give it to-day, and rule thereby his policy? And yet we no longer have even the laurel-branch for valour: nor the olive-branch or palm, but merely the industry-branch which shades the whole world now beneath the shelter of strategical appliances.

But what need have we of throwing further light upon this modern world, to discover that there is nothing to be hoped of it? Ever, and under every form, will it be hostile to such wishes as we cherish for the nurture of a noble art, because the very thing we will it *wills not.* It has been my privilege to moot this subject with many a princely head: to the best-meaning it was, or was made, impossible to thoroughly change inherited custom; only with regard to Friedrich Wilhelm IV. of Prussia, when in 1847 I wished to impart my ideas to that talented monarch, was I told that after hearing me he would probably advise me to discuss the matter with his operatic regisseur Stawinsky,—and Frederick the Great would surely not have gone so far as even that. But it came to neither an audience nor a word of counsel.

In such a state of utter hopelessness one finally might follow Faust, and say: "Alone I will!" Whereupon we certainly should have to go by Mephistopheles, who answers: "I'm glad to hear it." This Mephistopheles is in our midst, and if one turns to him he gives good counsel—in his own sense. At Berlin I was advised to build my Bühnenfestspielhaus in that city, which the whole Reich would surely not have held too shabby for its domicile. There every devil of straight or crumpled horns was to stand at my disposal if I would only let things go Berlin-wise, make due concessions to the shareholders, and gaily give my representations in the winter-season, when people like to stop at home, but in no case earlier than the hour of office-closing. I saw that I had been heard indeed, but not quite rightly understood. At Munich, the metropolis of German art, folk seemed to understand me better: they read my articles in a South-German newspaper, afterwards collected in my work on "German Art and German Policy," and brought about their discontinuance; plainly they feared lest I should talk my head off. But when I kept returning to the "Alone I will!" Mephistopheles himself at last must shrug his shoulders; his straight and crumpled devils left his service, and the saving host of angels summoned to replace them could only sound a hoarse and timid whisper in the chorus of redemption. I am afraid that even with a reinforced "Alone we will!" we shall not bring things much farther, perhaps not quite so far as I did then. And my doubt has good grounds: for who would stand by us, when it concerns the realising of an idea that can bring in nothing but inner satisfaction? Only a year after the Bühnenfestspiels I declared myself again prepared to "will." I placed my knowledge and experience at disposal for guidance and practice in the rendering of German works of musical and musico-dramatic art. In a word, something like a School. It required a little money: seeing that everything was to be voluntary, this might perhaps have been collected with a little patience, and it was not its momentary absence that scared me off. But there was an almost total dearth of applications from talented young people desirous of learning something from me. This circumstance explained itself upon reflection, for the young people who might have learnt with me would nowhere have found engagement, whether at a high or low School, in an orchestra (as conductor, we will say) or even at an opera-house as singers. I certainly had a right to assume that they did not expect to learn better elsewhere, since straight and crumpled devils alike had allowed that I conducted well and knew how to obtain a proper rendering; on the other hand I had made no promise to teach composition too, as I might take it that this branch was well looked after by those followers of Beethoven who write Symphonies à la Brahms. All my pupils would therefore have had to be provided with incomes for life, to move them to the daring step of becoming penniless "Wagnerians." Here again, then, money was wanted; very much money; enough to starve out every concert-institute and opera-house. Who could venture on such gruesome things? There lies my "School" idea, and here stand I, on the verge of my sixty-seventh birthday, and confess that the "Alone I will!" grows harder to me year by year.

Yet if Mephistopheles returned once more, with the assurance that he now knew means of getting all the needful money collected by his devils, and that without concessions to shareholders, subscribers or "habitués," after many an experience I still should ask if even with the help of tons of money my goal could yet be reached. Before us lies a yawning gulf, which we dare not hope to fill at once by never so many sacks of gold. The only thing I still could have at heart would be, *to give an unmistakable example of how the qualities of the German Spirit may be brought to a manifestation such as is possible to no other people, and to commend it to the lasting shelter of a ruling social power.*—I believed I was nigh to setting that example: with but a little hearty countenance from the German's public spirit, it might have been considered quite distinct. That never came: for our public spirit is prey to a heartless weighing of For and Against; we lack all inner *Must.* And quite in opposition to Lessing's most humane, but not over "wise" *Nathan*, the veritable sage perceives the only truth in *Man must must!*

What phases of development are appointed for the German nation, it is difficult to say; under the alleged dominion of Free-will much appears to be spoilt in it. For instance, whoever attends our present free discussions of Protective Duties will find it hard of comprehension how anything inherently essential to the nation can be the upshot: one free-willed man,* at the head of a Chamber of Deputies elected by a free-willed people, will do what he thinks fit, just as a few years back he did the seeming-profitable opposite. On the other hand what *must be* will shew itself when everybody must-s for once; though, to be sure, it then will appear as an outward obligation, whereas the inner Must can only dawn on a very great mind and sympathetically productive heart, such as our world brings forth no longer. Under the spur of this fully conscious inner Must, a man so equipped would gain a power no so-called Free-will—no choice of Free-trade or Protection, let us say—could possibly withstand. This, however, is the wondrous plight into which the German Folk has fallen: whilst the Frenchman and the Englishman know quite by instinct what they will, the German doesn't, and lets himself be managed as "one" wills.

I believe I may say without presumption that the thought worked out in that essay on "German Art and German Policy" was no idle caprice of a self-deluding fancy: it took shape within me from an ever plainer recognition of the powers and qualities peculiar to the German spirit, as witnessed by a lengthy roll of German masters all striving—in my way of feeling—for that spirit's highest manifestation in an Artwork national to the human race. The importance of such an Artwork for the very highest culture of this and all other nations, once it were tended as

* Bismarck.—TR.

a living, ever new possession of our people, must strike the mind of him who has ceased to expect aught beneficial from the working of our modern State and Church machinery. If with Schiller we call them both "*barbaric*," by singular good fortune it is another great German who has rendered us the meaning of this word, and that from Holy Writ itself. *Luther* had to translate the eleventh verse of the fourteenth chapter of the first epistle of Paul to the Corinthians. Here the Greek word "*barbaros*" is applied to him whose tongue we do not understand; the Latin translator—for whom the word had already lost its Greek significance and become a mere synonym for uncivilised and lawless foreign races—sets down a half unmeaning "*barbarus*", no longer to the point. All subsequent translators, in every language, have followed the Latin example; especially weak and formal seems the French translation of the text, "*Si donc je n'entends pas ce que signifient les paroles, je serai barbare pour celui à qui je parle; et celui qui me parle sera barbare pour moi*"—from which one might deduce a maxim that governs the French to this day, and not to their advantage, in their judgment of other nations. Even in this connection, on the contrary, Luther's rendering of "*barbaros*" by "*undeutsch*" gives a milder, unaggressive aspect to our attitude towards the foreign. To the dismay of all philologists he translates the verse as follows: "If I know not the meaning (*Deutung*) of the voice, I shall be *undeutsch* to him that speaketh, and he that speaketh will be *undeutsch* to me."—Anyone who carefully collates the Greek text with this frankly faithful rendering, will perceive that the latter gives us its inner meaning even more aptly than the original itself, for it sets "Deutung" and "Deutsch" in direct relation;* and, kindled to a deep sense of the treasure we possess in our language, he will surely be filled with unspeakable sorrow when he sees its value shamefully

* A further elaboration of the same idea will be found in the article "What is German?" in vol. IV.—Tr.

debased. Yet it was recently said * that it would have been better if Luther had been burned at the stake, like other heretics; the Romish renaissance would then have taken root in Germany as well, and raised us to the same height of Culture with our reborn neighbours. I fancy this wish will strike many as not only "undeutsch", but also "barbarous" in the sense of our Romanic neighbours. Despite it we will cling to one last hope, and take Luther's "un-German" for a translation of Schiller's "barbaric", as applied to our State-and-Church machinery; then, seeking for the German Spirit's *must*, we perhaps may even light upon a glimmer of its realising.

Beside the polish of these latinised nations of Europe, and suffering under the un-German-ness of all his higher social system (*Lebensverfassung*), is the German already tottering to his fall; or dwells there in him still a faculty of infinite importance for the redemption of Nature, but therefore only cultivable by endless patience, and ripening toward full consciousness amid most wearisome delays—a faculty whose full development might recompense a new and broader world for the fall of this old world that overshadows us to-day?

That is the question; and in its answer must we seek the "Must." To us it seems as if the unity and European power the Germans lost in their fights for Reformation had to be given up that they might keep the idiosyncrasies which mark them, not for rulers, but for betterers of the world. What we *must* not, neither *can* we be. With the aid of all related branches of the German stock, we might steep the whole world in art-creations peculiar to ourselves, without ever becoming world-rulers. The use made of our late victories over the French proves this: Holland, Denmark, Sweden, Switzerland—not one of them shews dread of our predominance, albeit after such successes a Napoleon I. would easily have yoked them to the "Reich." But unfortunately we also omitted to knit these neighbours to

* By Friedrich Nietzsche in the 237th aphorism of his "*Menschliches, Allzumenschliches.*"—Tr.

us by fraternal ties, and recently an English Jew has laid us down the law.* Great politicians, so it seems, we shall never be; but haply something far greater if we rightly gauge our faculties, and make the "must" of their employment a noble master to ourselves. Where our un-German barbarians sit, we know: as the elect of "*suffrage universel*" we find them in a Parliament which knows everything but the seat of German power. Who seeks it in our armies, may be deceived by the appearance they present at this instant: in any case he would be nearer the mark, to seek it in that force which feeds these armies; and this undoubtedly is German Labour. Who cares for it? England and America are busy shewing us what German Labour is: the Americans confess that German workmen are their best mechanics. It put new life into me, to hear this lately from the minute and personal experience of an educated American of English descent. What is our "*Suffrage-universel* Parliament" doing with these German workmen? It compels the ablest hands to emigrate, and leaves the rest to rot in squalor, vice and senseless crime. We are not wise; and when some day we *must* be, things perhaps will not look nice with us, since we did not "must" from our inner heart at the proper season, but let our Free-will lead our work and play.

But what place is this for Art, where the first and foremost life-force of a nation is never tended, but sopped at most with pappy alms? We get pictures painted for us: that is all; though our most talented painters both know and admit that, compared with the great artists of earlier periods, they can never quit the rank of bunglers,—presumably for reason of the Constant Progress in which we are engaged. And how should this "progress" care aught for us who have in mind a Highest in accordance with the German's deepest nature? But we who choose to flatter ourselves with the hope that a knowledge of his true qualities will make us masters of all the German's power, how

* The Earl of Beaconsfield (then Benj. Disraeli) at the Berlin Congress.—Tr.

powerless we are against those who mock our want, since alien to them [the Jews?], and turn a scornful back upon us in feeling of their might! It is not good to join with them, for they have all the lofty arrogance of the rich towards the beggar: what care they for the "déluge" haply coming after?

Against this strange and mutually-assuring loftiness of his opponents, which could but seem invincible and unassailable to poor weak wretches trodden to the dust, *Oliver Cromwell* devised a means. The London trainbands, composed of tapsters and apprentices, could make no stand against the trusted horsemen of the boastful Royalists. "We must have a troop," said Cromwell, "instinct with a still stronger sense-of-self than theirs: and that the fear of God and stout belief alone can lend us. Let me enlist my men, and I warrant they will not be beaten." Unconquerable squadrons soon were there, and England's history began afresh. Luckily we have not to pursue this example to the length of invoking the spirit to which a king's head fell as sacrifice: neither Gideon, Samuel or Joshua, nor the God Zebaoth of the fiery bush, do we need to help us when we call awake the German Spirit in our bosoms, and strive our best to do its work. We simply have to prove all habits and opinions ruling us, and clear them of what is "barbaric"—according to Schiller—according to Luther "undeutsch"; for in "German" alone can we be true to ourselves and sincere. Let us have no fear, for instance, of Herren *Perles* and *Schmelkes* in Vienna, even though their association with Dr. *Spitz* makes us deem those pretty names mere noms-de-plume (*Spitznamen*) and suspect beneath their masks a monstrous engine of the present day [the Jews again]: these gentry's "Organ for High Schools," lately sent us for our humbling, perhaps may inflame those Schools themselves, especially in Berlin, but not the healthy burghers of Vienna—notwithstanding its visible bait for the Austrian people—when it warns against the danger of our "German craze" ("*Deutschthümelei*").

If with some knowledge, and maybe its attendant sacrifice, we mean to stick fast to the saddle against our foeman's cavalry (in Cromwell's sense), we shall have at first to pay much closer attention to the effect of the Daily Press on ourselves.

Nature *wills*, but *sees* not. Had she foreseen that Man would some day call forth artificial light and fire (a vivid instance adduced by Schopenhauer), she would have endowed the poor insects, and other animals that rush on destruction in our flame, with an instinct safe against that peril. When she gave the German his special faculties, and thereby his vocation, she could not foresee that Journal-reading would one day be invented. Artificial fire and mechanical printing are neither of them unbeneficial in themselves; but the latter at least was to plunge the German into progressive confusion. With the printing of books he loftily began to latinise, to take unto himself translated names, neglect his mother-tongue and found a literature outlandish to the common Folk, which theretofore had talked the same as knight and prince. Luther was much plagued by the printing-press: the devil of Much-printing all around him he must try to ward off by the Beelzebub of Much-writing, to find in the long run that this people for whom he had toiled so hard would, rightly looked at, be quite well suited with a Pope. Words, words—and syllables at last, mere letters, but no living belief! Yet it dropped to the writing of newspapers, and what is still more horrible, their reading. Which of our great poets and sages has not felt and deplored with increasing anguish the constant diminution in the German public's power of judgment caused by journal-reading? And to-day things have gone so far that our statesmen pay less regard to the opinions of the people's deputies, the chosen of universal suffrage, than to the dreaded lucubrations of the leader-writer. This we at last must comprehend; wonderful as it is, that Governments cannot scrape enough money together to buy up the Press, if it is really so alarming; for all is on sale in the end. Our modern Press, however, appears itself to sit on all the money of the nation: in a certain sense one might say that the nation lives on what the Press allows it. That it mentally lives on the Press, must pass as undeniable: but we also see what this mental life is like, particularly in the "widened horizon" that opens before each tobacco-stung eye in the wretched beerhouse when once the tables are well strewn with papers!

What singular delirium is it, that unfits the German to see for himself, and fosters his passionate habit of fussing with things he doesn't understand, just because they are distant? For everything he does not know he trusts the leader-writer: the latter dupes him day by day, since he merely wills but does not wit; and that again delights the journal-reader, for he also is none too particular if only he can—get newspapers to read!

I believe that we here have the deadliest bane of our social life; and I presume that many of my friends have gained a like perception. But rarely, almost never, have I lit on a definite notion, even among my friends, of how to rob this poison of its harm. Wellnigh all are of opinion that nothing can be done *without* the Press—and consequently nothing against the Press. I seem as yet to be the only one on whom it has dawned that the Press is not to be heeded; a view to which I was led by imagining what satisfaction I should reap from a success obtained through its means. My failure in Paris did me good; could success have rejoiced me, had I had to purchase it with the selfsame coin as my quaking hidden antagonist?* These Messieurs Journalists—the only men who find appointments in Germany without having passed an examination!—they live upon our dread of them; disregard, which also means contempt, to them is most annoying. A few years ago in Vienna I had to tell the company of singers in my operas that I gave them a certain explanation concerning themselves by word of mouth, because I *despised* the Press. It all was reported verbatim in the newspapers, saving that in place of "I

* Meyerbeer.—Tr.

despise the Press" one had to read "I *hate*" it. With a thing like hate they are well content, for "naturally the only man who can hate the Press is one who fears the truth!"—But even such skilful fabrications should not prevent our staying without hate in our contempt; for myself at least, it suits me admirably. The maintenance of a proper attitude towards this Paper and Pamphlet Press would therefore cost us nothing more than the resistance of all temptation to regard it; though I almost fear that even this may still prove very hard to some of my friends: they still are under the delusion that they can refute, or at least must put things right before the journal-readers. Only, it is just these readers that constitute the evil: for where would the writers be without them? That we have become a nation of newspaper-readers, in this consists our ruin. How could it occur to those literary street-arabs to smirch the Noblest with sorry jests, if they did not know that they were thus affording us agreeable entertainment? Is not a people itself precisely what it lets itself be represented? The Deputies we delegate to any kind of Chamber are our own work: did we err from ignorance in their choice, that ignorance is our crime; did we abstain from voting, our own indifference is punished; if we are obliged to elect on an evil plan, it is our fault that such laws were laid on us. In short, 'tis we ourselves who talk to us and govern us. How then can we wonder that we so are talked to, and so governed, as to rouse our ire at last? How could this "power" of the Press continue, if we simply ignored it? And how little exertion that would cost us!

Yet without exertion we cannot do. We require the strength to form other habits. The readers of "German Art and German Policy" already know my ideal of a habit of German intellectual intercourse in the noblest national sense, and I therefore have no need to enlarge on it to-day. Only give this ideal a fruitful soil in your present habits, and thence must spring a new force which in time will quite disarm that power of joint-stock literature, in so far at least as it has withstood and shattered our heartfelt wishes for ennoblement of the German public's artistic spirit. But only a most earnest endeavour, steeled by great patience and endurance, can mould such habits to a veritable sinew of our life: from a strong inner Must alone can spring the Necessity of action; and without such Necessity no true and genuine thing can be set on foot.

May my friends not misjudge myself in particular, if I set them now the first example of patience and endurance.* The very fact of our forces being still in infancy, makes me chary of premature attempts conducting to no lasting issue. That I myself have not abandoned hope, I have proved by completing the music for my "Parsifal" within the past few days. As the boundless favour of my illustrious benefactor inspired me once to draft this work, my not yet forfeited trust in the German Spirit has warmed me in its carrying out. But much, much lies before me still, and thrusts itself between the composition of my work and its making over to the public. This must be overcome; yet he who hopes with me, let him hope in my meaning alone: can a fleeting show no more suffice him, he hopes with me.

* This should be taken in conjunction with the postponement of *Parsifal* announced in July of the same year; see page 30. The "sketch" of its music was completed on April 25, 1879, the full orchestration not till Jan. 13, 1882.—Tr.

ON POETRY AND COMPOSITION.

Über das Dichten und Komponiren.

Originally published in the Bayreuther Blätter *for July 1879.*

TRANSLATOR'S NOTE.

ERHAPS also, "On the Book and Music Trade"?—

To some that may seem too outward a view of the matter. Yet the departed Gutzkow has divulged to us the awful secret that the unbounded popularity of Goethe and Schiller is simply due to the energetic speculation of their publishers.* Though this explanation should not hold water in the present case, its very advancement will teach us at least that our writers hold it possible for their own publishers to manœuvre a like success. In this way it would take a largish capital to duly plant the German "Poets'-grove"; accordingly we need not be surprised if the publisher assigns to himself the lion's share in the production of poetic works, especially of such as aim at notoriety. And thus we may assume a queer relation between poets and their publishers, in which but little mutual esteem would figure. A famous poet once assured me that publishers were the most knavish of dealers, their commerce being with none but fantastic producers, whereas all other middlemen did business exclusively with folk as cunning as themselves. At anyrate the case seems pretty bad. To ensure renown, the poet or composer thinks best to seek the ægis of some great firm of publishers. Such a firm has to spend a fortune on enormous establishments for printing or note-engraving; these must be always kept at work, with result that the publisher is obliged to risk the manufacture of a deal of useless stuff; often no journalism in the world can help him to dispose of it: but for once he hits on a remarkably happy article, the work of a brain above the common. With the success of this one article the publisher recoups himself for all his previous losses; and if the author wants to have his portion

* See Glasenapp's article in the *Bayreuther Blätter* for March, 1879, already mentioned on page 116.—Tr.

of the profits, the publisher can coolly shake him off with the retort that he had borne no part in the expenses attending a perpetual output of rubbish. On the other hand, it is just this perpetual output that hoists the publisher to eminence. Everybody nowadays writes poetry or music, whilst the big firm must be constantly printing and issuing: the two habits and necessities complete each other; but the publisher has the advantage, in that he can shew his clients how much he loses and at like time prove his generosity by declaring himself quite ready to proceed with further issues, thereby making the "fantastic" author his very humble servant. Thus the book and music publisher, the poet and composer's wage-giver—nay, their populariser, under circumstances, as alleged of Schiller and Goethe—may with some reason be regarded as the patron-saint, if not the creator, of our poetic and musical literature.

Maybe it is this flourishing state of the book and music printing-house, to which we owe the strange phenomenon that almost every person who has heard or read a thing must promptly fly at poetry or composition. Often have I heard the complaint from university-professors that their students no longer will learn what they should, but mostly play at scribbling or composing. This was peculiarly the case at Leipzig, where the book-trade so closely elbows erudition that one almost might ask *which* strictly has our modern education most in hand, the University or the Book-mart; for plainly one can learn from books the same or even more than from professors, whilst these latter are so short-sighted as to print in low-priced monographs their whole stock-in-trade of information. The passion of our lecture-glutted students for writing verse and tunes, upon the other hand, we might compare with that extraordinary love of play-acting which from the dawn of German histrionic art to the commencement of our present century lured sons and daughters from the best-respected families. In the last regard our young people appear to have grown more philistine, perchance from fear of making themselves ridiculous upon the boards; a personal discomfiture now more and more relinquished to the Jews, who seem to take less account of unpleasant experiences. But poetry and composition can be plied quite quietly and peaceably at home: nor do we notice how foolish our lyric spoutings make us look in type, since luckily no reader finds us out. The thing does not become perceptibly absurd, till read aloud. In my time the Leipzig students made a butt of a poor devil whom they would get to declaim his poems in return for the settling of his score; they had his portrait lithographed, above the motto: "Of all my sufferings Love is cause." Some years ago I told the story to a well-known poet of our day, who since has taken a strange dislike to me: too late I learnt that he had a new volume of poems in the press at that very moment.

Touching the "German Poets'-grove," one latterly finds that, despite the need of keeping their machinery in constant motion, the publishers are growing more and more averse to lyric poems, since the lyrical musicians still keep composing nothing but "*Du bist wie eine Blume*" or "*Wenn ich dein holdes Angesicht*," and so forth. How matters stand with "epic poetry," is also difficult to judge: a mass of it is thrown upon the market, and moreover set to music for our Subscription-concerts by composers who still have a bone to pick with Opera—a course alas! found hitherto impossible with the "Trompeter von Säckingen." * —That all this "brings in" much, it is not easy to believe; for there still are very many dwellers in Germany who never subscribe to such concerts. "Dramatic poems," on the contrary, have certainly a larger public; that is to say, when they are produced on the stage. But among theatrical directors one meets the wildest craving for returns; here still prevails the barbaric justice of "God's verdict," and that is not so lightly "bought." Only to

* The poem by J. V. von Scheffel (1853), author also of the novel "Ekkehard," etc., etc. A stupid play was made from this poem by E. Hildebrandt and J. Keller, with vocal pieces by one Brenner; but not till the year after Wagner's death did Victor Nessler's washy but popular opera on the same subject appear.—Tr.

English publishers has it been possible to use the theatre for bold and most ingenious advertisement. The sole article of any service to the English music-trade is a "Ballad" modelled more or less on the street-singer's genre, which, fortune favouring, is sold in several hundred-thousand copies to all the colonies as "the very latest." To get this ballad duly famed the publisher spends money on the composition of an entire opera, pays the manager for its performance, and then proceeds to give the mounted ballad out to all the barrel-organs of the land, till every pianoforte yearns at last to have it in the house. Who calls to mind our native "Einst spielt ich mit Zepter," might think that German printers also were no fools, and knew what they were about with a full-fledged "Zar und Zimmermann":* the "Czar" finds work for the engravers, and the "Sceptre-player" pays them.

Nevertheless the penning of complete dramas appears to have a mighty charm for old and young, and it is remarkable how every author believes he has done wonders with the stalest subject, under the illusion, maybe, that it had never been rightly treated by his predecessors. The five-foot Iambic, jogging on in honour indestructible, must still confer upon the diction its true poetic flavour; though naked prose, the less select the better, affords more chance of the piece's acceptance by Directors. The five-footed dramatist has therefore to depend, in general, on the favour of the publisher who must always be printing; so that one may assume his only interest is "a hobby." I scarcely think that very great poets thus come to light: how Goethe and Schiller began, God only knows—unless some information could be gleaned from the firm of Cotta, who once declined to issue my Gesammelte Schriften because they still had their hands so full with Goethe and Schiller.—

But the above, are they not all mere foibles of our poets? Though a true inhabitant of our Poets' grove in

* By G. A. Lortzing, 1837.—Tr.

youth may twitter his verse and rhymes in childlike imitation of the songsters on the branches, with the *toga virilis* he blooms into a *novelist,* and learns at last his business. Now the publisher seeks out *him,* and he knows how to put his price up: he is in no such hurry to hand his three, his six or nine volumes to the lending-libraries; first comes the journal-reader's turn. Without a "solid" Feuilleton, with theatrical criticisms and thrilling romances, even a political world-sheet cannot well subsist; on the other side, what receipts these newspapers drag in, and what a figure they can pay! Engrossed in true creation, my friend *Gottfried Keller* forgot in his day to heed those paper birth-throes of his works; it was most obliging of an already-famous novelist, who regarded Keller as his equal, to instruct him how to make a novel bring in money: manifestly the officious friend beheld in the unbusinesslike poet a terrible case of wasted energy, on which he could not look without a pang. The incorrigible poet (in jest we called him "Auerbach's Keller") did not at anyrate get very far in the race for issues: it was only the other day that a second edition appeared of his romance "der grüne Heinrich," first published thirty years ago; in the eyes of our wideawake authors a manifest failure—in fact, proof positive that Keller had not risen to the level of the day. But they, as said, know better. And so the swarm in our Poets'-grove is so thick that one cannot see the trees for numberless editions.

In this highly prosperous activity of our modern poet-world, however, we light upon that element to which all poetry owes its source, its very name. The *narrator* in truth is the "poet" proper, whereas the subsequent elaborator of the narrative should rather be regarded as the *artist.* Only, if we are to accord to our flourishing novelists the boundless significance of genuine poets, that significance itself must first be somewhat more precisely defined.

The old world, speaking strictly, knew but one poet, and named him "*Homeros.*" The Greek word "*Poietes,*" which the Latins—unable to translate it—reproduced as "Poeta," recurs most naïvely among the Provençals as "Trouvère," and suggested to our Middle-high Germans the term of "Finder," Gottfried von Strassburg calling the poet of *Parzival* a "Finder wilder Märe" ("finder of strange tales"). That "poietes"—of whom Plato averred that he had found for the Greeks their gods—would seem to have been preceded by the "Seer," much as the vision of that ecstatic shewed to Dante the way through Hell and Heaven. But the prodigy of the Greeks' sole poet—"the" —seems to have been that he was seer and poet in one; wherefore also they represented him as blind, like Tiresias. Whom the gods meant to see no semblance, but the very essence of the world, they sealed his eyes; that he might open to the sight of mortals that truth which, seated in Plato's figurative cavern with their backs turned outwards, they theretofore could see in nothing but the shadows cast by Show. This poet, as "seer," saw not the actual (*das Wirkliche*), but the true (*das Wahrhaftige*), sublime above all actuality; and the fact of his being able to relate it so faithfully to hearkening men that to them it seemed as clear and tangible as anything their hands had ever seized—this turned the Seer to a Poet.

Was he "*Artist*" also?

Whoso should seek to demonstrate the *art* of Homer, would have as hard a task before him as if he undertook to shew the genesis of a human being by the laborious experiments of some Professor—supramundane, if you will —of Chemistry and Physics. Nevertheless the work of Homer is no unconscious fashioning of Nature's, but something infinitely higher; perhaps, the plainest manifestation of a godlike knowledge of all that lives. Yet Homer was no Artist, but rather all succeeding poets took their art from him, aad therefore is he called "the Father of Poetry" (*Dichtkunst*). All Greek genius is nothing else than an artistic réchauffé (*Nachdichtung*) of Homer; for purpose of this réchauffé, was first discovered and matured that "Techne" which at last we have raised to a general principle under name of *the Art of Poetry*, wrongheadedly including in it the "poietes" or "Finder der Märe."

The "*ars poetica*" of the Latins may rank as art, and from it be derived the whole artifice of verse-and-rhyme-making to our present day. If *Dante* once again was dowered with the Seer's eye—for he saw the Divine, though not the moving shapes of gods, as Homer—when we come to *Ariosto* things have faded to the fanciful refractions of Appearance; whereas *Cervantes* spied between the glintings of such arbitrary fancies the old-poetic world-soul's cloven quick, and sets that cleavage palpably before us in the lifelike actions of two figures seen in dream. And then, as if at Time's last stroke, a Scotsman's "second sight" grows clear to full clairvoyance of a world of history now lying lost behind us in forgotten documents, and its facts he tells to us as truthful fairy-tales told cheerily to listening children. But from that *ars poetica*, to which these rare ones owed no jot, has issued all that calls itself since Homer "Epic poetry"; and after him we have to seek the genuine epic fount in tales and sagas of the Folk alone, where we find it still entirely undisturbed by art.

To be sure, what nowadays advances from the feuilleton to clothe the walls of circulating libraries, has had to do with neither art nor poesy. The actually-experienced has at no time been able to serve as stuff for epic narration; and "second sight" for the never-witnessed does not bestow itself on the first romancer who passes by. A critic once blamed the departed Gutzkow for depicting a poet's love-affairs with baronesses and countesses, "things of which he certainly could never have had any personal experience"; the author most indignantly replied by thinly-veiled allusions to similar episodes that actually had happened to himself. On neither side could the unseemly folly of our novel-writing have been more cryingly exposed.—*Goethe*, on the other hand, proceeded in his "Wilhelm Meister" as the artist to whom the poet had refused his collaboration in discovery of a satisfactory ending; in his "Wahlverwandschaften" the lyric elegist worked himself into a seer of souls, but not as yet of living shapes. But what Cervantes had seen as *Don Quixote* and *Sancho Pansa*, dawned on Goethe's deep world-scrutiny as *Faust* and *Mephistopheles*; and these shapes beheld by his ownest eye now haunt the seeking artist as the riddle of an ineffable poet's-dream, which he thought, quite un-artistically but thoroughly sincerely, to solve in an impossible *drama*.

There may be something to learn from this, even for our members of the "German Poets'-grove" who feel neglected by their none too ardent publishers. For alas! one must say of their novels, their spirit's ripest fruits, that they have sprung from neither life nor tradition, but simply from theft and traduction. If neither the Greeks at their prime, nor any later great nation of culture, such as the Italians and Spaniards, could win from passing incidents the matter for an epic story, to you moderns this will presumably come a trifle harder: for the events they witnessed, at least were real phenomena; whilst ye, in all that rules, surrounds and dwells in you, can witness naught but masquerades tricked out with rags of culture from the wardrobe-shop and tags from the historical marine-store. The seer's eye for the ne'er-experienced the gods have always lent to none but their believers, as ye may ascertain from Homer or Dante. But ye have neither faith nor godliness.

So much for "Poetry."—Now let us see what "Art" can offer in our days of progressed Culture.—

We came to the conclusion that all Greek genius was but an artistic re-editing of Homer, whilst in Homer himself we refused to recognise the *artist*. Yet Homer knew the "Aoidos"*; nay, he himself perhaps was "*singer*" also?—To the sound of heroic songs the chorus of youths approached the mazes of the "imitative" dance. We know the choral chants to the priestly ceremonies, the dithyrambic choral dances of the Dionysian rites. What

* According to Liddell and Scott, "a singer, minstrel, bard; Homer, ἀοιδὸς ἀνήρ, Odyssey 3, 267. In the heroic age they are represented as inspired, and under divine protection."—Tr.

there was inspiration of the blind seer, becomes here the intoxication of the open-eyed ecstatic, before whose reeling gaze the actuality of Semblance dissolves to godlike twilight. Was the "musician" *artist?* I rather think he *made* all Art, and became its earliest lawgiver.

The shapes and deeds beheld by the blind poet-teller's second sight could not be set before the mortal eye save through ecstatic palsy of its wonted faculty of seeing but the physical appearance: the movements of the represented god or hero must be governed by other laws than those of common daily need, by laws established on the rhythmic ordering of harmonious tones. The fashioning of the tragedy belonged no more in strictness to the poet, but to the lyrical musician: not one shape, one deed in all the tragedy, but what the godlike poet had beheld before, and "told" to his Folk; merely the choregus led them now before the mortal eye of man itself, bewitching it by music's magic to a clairvoyance like to that of the original "Finder." The lyric tragedian therefore was not Poet, but through mastery and employment of the highest art he materialised the world the poet had beheld, and set the Folk itself in his clairvoyant state.—Thus "mus-ical" art became the term for all the gifts of godlike vision, for every fashioning in illustration of that vision. It was the supreme ecstasy of the Hellenic spirit. What remained when it had sobered down, were nothing but the scraps of "Techne"—no longer Art, but the arts; among which the art of versifying was to present the strangest sight in time, retaining for the position, length or brevity of syllables the canons of the musical Lyric, without an idea of how it had sounded. They are preserved to us, these "Odes"; with other prosaic conceits of the *ars poetica*, they too are labelled "poet-works"; and down through every age have people racked their brains with filling maps of verses, words and syllables, in the belief that if these only look a little glib in the eyes of others—and finally their own—they have really written "poetry."

We have no need to linger with this *ars poetica*, for we

shall never meet the *poet* there. With its practice *Wit* invaded poetry: the old didactic sentence—which still might run on lines of priest's or people's *melody*, as in the Pythia's oracles — became an Epigram; and here the artistic verse, with its really clever rhymes of nowadays, found fit employment. Goethe, who gave to everything a trial, down to his own disgust with the hexameter, was never happier in verse and rhyme than when they served his wit. Indeed one cannot find that the discardal of this artifice of verse has made our "poets" shine more: had it been applied to the "Trompeter von Säckingen," for instance, that epic would certainly not have gone through sixty editions, but probably would have made more dainty reading; whereas the jingling rhymes of H. Heine themselves still yield a certain pleasure. On the whole, our generation's love of verse-making appears to spring from an innate imbecility to which the attention of parents and tutors should be directed; if after thrashing through our youthful poets you light upon a young Ovid who really can write verses, by all means let him off, as we still prefer the witty epigrammist on our field of Literature, though not on that of—*Music.*

Music!—

Unutterably hard as is the task, we have already tried from time to time to throw some light on this, but not as yet upon the special point of "Composition."

Music is the most witless thing conceivable, and yet we now have wellnigh naught but witty composition. I suppose that this has come about for love of our dear littérateurs, Herr Paul Lindau in particular, who only asks amusement from all Art, as I am told, since otherwise it bores him. But strange to say, it is precisely our amusing music that is the greatest bore of all (just think of a piece entitled a "Divertissement" at any of our concerts), whereas—say what you will—a completely witless Symphony of Beethoven's is always too brief for every hearer. Methinks, at bottom lies a fatal error of our newspaper-reporters' system of Æsthetics. It is not to be expected that we shall win over our champions of musical amusement to another taste; nevertheless, quite among ourselves, we will once more devote a few words to the un-witty side of Music.

Have not the results of many an inquiry already plainly taught us that Music indeed has nothing to do with the common seriousness of life; that its character, on the contrary, is sublime and grief-assuaging radiance (*Heiterkeit*); ay—that it smiles on us, but never makes us laugh? Surely we may call the A-major Symphony of Beethoven the brightest thing that any art has e'er brought forth: but can we imagine the genius of this work in any but a state of loftiest transport? Here is held a Dionysos-feast such as only on the most ideal of suppositions can the Greek have ever celebrated: let us plunge into the rushing tumult, the frenzy of delight, we never leave the realm of lofty ecstasy, high as heaven above the soil where Wit rakes up its meagre fancies. For here we are in no masquerade, the sole amusement of our leathern world of Progress; here we accost no privy-councillor dressed up as a Don Juan, whose recognition and dismasking causes boundless fun: no, here appear those truthful shapes that shewed themselves in moving ranks of heroes to *blind* Homer, in ranks which now *deaf* Beethoven makes call aloud the mind's enraptured eye to see them once again.

But look! the amusement-hunting journal-cavalier sits there; his eyes are only for the quite material: he perceives nothing, nothing at all: to him the time grows long, whereas to us the time of respite from all which that man sees was far too short, too fleeting. So give him his amusement! Crack jokes, ye bold musicians too; disguise yourselves and put a mask on! Compose, compose, even though nothing occur to you! Why should it be called "composing"—putting together—if invention too is requisite? But the more tedious ye are, the more contrast must ye put into your choice of masks: 'twill amuse again. I know renowned composers you shall meet to-day at concert-masquerades in garb of a street-minstrel ("Of all my sufferings" etc.), to-morrow in the Hallelujah-perruque of a Händel, the day after as a Jewish tuner-up of Czardas, and later as solemn symphonist disguised in a number ten. You laugh:—and well you may, you witty hearers! But those gentlemen themselves take things so seriously, nay, strictly, that it became necessary to pick out one of them * and diploma him the Prince of Serious Music of our day, expressly to stop your laughter. Perhaps, however, that only adds to it? For this serious music-prince would long ago have struck you as most wearisome, had you sly ones not taken a peep behind the mask, and discovered that it hid no such mighty dignitary, but just a person like yourselves; so you now can go on playing masks again, pretending that you marvel at him, while it amuses you to see the mouths he makes as if he quite believed you. Yet what lies at deepest bottom of all this entertaining game of masks, should also be openly stated. The suave, but somewhat philistine *Hummel* once was asked what lovely landscape he had thought of when composing a certain charming Rondo: to tell the simple truth, he might have answered—a beautiful fugal theme of Bach's in C-sharp major; only, he was still more candid, and confessed that the eighty ducats of his publisher had swum before his eyes. The witty man; with him one might have dealings!

Taken strictly, however, the joke is not in the music, but in the composer's pretence of having written finely, with the resulting quid-pro-quo's. In the aforesaid masque one can scarcely consider *Mendelssohn* included. He was not always frank of speech, and liked evasion; but he never lied. When asked what he thought of Berlioz' music, he answered: "Every man composes as well as he can." If he did not compose his choruses to *Antigone* as finely as his Hebrides-overture—which I hold for one of the most beautiful musical works that we possess—the reason was, that it was the very thing he could not. In view of this instance, and alas! of many similar, his followers may inherit from Mendelssohn the *cold-blooded recklessness* with

* Johannes Brahms.—Tr.

which they have tackled every kind of composition, resembling that old General of Frederick the Great's who sang whatever was set before him to the tune of the Dessauer March; for the greatest itself they could but squeeze with calm indifference into the diminutive bed of their talent. It certainly was always their intention, to turn out something good; only, their fate has been the opposite to that of Mephistopheles, who ever willed the bad but did the good. Assuredly they each desired to bring to pass for once a real true *melody*, one of those Beethovenian *shapes* that seem to stand complete before us with every member of a living body. But what was the use of all *ars musicæ severioris*, nay, even of *musicæ jocosæ*, when the shape would not be conjured up, still less composed? All that we find recorded there looks so very like the shapes of Beethovenian music, as often to seem copied outright: and yet the most artful concoction declines to produce an effect even remotely approaching the almost ridiculously insignificant

which has not a word to say to art, but at every concert wakes from lethargy to sudden ecstasy an audience never so fatigued before! Plainly a little malice of the public's, which one must correct by strenuous application of the rod. My quondam colleague in the Dresden Kapellmeistership, Gottlieb Reissiger the composer of Weber's Last Thought, once bitterly complained to me that the selfsame melody which in Bellini's "Romeo e Giulia" always sent the public mad, in his own "Adèle de Foix" made no effect whatever. We fear that the composer of the last idea of Robert Schumann would have a like misfortune to bewail.—

It seems we here have quite a curious case: I am afraid, to fully fathom it would lead us to the edge of mystical abysses, and make those who chose to follow us seem

Dunces in the eyes of our enlightened music-world, as which—according to Carlyle's experience—the Englishmen regard all Mystics. Luckily, however, the sorrows of our present composing world are largely explicable in the sober light of sociology, which lets its cheering sunrays even pierce the cosy covert of our Poet-groves and Composer-hedges. Here everything is originally without guile, as once in Paradise. Mendelssohn's fine saying: "Every man composes as well as he can"—is deemed a wise provision, and really never overstepped. Guile first begins when one wants to compose better than one can; as this cannot well be, at least one gives oneself the air of having done so: that is the mask. Nor does that do so much harm: things worsen only when a number of good people—Principals and the like—are actually deluded by the mask, with Hamburg banquets, Breslau diplomas and so forth, as the outcome; for this illusion is only to be compassed by making folk believe that one composes better than others who really do compose well. Yet even this is not so very dreadful, after all; for we may generalise Mendelssohn's dictum into "Every man *does* what and how he can." Why make such fuss about the falsification of artistic judgment or musical taste? Is it not a mere bagatelle, compared with all the other things we falsify, wares, sciences, victuals, public opinions, State culture-tendences, religious dogmas, clover-seed, and what not? Are we to grow virtuous all of a sudden in Music? When a few years back I was rehearsing the Vienna company in two of my operas, the first tenor complained to a friend of mine about the unnaturalness of my request that he should be virtuous for six whole weeks, and regular in his habits, whilst he knew quite well that so soon as I had gone away he could only hold on by the common operatic vice of looseness. This artist was right in denouncing virtue as an absurd demand. If our composers' delight in the show of their excellence, their chastity and kinship to Mozart and Beethoven, were only possible without the need to vent their spite on others, one might grudge them nothing; nay, even this bad trait does not much matter in the long run, since the personal injury thus inflicted will heal in time. That the acceptance of the empty for the sound is cretinising everything we possess in the way of schools, tuition, academies and so on, by ruining the most natural feelings and misguiding the faculties of the rising generation, we may take as punishment for the sloth and lethargy we so much love. But that we should pay for all this, and have nothing left when we come to our senses—especially considering how we Germans pride ourselves on being somebodies—this, to be frank, is abominable!—

On the side last touched—the ethical, so to speak—of our poetising and composing, enough has been said for to-day. I am glad to think that a continuation of these notes will take me to a region of both art-varieties where we meet great talents and noble minds, and therefore have only to point out failings in the genre itself, not cant and counterfeiting.

ON OPERA POETRY AND COMPOSITION IN PARTICULAR.

Über das
Opern-Dichten und Komponiren
im Besonderen.

Originally published in the Bayreuther Blätter *for September 1879.*

TRANSLATOR'S NOTE.

PROPOS of sundry experiences, it has struck me how little the audience at opera-performances was acquainted with the matter of the plot. High-classic operas, like "Don Juan" and "Figaro's Hochzeit," came out of it very well with uncorrupted youthful hearers, especially of the female sex, protecting them from any knowledge of the frivolities in the text—a thing which guardians and teachers may probably have counted on when they expressly commended those works to their pupils as a model of pure taste. That the happenings in "Robert the Devil" and the "Huguenots" were intelligible to none but the inmost circle of initiates, had much in its favour; but that the "Freischütz" too should remain in shadow, as I lately discovered, amazed me till a little thought convinced me that, although I had conducted this opera any number of times in the orchestra, I myself was still quite hazy as to many a passage in the text. Some laid the blame on our singers' indistinctness of delivery; when I objected that in dialogic operas such as "Freischütz," "Zauberflöte," ay, and our German translations of "Don Juan" and "Figaro," everything that explains the action is simply spoken, I was reminded that the singers of our day speak indistinctly too, and also that, for this very reason perhaps, the dialogue is abridged to unintelligibleness. Nay, that here one passed from bad to worse; for with operas "composed throughout" one at least could arrive at sufficient understanding of the scenic action by assistance of the textbook, whereas in "aria-books" of dialogic operas such an aid was not forthcoming.—I have remarked that for the most part the German audience learns nothing at all of what the poet really meant with his libretto; often enough, not even the composer appears to know. With the French it is otherwise: there the first question is as to the "pièce"; the play must be entertain-

ing in and for itself, save perhaps with the lofty genre of "Grand Opera," where Ballet has to provide the fun. The texts of Italian operas, on the other hand, are fairly trivial as a rule, the virtuoso-doings of the singer appearing to be the main concern; yet the Italian singer cannot rise to the level of his task without a remarkably drastic enunciation, quite indispensable to his vocal phrasing, and we do the Italian operatic genre a great injustice when we slur the text of arias in our German reproduction. Mechanical as is the Italian type of operatic composition, I still have found that it all will have a better effect when the text is understood than when it isn't, since a knowledge of the situation and exact emotion will advantageously ward off the effect of monotony in the musical expression. Only with Rossini's "Semiramide" was even this acquaintance of no help to me; Reissiger's "Dido abandonata," which earned its composer the favour of a Saxon monarch, I do not know—any more than F. Hiller's "Romilda."

According to the above observations one might simply attribute the German public's love of opera-performances to its pleasure in hearing the separate 'numbers,' as purely melodic entities per se. Now, the Italians long ago attained great skill in manufacturing such pieces, so that it was very late before the German composer dared to vie with them. When Mozart had to compose the "Zauberflöte" he was worried by a doubt if he would do it right, as he "had composed no magic operas before." With what aplomb, on the contrary, he treated "*le nozze di Figaro*": on the set foundation of Italian *opera buffa* he reared a building of such perfect symmetry, that he well might decline to sacrifice a single note to his cut-demanding Kaiser. What the Italian threw in as banal links and interludes between the 'numbers' proper, Mozart here drastically employed to animate the situation, in striking harmony with just this exceptionally finished comedy-text that lay before him. As in the Symphony of Beethoven the very pause grows eloquent, so here the noisy half-closes and cadences which might well have held aloof from the

Mozartian Symphony give a quite irreplaceable life to the scenic action, where craft and presence of mind fight—lovelessly!—with passion and brutality. Here the dialogue becomes all music, whilst the music converses; a thing that certainly was only possible through the master's developing the orchestra to such a pitch as never before, and perhaps to this day, had been dreamt of. On the other hand the earlier isolated pieces became thereby fused into what appeared so complete a work of music's that the admirable comedy on which it stood might finally be altogether overlooked, and nothing heard but music. So it seemed to our musicians; and Mozart's "Figaro" was given more carelessly and indistinctly day by day, till at last we have dropped to a mode of performing this work itself that leaves our teachers no scruple about sending their pupils to the theatre on Figaro nights.

We will not discuss again to-day the effect of these instances of public vandalism on the German's sensibility to the genuine and correct; but it cannot be unimportant to note their misleading influence on the drafts and finished products of our operatic poets and composers. Forsaking all their native field, they first must seek an entrance to the ready-made Italian Opera; which could only lead to the nearest possible imitation of the Italian "cabaletta," with the abandonment of every broader mode of musical conception. Upon due "rhyme and reason" of the whole no weight was to be laid: had it done any harm to the "Zauberflöte," composed for a German text and spoken with German dialogue, that the villain was suddenly changed to a hero, the originally good woman to a bad one, making utter nonsense of what had happened in the first act? Only, it fell hard to the German genius to master the Italian "cabaletta." Even *Weber* in his earliest youth still tried in vain to make something of the "coloratura" aria, and it needed the heart-stirring years of the War of Liberation to set the singer of Körner's lays on his own feet. What we Germans received with the "Freischütz," has fallen to few nations' lot.

Yet we are not about to trace the historic evolution of German Opera—which I have already discussed at length elsewhere—but rather to explain the peculiar difficulty of that evolution by this Opera's fundamental faults. The chief of these I find in the criminal *vagueness* that has disfigured all our opera-performances from the beginning to this day, as I stated from personal experience in my prefatory words, and whose cause—the librettist's and composer's involuntarily accustomed standard for the degree of plainness needful to an operatic story—has been touched on in the previous paragraphs. The so-called "*Tragédie lyrique*," which reached the German from abroad, remained indifferent and unintelligible to him so long as the "Aria" did not take his fancy by its marked melodic structure. This Aria form of melody passed over into German Opera as the sole aim and end of the composer, and necessarily also of the poet. The latter felt that he might take his ease in the text for an aria, as the composer had his own musical scheme of extension, interchange and repetition of themes, and needed an entirely free hand with the words, which he would repeat at pleasure either as a whole or in part. Long lines could only hamper the composer, whilst a strophe of about four lines was ample measure for one section of an aria. The verbal repetitions necessary to fill out the melody, conceived quite apart from the verse, even gave the composer opportunity for pleasant variations of the so-called "declamation" through a shifting of accents. In Winter's "Opferfest" we find this rule observed throughout: there the "Inka," for instance, sings one after the other

> Mein *Leben* hab' ich ihm zu danken—
> mein Leben *hab'* ich ihm su danken ;

and repeats a question in the form of answer:

> Muss nicht der Mensch auch menschlich sein?—
> Der Mensch muss menschlich sein.

Marschner once had the grave misfortune, in his "Adolf

von Nassau," to triplicate the part of speech "hat sie" ("has she") on a particularly incisive rhythmic accent:

Even Weber could not avoid the temptation to vary the accent: his "Euryanthe" sings: "Was ist mein Leben gegen *diesen* Augenblick," and repeats it as: "Was ist mein Leben gegen diesen *Aug*enblick"! This sort of thing leads the hearer away from any serious following of the words, without affording adequate compensation in the purely musical phrase itself; for in most cases it is a mere question of musico-rhetorical flourishes, such as shew out the naïvest in Rossini's eternal "Felicità"s.

It seems, however, that it was not solely a delight in free command of flourishes, that prompted the composer to his arbitrary dealings with morsels of the text; no, the whole relation of our imaginary Verse to the truthfulness of musical Accent placed the composer from the first in the alternative of either declaiming the text in strict accordance with the accent of daily speech and common sense, which would have resolved the verse with all its rhymes into naked prose; or, regardless of that accent, completely subjecting the words to certain dance-schemes, and giving free rein to melodic invention. The results of this latter method were far less disturbing, or even destructive, with the Italians and French than with ourselves, because their speaking-accent is incomparably more accommodating and, in particular, not bound to the root-syllable; wherefore also, they do not weigh the feet in their metres, but simply count them. Through our bad translations of their texts, however, we had acquired from them that peculiar operatic jargon in which we now thought fit, and even requisite, to declaim our German lines themselves. Conscientious composers were certainly disgusted at last with this frivolous maltreatment of our tongue: but it never yet struck them that even the verse of our first-class poets was no true, no melody-begetting verse, but a mere elaborate sham. *Weber* declared it his duty to faithfully reproduce the text, yet admitted that, were he always to do so, he must say goodbye to his melody. In fact it was just this upright endeavour of Weber's to preserve the set divisions of the verse-text and thereby make the thought intelligible, which, coupled with his adherence to a melodic pattern for the resulting incongruences, led to that indistinctness whereof I promised an example from my experience. This occurs in Max's *Arioso* in the "Freischütz": "Durch die Wälder, durch die Auen." Here the poet had committed the egregious blunder of furnishing the composer with the following verse:

> "Abends bracht' ich reiche Beute,
> Und wie über eig'nes Glück—
> Drohend wohl dem Mörder—freute
> Sich Agathe's Liebesblick."

Now, Weber really takes the trouble to phrase these lines in strict accordance with their sense and sequence: he therefore makes a break after the parenthesis "drohend wohl dem Mörder," and begins the closing line with "freute"; but as that makes the line much longer, he feels obliged to employ the verb—so important for a connection with the second line—as a preliminary 'arsis' (*Auftakt*); whereas the pronoun "sich," merely introduced to supplement the verb, receives the stronger accent of the following beat. This certainly has resulted in an entrancing strain of melody:

Not only is the poet's verse as such, however, revealed as an absurdity, but, for all the distinctness of its musical phrasing, the *sense* has become so hard of understanding that, accustomed to merely hear it sung, it was only after this unintelligibleness had one day struck me, that I discovered the true connection of ideas. A similar difficulty arises in further course of the same aria through the favourite poetic trick of disassociating words for sake of rhyme; and here the composer unfortunately makes things worse by repeating the parenthesis:

> "Wenn sich rauschend Blätter regen,
> Wähnt sie wohl, es sei mein Fuss,
> Hüpft vor Freuden, wisskt entgegen—
> Nur dem Laub—nur dem Laub—den Liebesgruss."

Moreover "Fuss" and "Liebesgruss" are here intended to rhyme. The first time Weber accentuates thus:

the second time thus:

where the wrongful accent gives the rhyme, but the right discloses that these words do *not* rhyme. And so we have a flagrant instance of the utter folly of our whole literary scheme of Verse, which wellnigh always rests on end-rhymed lines, though it is only in the finest verses of our greatest and best-reputed poets that the rhyme, through being genuine, has a determinant effect. Nor has this genuineness or spuriousness much troubled our German composers heretofore; rhyme to them was rhyme, and they paired off their last syllables in true street-minstrel fashion. A striking example is offered by Naumann's melody, so popular at one time, to Schiller's Ode to Joy:

Now take *Beethoven*, the Truthful:

For sake of the imaginary rhyme, Naumann put the verse's accents all awry: Beethoven gave the proper accent, and, doing so, revealed the fact that in German compound words it falls on the first component, so that the hinder section, bearing the weaker accent, cannot be used for rhyme; if the poet does not hold by this, the rhyme is only present to the eye, a literature-rhyme: to the ear, and thus to both the feeling and a vital understanding, it vanishes away. And what a pother this wretched rhyme creates in all musical composition to verbal texts: twisting and disfiguring the phrases into utter gibberish, to be not so much as noticed in the end! In *Kaspar's* great aria I lately searched for a prior rhyme to correspond with the last line, "Triumph, die Rache gelingt," as I had never heard it in the singing, and therefore thought that Weber must have added this clause on his own authority: however, I succeeded in finding "im Dunkel beschwingt," which, hastily strewn between "umgebt ihn, ihr Geister" and "schon trägt er knirschend eure Ketten," without any musical cæsura, had never struck me as a rhyme before. In truth, what use had the composer for this rhyme, when he merely wanted words, eh! syllables, to give the singer his share in a tempestuous musical phrase that properly belongs to the characteristic orchestral accompaniment alone?

I believe this example, which I only hit upon at random, will afford the easiest introduction to a further inquiry into the mysteries of operatic melody. The meagre doggerel verse, often built of simply empty phrases; the verse whose sole affinity to music, its rhyme, destroyed the words' last shred of meaning, and thereby made its best conceits quite valueless to the musician—this verse compelled him to take the pattern and working-out of characteristic melodic motives from a province of music which had thitherto developed in the orchestral accompaniment to a lingua franca of the instruments. *Mozart* had raised this symphonic accompaniment to such high expressiveness that, wherever consistent with dramatic naturalism, he could let the singers merely speak to it in musical accents, without disturbance of the rich melodic woof of themes or break in the musical flow. And herewith disappeared that violence towards the word-text; whatever in it did not call for vocal melody, was understandably intoned. Yet the incomparable dramatic talent of the glorious musician only perfectly accomplished this in so-called *opera buffa,* not to the same degree in *opera seria.* Here his followers were left with a great difficulty. They could see nothing for it, but to keep the utterance of passion invariably melodious; since the threadbare text gave them little help, and wilful repetition of its words had already made them deaf to any claims of the librettist, they finally set the [prose part of the] text itself, with just as many repetitions as the purpose needed, to melodic-looking phrases such as Mozart had originally assigned to his characterising orchestral accompaniment. In this wise they thought to give their singers always "melody" to sing; and to keep it in perpetual motion they often buried all the text, if there was rather too much of it, beneath such a mass of scales and runs, that neither song nor text could be discerned.—Whoever wants a fairly striking instance, let him study the Templar's great air in *Marschner's* "Templer und Jüdin"; say the *allegro furioso* from "mich fasst die Wuth" onwards, where the composition of the final verses is specially instructive: for in one breath, without the smallest pause, stream forth the words:

"Rache nur wollt' ich geniessen;
Ihr allein mein Ohr nur leihend

Trennt' ich mich von allen süssen,
Zarten Banden der Natur,
Mich dem Templerorden weihend."

Here the composer halts; for the poet's having tacked on a

" Bitt're Reue fand ich nur."

after the full-stop, just to make a rhyme for "Natur," seemed really too bad: only after two bars of interlude does Marschner allow this strange addendum to appear, of course in breathless roulades as before.

Thus the composer believed he had "melodised" everything, even the wickedest. Nor was it better with the elegiac-tender, whereof the same air of the Templar affords us evidence in its Andante (3/4): "in meines Lebens Blüthezeit"—the second verse, "einsam in das dunkle Grab," being sung in Ballad fashion to the exact tune of the first, saving for that elegance of melodic embellishment which has brought this genre of German vocal music to the verge of the ridiculous. The composer opined that the singer would always like "something to sing": the great bravura fireworks of the Italians did not go off quite briskly with the German; on "Rache" at most, did one feel it incumbent to risk a run up and run down. In the "Cantabile," on the contrary, one found those minor prettinesses, particularly the "Mordente" and its derivative grace-notes, which would shew one had one's taste as well. *Spohr* brought the agrémens of his violin-solos into his singers' airs, and if the melody, apparently composed of these extras, turned out a nothing-saying weariness, at like time it strangled the verse that had been making signs of having something to say. With Marschner—beside the manifest traits of genius that occur so frequently (in that great Templar-air for instance) and now and then ascend to positive sublimity (for instance in the choruses introducing the second finale of the same opera)—we meet an almost preponderant mawkishness and an often astounding incorrectness, mostly due to the unfortunate delusion that things must always go "melodiously," i.e. must everywhere be "tuney." My departed colleague Reissiger complained to me of the failure of his "Schiffbruch der Medusa," in which, as I myself must admit, there was "so much melody,"—which I had at like time to take as a bitter allusion to the success of my own operas, in which, you know, there was "so little melody."—

This wondrous Wealth-of-melody, which emptied its horn of plenty on the just and unjust, made good its squandered riches by an—alas! not always skilful—annexation of all the musical gew-gaws current in the world, mostly filched from French or Italian operas and huddled up pell-mell. Against Rossini there was many an outcry: yet it was merely his originality that vexed us; for as soon as Spohr's violin-solo was exhausted for the trimming of the "Cantabile," Rossini's march-and-ballet rhythms and melismi flocked into the freshening *Allegro* almost of themselves: nothing again, but yards of "melody." The overture to the "Felsenmühle" still lives at our garden-concerts and change-of-guards, though we hear no more the March from "Mosé"; in this case German patriotism, to the shade of Reissiger's great satisfaction, would seem to have gained the victory.

Yet it was not solely those ineffective importations of Italian and French melismic and rhythmic nick-nacks, that feathered German operatic melody, but the sublime and hearty further taxed the four-part male chorus so passionately practised since the last half-century. Spontini attended a performance of Mendelssohn's "Antigone" in Dresden, against his will; he soon left it in contemptuous dudgeon: "*c'est de la Berliner Liedertafel*!" 'Tis a sad tale, the incursion of that miserably thin and monotonous beer-chant, even when raised to the rank of a Rhine-wine song, with which the Berlin composer of the opera "die Nibelungen"* himself could not dispense.—It was the genius of *Weber* that led the Opera into noble pathways of the National by introducing the German men's-chorus, to which he had given so splendid an impetus by his songs

* H. Dorn; see Vol. III. p. 261.—Tr.

of the War of Freedom. Its uncommon success moved the master to lend its character to the chorus that takes a dramatic part in the action: in his "Euryanthe" the dialogue of the principal characters is repeatedly arrested by the chorus, which unfortunately sings entirely in the strain of the four-part glee, by itself, unrelieved by any characteristic movement in the orchestra, almost as if these passages were intended to be cut out as they stand for the Liedertafel books. What here was most surely meant nobly, perhaps in opposition to the stereotyped employment of the Italian chorus to merely accompany the aria or ballet, led Weber's successors into that eternal nothing-saying "melodic" chorus-ing which, together with the aforesaid aria-tuning, makes out the entire substance of a German opera. Whole breadths are covered by this "melodic" general-muster, without a single striking moment to tell us the cause of the unbroken drench of melody. For an example I return to the operas of that else so highly talented Marschner, and point to his so-called Ensembles, such as the *Andante con moto* (9/8) in the second finale of his *Templer*, "lässt den Schleier mir, ich bitte"; as also (for a model) the introduction to the first act of the same work, with special reference to the first strophe of the male chorus: "wir lagern dort im stillen Wald, der Zug muss hier vorbei, er ist nicht fern, er nahet bald und glaubt die Strasse frei," sung to a hunting-tune; and in further progress of the piece, the extraordinary melodising of the strictest dialogue by aid of unimaginable repetitions. Here dramatic melodists may learn how long a fair number of men can indulge in an 'aside' on the stage; naturally it can only be done through their standing in rows with their backs to the forest, and facing the audience—which in its turn pays no heed to a man of them, but patiently waits for the end of the general "melody."

To the intelligent spectator the spoken dialogue in such an opera often comes as a positive relief. On the other hand this very dialogue betrayed composers into the belief that the musical numbers embedded in the prose must always be of lyric kind; an assumption quite justified in the "Singspiel" proper, for there one only wanted vocal "Intermezzi," while the piece itself was recited in intelligible prose, just as in Comedy. Here, however, it was "Opera"; the vocal pieces lengthened out, arias changed places with concerted "Ensemble" numbers, and at last the "Finale," with all the text, was put at the musician's disposal. And these separate "numbers" must all be telling in themselves; their "melody" must never flag, and the closing phrase must be rousing, clamorous for applause. Already the music-dealer had been taken in eye: the more effective, or merely pleasing single pieces that one could extract, the more valuable the work to the trade. Even the pianoforte-score must begin with a table-of-contents cataloguing the numbers under the rubric of "Aria," "Duet," "Trio," "Drinking-song," and so on throughout the whole length of the opera. This continued when "Recitative" already had ousted the dialogue, and the whole had been given a certain show of musical cohesion. To be sure, these recitatives weren't much to speak of, and contributed no little to the ennui of the opera-genre; while "Nadori" in Spohr's "Jessonda," for instance, delivered himself of the recitative: "still lag ich an des Seees Fluthen—

one simply was all impatience for re-entry of the full orchestra with definite tempo and a set "melody," let it be put together ("composed") as it might. At end of these redeeming numbers one must be able to applaud, or things looked black and the number would have to be left out in time. In the "Finale," however, quite a little tempest of delirium must be caused; a kind of musical orgy was needed, to bring the act to a satisfying close: so "Ensemble" was sung; every man for himself, all for the audience; and a jubilant burst of melody with a soaring final cadence, appropriate or not, must waft the whole into due ecstasy. If this also fell flat, the thing had failed, and the opera was withdrawn.—

Coupling the above considerations with the utterly chaotic vocalising of most of our singers—their want of finish aggravated by the want of style in such tasks—we must candidly admit that German Opera indeed is bungler's work. We must confess it even in comparison with French and Italian Opera; but how much more when we apply the requirements that should necessarily be met by a drama on the one hand, an independent piece of music on the other, to this pseudo-artwork kept in hopeless incorrectness!—In this Opera, taken strictly, everything is absurd, up to what a god-given musician offers up therein as original-melodist. For definitely so-called "German Opera" such a one was *Weber*, who sent to us his most enkindling rays of genius through this opera-mist, which Beethoven shook off in anger when he scored his diary with: "No more operas and such-like, but *my* way!" And who shall dispute our verdict on the genre itself, when he recalls the fact that Weber's finest, richest and most masterly music is as good as lost to us because belonging to the opera "Euryanthe"? Where shall we find this work performed to-day, when even Sovereign heads are more easily inclined to the "Clemenza di Tito" or "Olympia"—if something heavy must really be dug up for their wedding or jubilee festivities—than to this "Euryanthe" in which, 'spite all its name for tedium, each single number is worth more than all the *Opera seria* of Italy, France and Judæa? Such preferences, beyond a doubt, are not to be simply set down to the somnolent discrimination of the Prussian Operatic College of Directors; but, as everything there is governed by a certain dull but stiff-necked academic instinct, from such a choice we may gather that beside those works of undeniably firm-set style, though very cramped and hollow genus, the best of "German operas" must needs look incomplete and therefore unpresentable at Court. Certainly all the sins of the Opera genre come out most strongly in this work, yet solely because its composer was in mortal earnest this time, but still could do no more than try to cover up the failings, nay, absurdities of the genre by a supreme exertion of his purely-musical productiveness. To revive my old figure of speech, that in the marriage to beget the grand United Artwork the poet's work is the masculine principle, and music the feminine, I might compare the outcome of this penetration of the Euryanthe text by Weber's genius with the fruit of the union of a "Tschandala" with a "Brahminess"; for according to Hindu belief and experience a Brahmin might beget from a Tschandala woman a quite goodly child, though not one fitted for the rank of Brahmin, whereas the offspring of a Tschandala male from the superbly truth-bearing womb of a Brahmin female revealed the outcast type in plainest, and consequently in most revolting imprint. Moreover in the conception of this unlucky "Euryanthe," you must remember, the poet-father was a lady, the music in the fullest sense a Man! When Goethe thought that Rossini could have written quite passable music for his "Helena," it was the Brahmin casting his eye on a buxom Tschandala maiden; only in this case it is scarcely to be supposed that the Tschandala girl would have stood the test.—

In the first part of my larger treatise on "Opera and Drama" I long ago tried to expound the mournful, nay, heart-rending lessons to be drawn from Weber's work last-named; in particular I endeavoured to shew that even the most richly-gifted melodist was in no position to turn a collection of verseless German verses for a poetic-posing operatic text into a sterling artwork. And Weber, beyond being one of the most pre-eminent of melodists, was a bright-witted man with a keen eye for all trash and humbug. With the young musicians who came after, he soon fell into a certain disesteem: God knows what mixtures of Bach, Händel and so forth, they concocted as the very newest recipes: but none of them ventured to face the problem which Weber seemed to have left unsolved; or if any did, he gave it up after a brief but laboured attempt. Only Kapellmeisters went gaily on composing "operas." In their installation-contracts it was written that they must enrich the Court-opera conducted by them with a new product of their fancy every year. My operas "Rienzi," "der fliegende Holländer," "Tannhäuser" and "Lohengrin," are given gratis at the Dresden Court-theatre to this day, because they are reckoned to me as Kapellmeister-operas from the period of my life-appointment there; I therefore have to pay a curious penalty for these operas having fared better than those of my colleagues. Happily this calamity affects myself alone; I know of no other Dresden opera-composer whose works have survived his Kapellmeister-ship, except my great predecessor *Weber*; but from him they asked no opera expressly written for the Court-theatre, as in his time Italian Opera alone was deemed compatible with human dignity. His three famous operas Weber wrote for theatres elsewhere.

Apart from this nice enrichment of the Royal Saxon Court-theatre's repertoire by my modest, but now over-thirty-years-enduring works, not one of the afterbirths of Weberian Opera has had any real subsistence at the other Court-theatres either. Incomparably the most significant of them, were the first operas of Marschner: for some time their author was kept erect by the great unconcern with which, untroubled by the problem of Opera itself, he let his melodic talent and a certain idiomatic trick of maintaining his music, not always very new, in constant active flow, work out their own salvation. But the contagion of the new French Opera caught him as well, and soon he lost himself past rescue in the shallows of the poorly-schooled Not-highly-gifted. In face of Meyerbeer's successes one and all stood still and timid, were it only for good manners: not until recent times did one dare to follow up the creations of his style with Old-testament abortions.* "German

* Goldmark's "Königin von Saba," for instance.—Tr.

Opera," however, was on its deathbed till it happened at last that the still opposed, but less and less disputed successes of my own works seemed to have set pretty well the whole German composer-world in alarm and eager competition.

Long years ago I noticed symptoms of this movement. My successes at the Dresden Court-theatre even then drew F. Hiller, and later R. Schumann also, into my vicinity; at first, no doubt, just to see how it arrived that on an important German stage the operas of a thitherto entirely unknown German composer could lastingly attract the public. That I was no remarkable musician, both friends believed they had soon detected; so that my success appeared to be founded on the texts I had penned for myself. Indeed I also was of opinion that, as they now were brooding operatic plans, they should first of all procure good poems. For this they begged my help; but declined it again when things came to the point—I presume for fear of shabby tricks that I might play them. Of my text for "Lohengrin" Schumann remarked that it could never be composed as an opera; wherein he differed from Upper-Kapellmeister Taubert of Berlin, who later on, after my music also had been finished and performed, declared that he should like to set its text all over again for himself. When Schumann was compiling the book of his "Genovefa" no argument of mine could dissuade him from retaining the lamentably foolish third act as he had framed it; he took offence, and certainly imagined that I wished to spoil his very best effects. For *effect* he aimed at: everything "German, chaste and pure," but with a piquant dash of mock unchastity, to be harrowingly supplied by the most un-human coarsenesses and lownesses of the second finale. A few years ago I heard a most carefully prepared performance of this "Genovefa" in Leipzig, and could but find that the revolting and offensive scene which ends the third act of Auber's "Bal masqué," founded on similar motives, was quite a dainty *bon mot* compared with this sickening brutality of the chaste German effect-composer and librettist. And—marvellous! Never have I heard a solitary complaint about it.* With such energy does the German control his inborn purer feelings when he means to pit one man—Schumann for instance—against another—e.g. myself.—For my part, I perceived that I could have been of no earthly use to Schumann.

But—this was in the good old times. Since then the Thirty-years' Zukunftsmusik War broke out, as to which I cannot quite ascertain whether it is yet deemed ripe for a Westphalian treaty. At anyrate there was a fair amount of opera-composing again in the years of war themselves, prompted perhaps by the very circumstance that our theatres were doing less and less business with the French and Italian wares they used to live on, whereas a number of German texts from my dilettantish pen, and actually composed by my own unaided self, for long had furnished them with good receipts.

Unfortunately I have been unable to gain any closer acquaintance with the creations of the neo-German Muse. They tell me that the influence of my "innovations" in the dramatic style of music may there be remarked. Notoriously I am credited with a "manner" [or "line"—"*Richtung*"], against which the deceased Kapellmeister Rietz of Dresden was predisposed, and the departed Musikdirektor Hauptmann of Leipzig directed his choicest sallies; I fancy they were not the only ones, but quite a number of masters of all sorts were, and probably still are, unfriendly toward this "line." In the Music-schools and Conservatoria it is said to be sternly tabooed. What "line" may be taught there, is not clear to myself; all I know is, that mighty little is learnt: someone who had studied composition for six whole years at one of these establishments, gave it up at the end. It almost seems that the learning of Opera-composition must proceed in secret, outside the High Schools; so that he who falls into my "line," had best keep a look out! But it is less a

* In England they give it to Academy young ladies and gentlemen to perform!—Tr.

study of my works, than their success, that appears to have sent many an academically-untaught to my "manner." In what the latter consists, to myself is most unclear of all. Perhaps in the recent predilection for medieval subjects; the Edda and the rugged North, in general, have also been taken in eye as quarries for good texts. Yet it is not only the choice and character of its opera-texts that seems to have been of weight to the by all means "new" line, but several things besides; in particular that "composing-throughout," and above all a never-ceasing interference of the orchestra in the singers' affairs—a mode with which one was the more liberal as a good deal of "manner" had lately arisen in the instrumenting, harmony and modulation of orchestral compositions.

I scarcely think that in all these things I could give much useful instruction; as I luckily am neither asked for it by anyone, at most I might give—unbidden—the following little counsel out of pure good-nature.

A German prince with a turn for composing operas* once asked friend Liszt to procure my aid in the instrumenting of a new opera by his Highness; in particular he wanted the good effect of the trombones in "Tannhäuser" applied to his work, in which regard my friend felt bound to divulge the secret that something always occurred to me, before I set it for the trombones.—On the whole it would be advisable that sundry composers adopted this "manner": to myself, indeed, it is of scanty profit, for I never can compose at all when nothing "occurs" to me; and perhaps the generality are wiser not to wait for such "ideas." With regard to the dramatic branch, however, I would indicate the best device for positively forcing such "occurrences."

A young musician whom I also once advised to wait for ideas, asked sceptically how he was ever to know that the idea he might get, under circumstances, was really his own. This doubt may arrive to the absolute Instrumental-composer: in fact our great Symphonists of the "now-

* The Late Duke of Coburg.—Tr.

time" might be counselled to turn any doubt as to the ownership of their stray ideas into downright certainty, ere others do it for them. *Dramatic* composers of my "manner," on the other hand, I would recommend to never think of adopting a text before they see in it a plot, and characters to carry out this plot, that inspire the musician with a lively interest on some account or other. Then let him take a good look at the one character, for instance, which appeals to him the most this very day: bears it a mask—away with it; wears it the garment of a stage-tailor's dummy—off with it! Let him set it in a twilight spot, where he can merely see the gleaming of its eye; if that speaks to him, the shape itself will now most likely fall a-moving, which perhaps will even terrify him—but he must put up with that; at last its lips will part, it opens its mouth, and a ghostly voice breathes something quite distinct, intensely seizable, but so unheard-of (such as the "Guest of stone," and surely the page Cherubino, once said to Mozart) that—he wakes from out his dream. All has vanished; but in the spiritual ear it still rings on: he has had an "idea" ("*Einfall*"), a so-called musical "Motiv"; God knows if other men have heard the same, or something similar, before? Does it please X.Y, or displease Z? What's that to him? It is *his* motiv, legally delivered to and settled on him by that marvellous shape in that wonderful fit of absorption.

But one only gets these inspirations when one doesn't ply for opera-texts with theatre-dummies: to invent "new" tunes for such, is uncommonly hard. We may take it that Mozart has exhausted all the music for those same dramatic masquerades. Clever men have praised his texts, that of "Don Juan" for instance, as the half-sketched programmes for a stage masque, with which they say his music corresponds so admirably because it reproduces even the most passionate of human situations as an always pleasantly diverting game. Though this view is easy of misconstruction, and above all may wound as derogatory, it was seriously meant, and involved that widely-accepted verdict of our Æsthetes on Music's true office which it is so hard to combat till this day. Only I think that Mozart, while elevating this art—exposed, in a certain and very deep sense, to the charge of frivolity—to an æsthetic principle of Beauty, at like time completely exhausted it; it was his own: whoever thought to follow him, merely bungled and bored.

The stock of "pretty melodies" is out, and without "new ideas" there cannot be much originality remaining. Wherefore I advise the "new-mannered" to keep a keen eye on his text, his plot and characters, for inspirations. But whoso has no time to wait for the results of such a scrutiny (to many it has so happened with their "Armin"s and "Konradin"s!), and finally contents himself with stage-dummies, processions, shrieks of vengeance, storms in a teacup, and all the dance of death and devils, at least I warn him not to employ for the musical outfit of such mummery those attributes of the "manner" which have issued from communion with the true-dream shapes I spoke of above, as he would only make a muddle of it. For he who has looked those figures in the face, has had a difficulty in drawing on the store-room of our masking music to plainly re-compose the motive they had given him: frequently there was nothing to be done with the squaring of rhythm and modulation, since it is somewhat different to say "It is," from "Let us say" or "He believes so." Here the straits (*Noth*) of the Unheard-of bring often new necessities to light, and the music may haply weave itself into a style that might much annoy our Quadrature musicians. Not that that much matters: for if he who makes strange and startling modulations without that Want is certainly a bungler, so he who does not recognise the compulsion to modulate forcibly in the proper place is a—"Senator." The worst of it is, that the "new-mannerist" assumes that those occasional unheard-of-nesses have now become the common property of all who have footed the "line," and that if only he lays them on thick enough, his dummies will at once look something like. But they look very bad, and I can't blame many an honest soul of the German Reich for still preferring to hear masque-music correctly built according to the lines of Quadrature. If only there were *Rossinis* to be had ! I am afraid, however, they have come to an end.—

After all, there won't be much to learn from my jottings of to-day ; my counsels, in particular, will prove quite useless. Indeed under no conditions would I pretend to teach how men should make, but merely to guide them to a knowledge of how the made and the created should be rightly understood. Even for this a really lasting intercourse were requisite ; for only by examples, examples, and again examples, is anything to be made clear, and eventually something learnt: but effectually to set examples, in our domain, we need musicians, singers, finally an orchestra. All these the minions of our Culture-ministries have at their hand in schools of the great cities: how they have contrived that nothing right will yet come of our music, and that even at the change-of-guard the pieces played grow daily worse, must remain a modern mystery of State. My friends are aware that two years back I thought it would be useful if I mixed a little in the thing myself; what I wished, however, seemed to be viewed as undesirable. I have been left in peace, for which I may be thankful in some respects. Only I regret to have to remain so incomplete and hard of understanding when I feel moved at times, as with the above, to throw a ray of light on much that touches our world of music. May it be adjudged to this evil, if the present article is found more agitating than instructive: luckily it is written for neither the *Kölnische*, the *National-*, nor any other world-*Zeitung*, and whatever is amiss in it thus stays among ourselves.

ON THE APPLICATION OF MUSIC TO THE DRAMA.

Über die
Anwendung der Musik auf das Drama.

This article originally appeared in the Bayreuther Blätter *for November 1879.*

TRANSLATOR'S NOTE.

Y last article on Opera-writing contained an allusion to the necessary difference in musical style between a dramatic and a purely-musical composition. I now should like to put this plainer, as it seems to me that one thus might rectify great misconceptions both in the judgment of music and, more particularly, in our composers' ideas of production. I spoke of "bunglers" who needlessly indulge in strange and startling modulation, and of "senators" who are unable to perceive the necessity of apparent extravagances in that department. The euphemism "Senator" was furnished me at a critical moment by Shakespeare's "Iago," who wished to avoid the application of an epithet from the animal world to a person of official status *; in a similar predicament of respect towards art-scientific worthies I will in future employ the more becoming term "Professor." The weighty question here involved, however, had better be discussed without any reference to "Professors," purely among artists and true, i.e. unsalaried friends of art; to such alone I therefore propose to address the following upshot of my experiences and meditations in the exercise of my artistic calling.

As Example always teaches best, I at once adduce a speaking instance from art-history: namely that Beethoven shews such daring in his symphonies, such caution in his (only) opera, "Fidelio." The cramping structure then accepted as the mould of Opera I assigned in my preceding essay as the reason of the master's turning a sullen back on further attempts with the dramatic genre. Why he did not seek to broaden the whole style of Opera itself into correspondence with his mighty genius, was manifestly that he found no instigation in the only case that

* *Othello*, Act I., scene i. :—BRABANTIO, "Thou art a villain." IAGO, "You are—a senator."—Tr.

lay before him; that he did not strive to gain him such a stimulus by hook or crook, we must explain by the all-unknown New having already opened up to him as Symphonist. If we watch him in the fulness of his innovating force, we can but recognise that he fixed for once and all the character of independent Instrumental-music by the plastic barriers his impetuous genius never overstepped itself. Let us now endeavour to perceive and understand these barriers, not as limitations, but conditions of the Beethovenian Artwork.

I have called these barriers plastic: I will further denote them the pillars through whose ordering, as symmetrical as to the purpose, the Symphonic edifice is bounded, borne, and made distinct. In the construction of the symphonic Movement, all ready-planned by Haydn, Beethoven altered nothing; and for the same reason that forbids an architect to displace the columns of a building at discretion, or to use forsooth the horizontal parts as vertical. If it was a conventional order, the very nature of the artwork had dictated that convention; for the basis of the Symphonic artwork is the Dance-tune. It is impossible for me to here repeat what I have said upon this theme in earlier essays, and, as I believe, established. Merely I would point once more to the character stamped for good and all on the Haydn and Beethoven Symphony by that foundation. Dramatic pathos is completely excluded, so that the most intricate involvements of the thematic motives in a symphonic movement could never be explained on the analogy of a dramatic action, but solely by the mazes of an ideal dance, without a suspicion of rhetorical dialectics. Here there is no "conclusion," no problem, no solution. Wherefore also these Symphonies bear one and all the character of lofty glee (*Heiterkeit*). Never are two themes of diametrically opposite character confronted here; diverse as they may seem, they always supplement each other as the manly and the womanly element of one whole character. Yet the undreamt variety in which these elements may break, re-form, and re-unite with one another, is proved to demonstration by such a Beethovenian Movement: the first in the Eroica reveals this to the absolute bewildering of the uninitiate, although to the initiate this movement bares the unity of its root-character the most convincingly of all.

It has been very rightly remarked that Beethoven's innovations are far rather to be sought on the field of rhythmic distribution, than on that of harmonic modulation. Remote changes of key are scarcely used except in wanton fun, whereas we find an invincible power of constantly reshaping rhythmic-plastic motives, of ordering and ranging them in ever richer piles. Here we light, so it seems, on the line of cleavage of the Symphonist from the Dramatist. Mozart was new and startling to his cotemporaries through his love of daring flights in modulation, inspired by deepest need: we know their horror at the harmonic acridities in the introduction to that Quartet which he dedicated to Haydn. Here, as in so many characteristic passages, where the contrapuntal theme is raised to the expression of anguished yearning through an ascending series of accented suspending-notes, the craving to exhaust all Harmonic possibilities appears to border on dramatic pathos. In effect it was from the realm of dramatic music, already widened by himself to undreamt capability of expression, that Mozart first entered on the Symphony; for those few symphonic works of his whose peculiar worth has kept them living to this day, we owe to that creative period when he had fully unfolded his genius as Opera-composer. To the composer of "Figaro" and "Don Giovanni" the framework of the symphonic movement only offered a curb on that mobile love of figure-painting (*gestaltungsfrohe Beweglichkeit*) which had found such congenial scope in the passionately changeful situations of those dramatic drafts. Viewing his art as Symphonist a little closer, we observe that here he shines by wellnigh nothing save the beauty of his themes, whilst in their application and refashioning he distinguishes himself merely as a practised contrapuntist; to breathe life into connecting links he missed the accustomed dramatic stimulus. Now, his dramatic art of music had really fed on nothing but the so-called *Opera buffa*, the melodic comedy; true "Tragedy" was still a stranger to him, and only in single lofty features, as *Donna Anna* and the *Marble Guest*, had she turned on him her quickening countenance. Was he seeking for it in the Symphony? Who shall answer for the latent parts and possible developments of a genius who passed his earthly life, itself so brief, beneath the scalpel of the vivisector?

But now the Tragic Muse has actually laid hands on Opera. Mozart knew her only in the mask of Metastasio's "*Opera seria*": stiff and arid—"*Clemenza di Tito*." Her true visage she appears to have but gradually unveiled to us: Beethoven saw it not yet, and abode by "*his way*." I believe I may aver that, with the advent of full earnestness in the conception of Tragedy and the realising of the Drama, quite new necessities arose for Music; requirements which we must accurately measure against those demanded of the Symphonist in preservation of the pureness of his art-style.

Though the absolute Instrumental-composer found no musical forms to hand save those in which he originally had had to "strike up," more or less, for the enlivenment or even the encouragement of others at festal dances and marches; and if this formed the basal character of the Symphonic artwork, at first compounded of such Dance and March tunes, which dramatic pathos could only confuse by the posing of questions without a possibility of answers: yet certain vividly-gifted instrumentalists nursed the irrepressible desire to enlarge the bounds of musical form and expression by superscribing their pieces with a dramatic incident, and endeavouring to present it to the imagination through purely musical means. The reasons why a pure artistic style could never be attained on this path, have doubtless been discerned in course of the manifold attempts thereon; but to us it seems that the admirable service thus rendered by exceptionally gifted musicians has not yet been sufficiently regarded. The excesses to which his guardian dæmon drove a Berlioz were nobly tempered by the incomparably more artistic genius of Liszt to the expression of soul and world events too great for words; and to the disciples of their art it might appear that a new order of composition was placed at their immediate disposal. In any case it was astonishing to see what boundless faculties sheer Instrumental-music had acquired under guidance of a dramatic synopsis. Theretofore the Overture to an opera, or play, alone had offered occasion for the employment of purely musical means of expression in a form departing from the Symphonic movement. Beethoven himself had here proceeded very circumspectly: feeling impelled to introduce an actual stage-effect in the middle of his Leonora-overture, he still repeated the first section of the tone-piece, with the customary change of key, exactly as in a symphonic movement—heedless that the dramatic excitement of the middle section, reserved for thematic working-out, had already led us to expect the dénouement; a manifest drawback to the receptive hearer. Far more concisely, and in a dramatic sense correctly, did Weber plan his Freischütz-overture, where the so-called middle section rushes on at once to the conclusion through a drastic climax in the thematic conflict. Now, though in the larger Programme works of the more recent tone-poets named above we find clear traces of the Symphony-construction proper—indelible for natural reasons,—in the fashioning of the themes, their contrast and remodelling, there already appears a passionate and 'eccentric' character such as pure Symphonic instrumental-music seemed called to hold entirely aloof; indeed the Programmist felt bound to give this eccentric characterisation particularly high relief, as a poetic shape or episode was always present to his mind, and he believed he could not set it plain enough before, as it were, the eye. At last this obligation led to downright melo-drama-music, with pantomime to be supposed, and quite consistently to instrumental recitatives—whilst horror at the pulverising formlessness filled all the critical world; so that nothing really remained, but to help the new form of Musical Drama itself to light of day from such birth-agonies.—

This latter is as little to be compared with the older Operatic form, as the newer instrumental-music conducting to it is to be likened with the Classic Symphony, become impossible to our composers. But we will defer for a while our inquiry into that so-called "Musikdrama," and first cast a glance on the "classical" instrumental-composition of our latest times, all unaffected by that process of gestation; we shall find that this "classic survival" is an empty pretence, and has planted beside our great Classic masters a highly unattractive hybrid from "I would" and "Yet I cannot."

That Programme-music, on which "we" looked with timid glances from the corner of our eye, had imported so much novelty in harmonisation, theatrical and landscape effects, nay, historical painting; and had worked it all out with such striking brilliance, in power of an uncommonly virtuosic art of instrumenting, that to continue in the earlier style of Classic Symphony one lacked alas! the Beethoven who would have known how to make the best of it. "We" held our tongues. When at last we took heart to open our symphonic mouth again, just to show what still was in us, we found we had grown so turgid and wearisome that there was nothing for it but to deck ourselves with fallen feathers from the Programme petrel. In our symphonies, and that sort of thing, all now goes world-distraught and catastrophic; we are gloomy and grim, then mettlesome and daring; we yearn for the fulfilment of youthful dreams; dæmonic obstacles encompass us; we brood, we even rave: and then the world-ache's tooth is drawn; we laugh, and humorously shew the world its gaping gum; brisk, sturdy, blunt, Hungarian or Scotch,*—alas! to others dreary. To

* Brahms again.—Tr.

be serious: we cannot believe that a happy future has been secured to instrumental music by the creations of its latest masters; above all, it must be bad for us to recklessly tack on these works to the legacy of Beethoven, in view of the utter un-Beethovenism which we ought, on the contrary, to be taught to discern in them — a lesson that should not come so very hard in the matter of kinship to the Beethovenian spirit, in spite of all the Beethovenian themes we here meet once again; though in the matter of form it could scarcely be easy to the pupils of our Conservatoires, as under the rubric of "Æsthetic Forms" they are giving nothing but a list of different composers' names, and left to form a judgment for themselves without further comparison.

The said symphonic compositions of our newest school —let us call it the Romantic-classical—are distinguished from the wild-stock of our so-called Programme-music not only by the regretted absence of a programme, but in especial by a certain clammy cast of melody which its creators have transplanted from their heretofore retiring "Chamber-music." To the "Chamber," in fact, one had withdrawn. Alas! not to the homely room where Beethoven once poured into the ears of few and breathless friends all that Unutterable he kept for understanding here alone, instead of in the ample hall-space where he spoke in none but plastic masses to the Folk, to all mankind: in this hallowed "chamber" silence long had reigned; for one now must hear the master's so-called "last" Quartets and Sonatas either badly, as men played them, or not at all—till the way at last was shewn by certain outlawed renegades, and one learnt what that chamber-music really said. No, those had already moved *their* chamber to the concert-hall: what had previously been dressed as Quintets and the like, was now served up as Symphony: little chips of melody, like an infusion of hay and old tea-leaves, with nothing to tell you what you are swallowing but the label "Best"; and all for the acquired taste of World-ache.—On the whole, however, the newer tendency to the eccentric, the requiring-a-programme, retained the upper hand. With fine discernment Mendelssohn had gone to Nature for his subjects, and executed them as a kind of landscape epic: he had travelled much, and brought home many a thing that others could not lightly come by. But the latest phase, is to take the cabinet-pictures of our local Exhibitions and set them to music straightway; enabling one to seize those quaint instrumental effects which are now at everyone's command, disguise embezzled melodies in harmonisations that are a constant surprise, and play the outcome to the world as Plastic music.

The results of our survey may be summed up as follows:—

Pure Instrumental-music, no longer content with the legalised form of the Classical Symphonic Movement, sought to extend her powers in every respect, and found them easily increased by poet's fancies; the reactionary party was unable to fill that Classic form with life, and saw itself compelled to borrow for it from the wholly alien, thereby distorting it. Whilst the first direction led to the winning of new aptitudes, and the second merely exposed ineptitudes, it became evident that the further evaluation of those aptitudes was only to be saved from boundless follies, threatening serious damage to the spirit of Music, by openly and undisguisedly turning that line itself towards the *Drama.* What there remained unutterable, could here be spoken definitely and plainly, and thereby "Opera" redeemed withal from the curse of her unnatural descent. And it is here, in what we may call for short the "Musical Drama," that we reach sure ground for calmly reckoning the application of Music's new-won faculties to the evolution of noble, inexhaustible artistic forms.

The science of Æsthetics has at all times laid down Unity as a chief requirement from the artwork. In the abstract this Unity is difficult to dialectically define, and its misapprehension has led to many and grave mistakes.

It comes out the plainest in the perfect artwork itself, for it is it that moves us to unbroken interest, and keeps the broad impression ever present. Indisputably this result is the most completely attained by the living represented drama; wherefore we have no hesitation in declaring the Drama the most perfect of artworks. The farthest from this artwork stood the "Opera," and perhaps for very reason that she made a pretence of drama, but split it into countless disconnected fragments for sake of the Aria form: in Opera there are pieces embracing all the structure of a symphonic Movement in briefest lapse of time, with first and second themes, return, repetition and so-called "Coda"; but, self-included, they remain without one whit of reference to all the other pieces like them. In the Symphony, on the contrary, we have found this structure so developed and enlarged, that its master turned in anger from the cramping form of Operatic numbers. In this Symphonic Movement we recognised the unity that has so determinant an influence on us in the perfect drama, and the downfall of that art-form so soon as foreign elements, all unassimilable with that unity, were introduced therein. But the element most foreign to it was the Dramatic, which needed infinitely richer forms for its unfolding than could naturally present themselves on the basis of the Symphonic movement, i.e. Dance music. Nevertheless, to be an artwork again quâ music, the new form of dramatic music must have the unity of the symphonic movement; and this it attains by spreading itself over the whole drama, in the most intimate cohesion therewith, not merely over single smaller, arbitrarily selected parts. So that this Unity consists in a tissue of root-themes pervading all the drama, themes which contrast, complete, re-shape, divorce and intertwine with one another as in the symphonic movement; only that here the needs of the dramatic action dictate the laws of parting and combining, which were there originally borrowed from the motions of the dance.—

Upon the new form of musical construction as applied

to the Drama I have expressed myself sufficiently in earlier articles and essays, yet sufficiently merely in the sense that I imagined I had plainly pointed out the road on which a true, and alike a useful judgment of the musical forms now won from Drama by my own artistic labours might be attained by others. To the best of my knowledge, that road has not been trodden yet, and I can remember nothing but the studies of one of my younger friends * who has viewed the characteristics of what he calls my "Leitmotive" rather in the light of their dramatic significance, than in that of their bearing on musical construction (since the specific art of music was not the author's province). On the contrary, I have lived to see our Music-schools all inculcating horror at the wild confusion of my periods, while young composers, fired by the success of public representations of my works, and guided by a superficial private reading of my scores, have unintelligently tried to copy me. As the State and Parish only pay for un-teachers of my art, such as Professor Rheinberger of Munich (to remain within the circle of my supposititious influence), instead of founding something like a Chair for it, as may some day happen in England or America,—the present little article will not have been labour thrown away if only it gives those said composers an inkling of what they might learn and copy from my works.

So, whoever till now has trained himself by listening to our newest Romantic-classical instrumental-music, and wants to try his skill with the dramatic genre, I would above all advise him not to aim at harmonic and instrumental Effects, but to await sufficient cause for any effect of the kind, as otherwise they will not come off. You could not insult Berlioz more profoundly, than by bringing him abortions of this sort on paper, and expecting them to please the composer of Witches' Sabbaths and the like. Liszt used to polish off these stupid suggestions with the remark that cigar-ash and sawdust steeped in aqua fortis

* Freiherr Hans von Wolzogen.—Tr.

did not make pleasant soup. I have never yet made the acquaintance of a young composer who did not think to gain my sanction for "audacities" before all things. On the other hand it has been a real surprise to me, that the restraint I have striven for with increasing vigilance in the modulation and instrumenting of my works has not met the smallest notice. In the instrumental introduction to "Rheingold," for instance, it was impossible to me to quit the fundamental note, simply because I had no reason for changing it; a great part of the not un-animated scene that follows for the *Rhine-daughters* and *Alberich* would only permit of modulation to keys the very nearest of kin, as Passion here is still in the most primitive naïvety of its expression. I do not deny that I certainly should have given to the first entry of *Donna Anna*—denouncing the shameless seducer *Don Juan* in the height of passion—a stronger colouring than Mozart held appropriate to the conventions of the operatic style and those means of expression he himself was the first to enrich. But there sufficed that simple austerity, which I had as little to abandon when the "Walküre" was to be introduced with a storm, the "Siegfried" with a tone-piece conducting us into the silent depths of Nibelheim's Hoard-smithy by a reminiscence of certain plastic motives from the previous dramas: all three were *elements* from which the drama had to quicken into life. Something different was demanded for an introduction to the Norns' scene of "Die Götterdämmerung": here the destinies of the ure-world are weaving themselves into that rope we must see the hooded sisters swing, when the curtain rises, to understand its meaning: wherefore this prelude could only be brief and preparatory, though the expectant use of motives made intelligible in the earlier sections of the work allowed a richer harmonic and thematic treatment. And it is important, how one commences. Had I used in an Overture a motive cast like that which is heard in the second act of "Die Walküre" at *Wotan's* surrender of world-sovereignty to the possessor of the Nibelungen-hoard:

according to my notions of distinctness of style I should have perpetrated a piece of downright nonsense. But after in course of the drama the simple nature-motive

had been heard at the earliest gleam of the shining Rhinegold; at the first appearance of the Gods'-burg "Walhall," shimmering in the morning's red, the no less simple motive

and each of these motives had undergone mutations in closest sympathy with the rising passions of the plot,—with the help of a digression in the harmony I could present them knit in such a way that, more than Wotan's words, this tone-figure should give to us a picture of the fearful gloom in the soul of the suffering god. Again, I am conscious of having always endeavoured to prevent the acerbity of such musical combinations from making a striking effect as such, as a special "audacity" we will say; both by my marks of expression and by word of mouth I sought to so tone down the change, whether by a timely slackening of tempo or a preliminary dynamic compensation, that it should invade our willing Feeling as an artistic moment in strict accordance with the laws of nature. So that it may be imagined how nothing more enrages me, and keeps me away from strange performances of my music, than the insensibility of most of our conductors to the requirements of Rendering in such combinations in particular; needing the most delicate treatment, they are given to the ear in false and hurried tempo, without the indispensable dynamic shading, and mostly unintelligible. No wonder they are a bugbear to our "Professors."

I have dealt at some length with this example because it has an application to all my dramas, only far more extended, and shews the characteristic distinction between the Dramatic and the Symphonic use and working-out of motives. But I will take a second of like nature, and draw attention to the metamorphoses in that motive with which the *Rhine-daughters* greet the glancing Gold in childish glee:

One would have to follow this uncommonly simple theme—recurring in manifold alliance with almost every other motive of the drama's wide-spread movement—through all the changes it receives from the diverse character of its re-summoning, to see what type of variations the Drama can engender; and how completely the character of these variations departs from that of those figured, rhythmic or harmonic alterations of a theme which our masters ranged in immediate sequence to build up pictures of an often intoxicatingly kaleidoscopic effect. This effect was destroyed at once, and with it the classic form of Variation, so soon as motives foreign to the theme were woven in, giving something of a dramatic development to the Movement's progress, and fouling the purity, or let us say self-evidence of the tone-piece. But neither a mere play of counterpoint, nor the most fantastic art of figuration and most inventive harmonising, either could or should transform a theme so characteristically, and present it with such manifold and entirely changed expression—yet leaving it always recognisable—as true dramatic art can do quite naturally. Hardly anything could afford a plainer proof of this, than a pursuit of that simple motive of the "Rhine-daughters" through all the changing passions of the four-part drama down to *Hagen's* Watch-song in the first act of the "Götterdämmerung," where it certainly takes on a form which—to me at least—makes it inconceivable as theme of a Symphonic movement, albeit it still is governed by the laws of harmony and thematism, though purely in their application to the Drama. To attempt to apply the results of such a method to the Symphony, however, must lead to the latter's utter ruin; for here would appear as a far-fetched Effect what follows there from well-found motives.

It cannot be my present purpose to repeat what I have said at length in earlier writings about the application of Music to the Drama, even though regarded from a fresh point of view; rather, my main object has been to mark the difference between two modes of music from whose commingling have sprung disfigurement of the one variety of art, false judgment of the other. And to me this seemed of weight, if we are ever to arrive at a proper æsthetic estimate of the great events in the evolutionary career of Music—the one still truly living and productive art of our era,—whereanent the greatest confusion prevails to this day. Starting from the structural laws of the Symphony, Sonata, or the Aria, when we hitherto have made for Drama we never got beyond that Operatic style which trammelled the great symphonist in the unfolding of his faculties; on the other hand, in our amazement at the boundlessness of these faculties when unfolded in right relation to the Drama, we confound those laws if we transfer the fruits of musical innovations on the dramatic field to the Symphony and so forth. However, as I have said that it would lead us too far, to display these innovations in all their mutual bearings; and as that task would also fall more fitly to another, I will conclude with one more illustration—namely of the characteristics demanded by the Drama, forbidden by the Symphony, not only in the use and transformation, but also in the first modelling of the Motive itself.

Properly speaking, we cannot conceive of a chief-motive of a Symphonic movement as a piece of eccentric modulation, especially if it is to present itself in such a bewildering dress at its first appearance. The motive which the composer of "Lohengrin" allots as closing phrase of a first arioso to his *Elsa* plunged in memory of a blissful dream, consists almost solely of a tissue of remote harmonic progressions; in the Andante of a Symphony, we will say, it would strike us as far-fetched and highly unintelligible; here it does not seem strained, but quite arising of itself, and therefore so intelligible that to my knowledge it has never been decried as the contrary. This has its grounds, however, in the scenic action. *Elsa* has slowly approached, in gentle grief, with timid down-bent head; one glance at her transfigured eye informs us what is in her soul.

Questioned, she replies by nothing save the vision of a dream that fills her with a sweet belief: "With signs so soft and courteous he comfort gave to me";—that glance had already told us something of the kind. Now, boldly passing from her dream to assurance of fulfilment in reality, she adds: "That knight I will await then; he shall my champion be." And after all its wanderings, the musical phrase now passes back to its mother-key.

At the time a young friend of mine,* to whom I had sent the score for arrangement of a pianoforte edition, was much astonished by the look of this phrase which had so many modulations in so few bars, but still more when he attended the first performance of "Lohengrin" at Weimar and found that this selfsame phrase appeared quite natural —which at anyrate was due in part to the musical conducting of Liszt, who by a proper rendering had turned the transient eye-sore into a well-favoured shape of Tone.

It seems that already a very large portion of the public finds much, nay, almost everything in my dramatic music quite natural, and therefore pleasing, at which our "Professors" still cry Fie. Were the latter to seat me on one of their sacred chairs, however, they perhaps might be seized with even greater wonder at the prudence and moderation, especially in the use of harmonic effects, which I should

* Theodor Uhlig.—Tr.

enjoin upon their pupils; as I should have to make it their foremost rule, never to quit a key so long as what they have to say, can still be said therein. If this rule were complied with, we possibly might again hear Symphonies that gave us something to talk about; whereas there is simply nothing at all to be said of our latest symphonies.

Wherefore I too will be silent, till some day I am called to a Conservatorium—only, not as "Professor."

AGAINST VIVISECTION.

Offenes Schreiben

an

Herrn Ernst von Weber,

Verfasser der Schrift:

"Die Folterkammern der Wissenschaft."

The following article originally appeared in the Bayreuther Blätter *for October 1879. A translation of its full title would be:* "An open letter to Herr Ernst von Weber, author of the work: '*The Torture-chambers of Science.*'"

TRANSLATOR'S NOTE.

Very dear Sir!

OU believe that my word may be of help to the crusade you have recently undertaken against Vivisection, and probably are counting on the perhaps not insignificant number of friends my art has won me. Whilst I unconditionally accept the challenge to follow your forcible example, it is less from any confidence in my ability to vie with you, than from a dim feeling of the necessity to test on a field apparently so distant from æsthetic interests the character of that artistic influence which has been attributed to me in many quarters.

As on the threshold of the present case we meet again that "Scientific" spectre which in our un-souled age has mounted from the dissecting-table to the small-arms factory, and made itself the patron spirit of that Utilitarian cult on which alone the State looks kindly, I can but deem it of great advantage to my own intervention that such considerable and authoritative voices have made themselves heard upon your side, laying the assertions of our opponents bare to sound common-sense as erroneous, if not intentionally misleading. On the other hand, mere "feeling" has certainly been made so much of in our cause that we have given the scoffers and witlings, who almost exclusively furnish our public entertainment, a welcome opportunity of upholding the interests of "Science." Nevertheless the most earnest concern of humanity, in my way of thinking, has here been so strongly called in question, that the deepest knowledge is only to be gained on the path of an exact analysis of that mocked-at "feeling." Gladly will I attempt to set my humble powers on that path.—

What hitherto has kept me from joining any of the

existing societies for the Protection of Animals, has been that I found all their arguments and appeals based well-nigh exclusively on the Utilitarian principle. It may have been a first necessity of the philanthropists who have heretofore concerned themselves with the protection of dumb animals, to prove to the people the usefulness of a merciful treatment of the beasts, since our modern civilisation does not empower us to count on any other motives than that of utility in the actions of State-ruled mankind. How far we thus have wandered from the only ennobling reason for kindness toward dumb animals, and how little could be really attained on the path here struck, is shewn quite palpably in recent days; for the advocates of the time-honoured tendence of societies for the Protection of Animals can advance no valid argument against the most inhuman cruelty to beasts, now practised in our licensed vivisection-chambers, as soon as it is defended on the plea of usefulness. Almost we are restricted to calling this Utility in question; and were it proved beyond all doubt, it would be precisely that union which had given a foothold to the most man-degrading barbarism towards its protégés by its hitherto promoted tenets. According to these, nothing but a State-acknowledged demonstration of the *in*utility of those scientific tortures could help us to preserve our benevolent aims: let us hope that such a thing may come to pass. But even supposing our efforts on this side were crowned with the most complete success, so long as the torturing of animals was abolished solely on the ground of inutility there would have been no lasting good accomplished for mankind, and the true idea that has prompted us to combine for the protection of animals would remain deformed and, out of cowardice, unuttered.

Who needs another motive for the protection of an animal from wilfully protracted sufferings, than that of pure humanity,* can never have felt a genuine right to stop another man's beast-torture. Everyone who revolts at the sight of an animal's torment, is prompted solely by

* "*Mitleid*" = "Compassion" or "Pity."—Tr.

compassion; and he who joins with others to protect dumb animals, is moved by naught save pity, of its very nature entirely indifferent to all calculations of utility or the reverse. But, that we have not the courage to set our only motive, this of Pity, in the forefront of our appeals and admonitions to the Folk, is the curse of our Civilisation, the attestation of the un-God-ing of our established Church-religions.

In our days it required the instruction of a philosopher who fought with dogged ruthlessness against all cant and all pretence,* to prove the *pity* deeply-seated in the human breast the only true foundation of morality. It was mocked at, nay, indignantly repudiated by the senate of a learned Academy; for virtue, where not enjoined by Revelation, was only to be based on Logic (*Vernunft-Erwägung*). Viewed logically, on the other hand, this Pity was pronounced a sublimated egoism: that the sight of others' sufferings caused pain to ourselves, was said to be compassion's ground-of-action, and not that foreign suffering itself, which we merely sought to do away with so as to obliterate the painful effect on our own selves.†

* Schopenhauer.—Tr.

† Again the master is obviously alluding to Friedrich Nietzsche and his *Menschliches, Allzumenschliches*, from which latter work I may quote the following, out of many passages of similar nature: "La Rochefoucauld is surely right when he warns all men-of-reason against pity, advising them to leave it to the people, who (not being led by reason) need passions to bring them to the point of helping the sufferer and actively intervening in misfortune; for in his opinion (and that of Plato) pity enfeebles the soul. Certainly one should *shew* pity, but pay heed not to *have* it: for the unfortunate are really so *stupid* as to take a show of pity for the greatest good in the world" —*Aphorism* 50. "The 'doing of harm for its own sake' *does not exist*, save in the brain of the philosopher, and just as little the 'doing of good for its own sake' (Pity, in the Schopenhauerian sense)"—*Aph.* 99. "All pleasure in one's self is neither good nor bad; whence comes the dictate that, to have pleasure in oneself, one must cause no grief to others? Merely from the utilitarian point of view, that is to say, from a calculation of *consequences*, the eventual unpleasantness to oneself from the aggrieved person or his representative, the State, wreaking punishment or vengeance: this can have been the only original ground for denying oneself such actions.—Pity aims as little at the pleasure of others, as wickedness at their hurt: for it bears in it at least two (perhaps many more) elements of a personal pleasure, and thus is self-

How ingenious we had become, in the slime of basest selfishness to guard ourselves against disturbance by the pangs of fellow-feeling! Again, this Pity was despised because most often met with as a quite inferior grade of human utterance, and in the very lowest classes: here one diligently confused it with that "regret" which is so readily shewn by onlookers in every case of domestic or civic misfortune, and, seeing the unmeasured frequency of such events, finds expression in a head-shake, a shrug of the shoulders, and departure,—till haply one steps forward from the crowd, a man impelled to active help by true compassion. He in whom no more of pity is ingrained, than just that cowardly "regret," may cheaply find his satisfaction in its warding off, and a full-bodied but well-dressed contempt for mankind will fitly serve his turn. In effect it will be hard to send such a person to his fellow-men themselves for his lessons in the exercise of pity, as, taking our law-abiding State and Burgher world in bulk, there is a sorry prospect of fulfilment of our Saviour's behest: "Thou shalt love thy neighbour as thyself." Our neighbours are not very loveable as a rule, and in most cases we are warned by prudence to first await proof of the neighbour's love, since we are not justified in relying much on his bare profession of it.* Viewed strictly, our State and our Society are so planned by the laws of mechanics as to manage quite supportably

gratification: the first is the pleasure of emotion, its type in compassion at a tragedy; the second, when it drives a man to action, the pleasure of exerting his power. Moreover if a suffering person is very near to us, by the exercise of compassionate deeds we remove from ourselves a smart.—Apart from a few philosophers, men have therefore placed Pity somewhat low in the scale of moral sentiments: and rightly"—*Aph.* 103. "We *judge* by analogy that something hurts a person, and our own memory and strength of fancy may make it painful to ourselves. But what a difference between the tooth-ache and the pain (Mitleiden) the sight of toothache conjures up!"—*Aph.* 104. Upon comparing the last little touch with page 180 *antea* it will be evident that Wagner had this very section of Nietzsche's work in mind.—Tr.

* Referring to Nietzsche's "All that one promises is the duration of a show of love, when, without self-blinding, one declares eternal love to another"—*Menschliches*, Aphorism 58.—Tr.

without either pity or neighbourly love. We fancy the apostle of Pity will have great trouble in getting his doctrine practised from man to man in the first place, as even our family-life of to-day is so degenerated by the pressure of care and the craze for distraction, that it would yield him no sound leverage. It is even to be doubted that his teachings will find ardent acceptance by the Army-control—which, with exception of the Bourse, keeps wellnigh all our public life in order—for here it would be proved to him that Pity is to be understood in quite another sense than his, namely *en gros*, summarily, the abridgment of life's inutile sufferings by surer and yet surer projectiles.

"Science," on the contrary, seems to have official sanction for taking over the business of Pity in civic society, by application of her fruits to professional practice. We will not here pry into the issues of that Theologic science which equips the soul-physicians of our parishes with knowledge of divine inscrutabilities, and we provisionally assume that the exercise of their unrivalledly beautiful calling will not have made her pupils unappreciative of efforts such as ours. Unfortunately it will sorely strain the strict ecclesiastic dogma, which still reposes on the First Book of Moses, if the pity of God is to be claimed for beasts created merely for the use of man. Yet nowadays one bridges over many a difficulty, and the good heart of a humane incumbent has doubtless found much else in his cure-of-souls to favourably incline his dogmatic reason to our cause. Hard as it may nevertheless remain to claim Theology for the exclusive service of Pity, our outlook should brighten at once when we turn to Medical science, which trains its students solely for the ministry of human suffering. The physician ought to seem to us the daily saviour of our life, with whose calling no other can be compared in point of directly visible beneficence. What provides him the means of healing us from grave afflictions we have to honour in all trust, and therefore is the Medical regarded as the most useful and precious of all the sciences, for whose requirements and exercise we are ready to make every sacrifice; for from it proceeds the true diploma-ed officer of personally active pity, so seldom to be met among us else.

When Mephistopheles warns us of the "hidden bane" of Theology, we may take that warning for just as sinister as his suspicious praise of Medicine, whose practical results, for the comfort of doctors, he commits to the "pleasure of God." Yet this very gloating over medical science makes us fear lest in *it* there lies no "hidden," but some quite obvious "bane," which the rascal merely tries to cloak from us by his instigative praise. At anyrate it is astonishing that the more this reputedly most useful of the "sciences" withdraws from practical experience, to seek a positive infallibility on fields of speculative operation, the more clearly does she demonstrate that she strictly is no science at all. It is from practising doctors themselves, that we gain this information. Their experimenting confrères of Speculative Physiology may call them vain, for imagining that the art of healing depends more on experiences open to none but the practitioner, on the eye of the born physician, and finally his eagerness to help his trusting invalid to the utmost of his power. When Mahomet had run through all the wonders of creation, he recognised it as the greatest, that men should pity one another; this we unconditionally presuppose of the doctor to whom we entrust our case, and we therefore believe him rather than the speculative physiologist who aims at fame and abstract knowledge with the tools of the dissecting-room. But this last trust will be robbed us if we hear, as recently, that an assembly of practising doctors allowed their fear of "science" and dread of being classed as hypocrites or heretics to make them disown those only qualities which inspire the sick with confidence, and brand themselves the humble servants of speculative outrage, by declaring that without the constant dissection of living animals by Messrs the Students the medical practitioner would soon be powerless to aid his patients.

Luckily the few data we have already received on the truth of this matter are so entirely convincing, that the cowardice of those other gentlemen can no longer tempt us to enthusiasm for the animal-torture they so philanthropically approve; on the contrary, it will make us cease committing our health and life to a doctor who gains his learning thence, for we shall regard him not only as a man insensible to pity, but also as a dunce in his profession.

Though that "science" is commended to the particular esteem of our "great public," the inviolable sanctuary of our ministers and privy councillors, its ghastly bungling has lately been so instructively exposed to us by the writings of several practical doctors—distinguished by the very purity of their German style in composition—that we may hold ourselves justified in the hope that the spectre of a "usefulness" of Vivisection will no longer vex us in our further efforts; so that henceforth we should only have to try to win a fruitful soil for fresh culture of the *Religion of Pity*, in defiance of all confessors of the Utilitarian creed. Unfortunately our review of human things has shewn us Pity struck from off the laws of our Society, since even our medical institutes, pretending care for man, have become establishments for teaching ruthlessness, which naturally will be extended—for sake of "science"—from animals to any human beings found defenceless against its experiments.

Or may our very indignation at the shocking sufferings inflicted wilfully on animals point out to us the pathway to the kingdom of pity toward all that lives, the Paradise once lost and now to be regained with consciousness?—

When first it dawned on human wisdom that the same thing breathed in animals as in mankind, it appeared too late to avert the curse which, ranging ourselves with the beasts of prey, we seemed to have called down upon us through the taste of animal food: disease and misery of every kind, to which we did not see mere vegetable-eating men exposed. The insight thus obtained led further to the consciousness of a deep-seated guilt in our earthly being: it moved those fully seized therewith to turn aside from all that stirs the passions, through free-willed poverty and total abstinence from animal food. To these wise men the mystery of the world unveiled itself as a restless tearing into pieces, to be restored to restful unity by nothing save compassion. His pity for each breathing creature, determining his every action, redeemed the sage from all the ceaseless change of suffering existences, which he himself must pass until his last emancipation. Thus the pitiless was mourned by him for reason of his suffering, but most of all the beast, whose pain he saw without knowing it capable of redemption through pity. This wise man could but recognise that the reasonable being gains its highest happiness through free-willed suffering, which he therefore seeks with eagerness, and ardently embraces; whereas the beast but looks on pain, so absolute and useless to it, with dread and agonised rebellion. But still more to be deplored that wise man deemed the human being who consciously could torture animals and turn a deaf ear to their pain, for he knew that such a one was infinitely farther from redemption than the wild beast itself, which should rank in comparison as sinless as a saint.

Races driven to rawer climates, and hence compelled to guard their life by animal food, preserved till quite late times a feeling that the beasts did not belong to them, but to a deity; they knew themselves guilty of a crime with every beast they slew or slaughtered, and had to expiate it to the god: they offered up the beast, and thanked the god by giving him the fairest portions of the spoil. What here was a religious sentiment survived in later philosophers, born after the ruin of religions, as axiom of humanity: one has only to read Plutarch's splendid treatise "On Reason in the Beasts of Land and Sea," to return with a tingle of shame to the precepts of our men of science.

Up to here, but alas! no farther, can we trace the religious basis of our human forbears' sympathy with animals, and it seems that the march of civilisation, by making him indifferent to "the God," turned man himself into a raging beast of prey; in fact we have seen a Roman Cæsar, clad wholly in the fell of such a beast, repeat its actions for the public eye. The monstrous guilt of all this life a divine and sinless being took upon himself, and expiated with his agony and death. Through this atonement all that breathes and lives should know itself redeemed, so soon as it was grasped as pattern and example to be followed. And this was done by all the saints and martyrs whom it drew to free-willed suffering, to bathe them in the fount of Pity till every worldly dream * was washed away. Legends have told us how wild beasts allied themselves in friendship with these holy ones—perchance not merely for the shelter thus ensured, but also driven by a possible first gleam of deep instinctive sympathy: here were wounds, and finally the kind protecting hand, to lick. In these legends, as of Genovefa's doe and many another, there surely lies a sense that leaves the Old Testament far behind.—

Those legends now are dumb: the Pentateuch has won the day, and the prowling has become the "calculating" beast of prey. Our creed is: "Animals are useful; particularly if, trusting in our sanctuary, they yield themselves into our hands. Come let us therefore make of them what we deem good for human use; we have the right to martyr a thousand faithful dogs the whole day long, if we can thereby help one human creature to the cannibal well-being of five-hundred swine."

Our horror at the consequences of this maxim, however, could not attain its true expression until we had been more precisely informed of the scandals of the scientific torture-chamber, which now at last have driven us to the question: How is our broader relation to animals to be made a moral one and easing to the conscience, since we can find no essential support in our churchly dogmas?

* *Weltenwahn*—cf. "Oh, Weltenwahn's Umnachten: in höchsten Heiles heisser Sucht, nach der Verdammniss Quell zu schmachten!" *Parsifal*, act ii.—Tr.

The wisdom of the Brahmins, nay, of every cultured pagan race, is lost to us: with the disowning of our true relation to the beasts, we see an animalised—in the worst sense—and more than an animalised, a devilised world before us. There's not a truth to which, in our self-seeking and self-interest, we are not ready to shut our eyes even when able to perceive it: herein consists our Civilisation. Yet this time it would seem as if the measure filled too full were brimming over; wherein one might see a good result of active Pessimism, in the sense of Mephistopheles the "good-doing." Apart from, but almost simultaneously with the outcrop of that torturing of animals in the name of an impossible science, an honest inquirer, a careful breeder and comparer, a scientific friend of beasts, laid once more open to us men the teachings of primeval wisdom, according to which the same thing breathes in animals that lends us life ourselves; ay, shewed us past all doubt that we descend from them. In the spirit of our unbelieving century, this knowledge may prove our surest guide to a correct estimate of our relation to the animals; and perhaps it is on this road alone, that we might again arrive at a real religion, as taught to us by the Redeemer and testified by his example, the religion of true Human Love. We have already touched on what has made compliance with this teaching so extremely hard to us slaves of Civilisation. As we have used dumb beasts not merely for our sustenance and service, but to shew us in their art-dealt sufferings what we ourselves may haply lack when, cankered by unnatural modes of life, excess and vice of every kind, our body is seized at last with sickness,—we now might fitly use them for improvement of our morals, ay, in many respects for our self-discipline, as Nature's never-lying witnesses.

A clue to this is given us by friend Plutarch. He had the daring to invent a dialogue between Ulysses and his companions turned to beasts by Circe, in which they refused for the soundest of reasons to be turned back to men. He who has carefully followed this wonderful dialogue, will find how hard it is to-day to exhort mankind, transformed into monsters, to return to paths of human dignity. An actual success might perhaps be only expected if man were first to learn his nobler self by observation of the beast. From the suffering and death of beasts we well might win a measure for the higher dignity of man, who is capable of taking sorrow as his most fruitful lesson, and death as a transfiguring atonement, whereas the beast must always smart and die without an object to itself. We despise the man who does not bear his tale of suffering stoutly, who falls into a quaking fear of death: but it is for him our physiologists vivisect animals, inoculate them with the poison he has bred through vice, and cunningly protract their torments to learn how long they haply might defend the wretch from his last agony! Who shall behold in that disease, or in this remedy, a moral factor? Would all these scientific wiles be plied to help the poor mechanic suffering from hunger, want and overtaxing of his powers? Why, we hear that just on him—who fortunately does not hanker after life, and gladly leaves it—the most interesting of all attempts at objective scrutiny of physiological problems are often made; so that even in his death the poor is made to serve the rich, as in his life by the so-called "airing" of fine mansions too newly-built for healthy habitation, and so forth. Yet this befalls the poor in dull unconsciousness. The animal, on the contrary, we may assume would willingly be plagued and tortured for its master in full knowledge, if we could make plain to its intellect that the welfare of its human friend was at stake. That this is not saying too much, we may judge from the fact that horses, dogs, and almost all domesticated animals, can only be trained by making it clear to their understanding what performances we want of them; once they understand it, they are willing and eager to do what we wish. Rough and brutal men believe they must convey their orders to the unenlightened animal by menaces, whose object it does not understand, and therefore fails in—which leads to fresh mishandling such as might be usefully applied to the master who knows the meaning of punishment; yet the love and fidelity of the grossly maltreated animal to its tormentor are not thereby diminished. That even in its sharpest pangs a dog can still caress its master, we have learnt from the studies of our vivisectors: but in the interest of human dignity the lesson to be drawn from such discoveries should be laid more seriously to heart than hitherto; to which end it might be profitable to first consider what we have already learnt from the brute beasts, and then the lessons still remaining to be won from them.

To the beasts, who have been our schoolmasters in all the arts by which we trapped and made them subject to us, man was superior in nothing save deceit and cunning, by no means in courage or bravery; for the animal will fight to its last breath, indifferent to wounds and death: "it knows nor plea nor prayer for mercy, no avowal of defeat." To base man's dignity upon his pride, compared with that of animals, would be mistaken; and our victory over them, their subjugation, we can only attribute to our greater art of dissembling. That art we highly boast of; we call it "reason" ("*Vernunft*") and proudly think it marks us from the animals: for look you! it can make us like to God himself—as to which, however, Mephistopheles has his private opinion, concluding that the only use man made of reason was "to be more bestial than any beast." In its great veracity and naïveness the animal is unable to estimate the moral meanness of the arts through which we cowed it; in any case it finds something dæmonic in them, which it obeys in timid awe: but if its master exercises kindness toward the daunted beast, we may assume that it recognises something divine in him, which it reveres and loves so strongly that it devotes its natural gifts of bravery entirely to the service of fidelity, to the point of agonising death. Just as the saint is driven irresistibly to attest his loyalty to God by martyrdom and death, so the animal with its love to a master adored as god. One only tie, which the saint has been able to break, still binds the animal to Nature, since it cannot be aught but sincere:

compassion for its young. In resulting dilemmas, however, it knows how to choose for the best. A traveller once left his brach behind him in the stable of an inn, as she had just brought forth young, and pursued alone the three-leagues journey to his house; next morning he finds on the straw in his yard the four sucklings, and beside them their dead mother: four times had she run the distance to and fro in haste and anguish, carrying home her litter one by one; only when she had brought the last pup safely to her master, whom she now had no more need to leave, did she yield to the lingering pains of death.—This the "free" burgher of our Civilisation calls "houndish fidelity," with a contemptuous accent on the "hound." * Yet in a world from which all *reverence* has vanished, or tarries but as hypocritical pretence, is there no example for us to take from the affecting lesson of the animals we govern? Where devotion true till death is met between man and man, we need not be ashamed to regard it as already a noble bond of kinship with the animal kingdom, since there is good reason for believing that this virtue is purer, eh! diviner in its exercise by animals than by man: for, quite apart from their value in the eyes of the world, in his sufferings and death man is able to recognise a blessed expiation; whereas the beast, without one ulterior thought of moral advantage, sacrifices itself wholly and purely to love and lealty—though this also is explained by our physiologists as a simple chemical reaction of certain elementary substances.

* At the end of vol. ii. of Nietzsche's *Menschliches* there is an imaginary dialogue between the "Wanderer" (the author) and his shadow, in which the Wanderer remarks: "I will have no slaves about me: not even the dog, that lazy tail-wagging parasite, who never was 'houndish' till he became the serf of man, and of whom they are even wont to boast that he is faithful to his master and follows him like his—"; the Shadow completes the sentence, with wounded pride.—This "Wanderer and his Shadow" is said by the editor of Nietzsche's Works not to have been printed till November 1879, or published till the end of that year; but there must be a slight mistake here, for Wagner is distinctly quoting from it, as above, in the *Bayreuther Blätter* of October 1879.—There is a good deal more about animals in Aphorism 57 of this "Wanderer" section, where Nietzsche attributes their humane treatment by man primarily and chiefly to a sense of their usefulness.—Tr.

These monkeys scuttling up the tree of knowledge in dread of their lives might be recommended not to look so much into the mangled entrails of a living animal, but rather with some calm and penetration into its eye; here perchance the scientific searcher would for the first time find expressed the thing most worthy man: namely *truthfulness*, the impossibility of a lie; and peering deeper, he might catch the lofty accents of Nature's grief at his own deplorably sinful presumption; for the scientific jokes he cracks the poor beast takes in bitter earnest. Thence let him look upon his truly suffering fellow-man, born in naked indigence, misused from tenderest childhood for toil that undermines his strength, ailing before his time through evil food and heartless treatment of all kinds, and lifting up to him sad eyes of pitiful inquiry: perhaps he then may tell himself that this at least is a man like him. 'Twere a result indeed. Next, if ye cannot imitate the pitying beast that hungers gladly with its human master, go seek ye to outvie it, by helping your hungering fellow-man to necessary food! And that might come quite easy to you, if ye but put him on the selfsame diet as the rich, allowing him just so much of the surplus food, that makes the rich man sick, as to give him back to health—not that there would be any need to think of delicacies such as larks, which certainly look better in the sky than in your stomachs. 'Twere to be wished your art could reach so far. But all the arts ye learn are useless. Upon the postponement of the death of a Hungarian magnate to a certain distant day, depended the recovery of enormous family interests: the beneficiaries offered gigantic fees to doctors who should let the dying noble see that day; they came: fine times were those for "science"; God only knows what all was bled and poisoned: triumph! the inheritance was ours, and Science was brilliantly remunerated. Now, it is not to be expected that so much science could be disbursed on our poor labourers. But perhaps something else: the outcome of a deep conversion in our inner hearts.

Should not the horror surely felt by everyone at the employment of the most unimaginable animal-tortures for the fancied good of our health—the worst thing we could possess in such a heartless world!—have already effected such a conversion altogether of itself; or do we first need to be informed that this utility is erroneous, if not mendacious, as the true object is nothing but the satisfaction of a virtuoso-vanity, with perhaps a touch of vulgar curiosity? Are we to wait for the victims of "utility" to comprise a vivisected man? Is the Use of the State indeed to rank before that of the Individual? A Visconti, Duke of Milan, once issued an edict against political offenders, whereby the delinquent's death-agonies were to be reckoned to last for forty days. This man appears to have scaled the studies of our physiologists in advance; with luck they also are able to prolong the torture of a good tough animal to exactly forty days, though it was there a case of cruelty, here more of calculating parsimony. Visconti's edict was approved by State and Church, for nobody objected to it; only those who did not deem the threatened torture the worst they could endure, found themselves moved to seize the State by the windpipe, in the person of my lord Duke. Would that the modern State itself would step into the shoes of those "offenders," and hurl our man-disgracing Messieurs Vivisectors clean out of their laboratories! Or are we to leave this again to "enemies of the State," as which the so-called "Socialists" are styled in the latest laws?—In fact, while State and Church are racking their brains as to whether they shall give way to our representations and brook the dreaded anger of offended "Science," we hear that a violent irruption into one of these vivisection-theatres in Leipzig, with a speedy despatch of animals trussed up and hacked and put aside for weeks of torture—as also, we may hope, a good sound thrashing administered to the careful guardians of that chamber of abominations—has been ascribed to a vulgar outburst of subversive socialist intrigues against the rights of property. Who would not turn Socialist, were he to find that State and Reich reject our steps against continuance of Vivisection, our demands that it be abolished unconditionally? But only an *unconditional abolishing*, not a mere "restricting as much as possible" under "State-supervision," would meet requirements; and the only thing to be understood by State-supervision, should be the attendance of a duly instructed Gens-d'armes at every physiological conference of these Messrs. Professors with their precious "spectators."

For our conclusion should be couched as follows:—That **Human dignity** *begins to assert itself only at the point where Man is distinguishable from the Beast by pity for it, since pity for man we ourselves may learn from the animals when treated reasonably and as becomes a human being.*

If we are to be mocked for this, disclaimed by our National Intelligence, and Vivisection is to continue to flourish in public and private as before, at least there is one good thing for which we might thank its defenders: that a world in which "no dog would longer care to live" we can gladly leave as Men, though no "German Requiem" be played to our ashes!

RICHARD WAGNER.

Bayreuth, October 1879.

RELIGION AND ART.

Religion und Kunst.

Ich finde in der christlichen Religion virtualiter die Anlage zu dem Höchsten und Edelsten, und die verschiedenen Erscheinungen derselben im Leben scheinen mir bloss desswegen so widrig und abgeschmackt, weil sie verfehlte Darstellungen dieses Höchsten sind.

Schiller, an Goethe.

"*Religion and Art*" *originally appeared in the* Bayreuther Blätter *for October 1880, constituting the whole of that number of the journal. The nearest translation of the motto taken from Schiller, would be:—*

> "*In the Christian religion I find an intrinsic disposition to the Highest and the Noblest, and its various manifestations in life appear to me so vapid and repugnant simply because they have missed expression of that Highest.*"

TRANSLATOR'S NOTE.

I.

NE might say that where Religion becomes artificial, it is reserved for Art to save the spirit of religion by recognising the figurative value of the mythic symbols which the former would have us believe in their literal sense, and revealing their deep and hidden truth through an ideal presentation. Whilst the priest stakes everything on the religious allegories being accepted as matters of fact, the artist has no concern at all with such a thing, since he freely and openly gives out his work as his own invention. But Religion has sunk into an artificial life, when she finds herself compelled to keep on adding to the edifice of her dogmatic symbols, and thus conceals the one divinely True in her beneath an ever growing heap of incredibilities commended to belief. Feeling this, she has always sought the aid of Art; who on her side has remained incapable of higher evolution so long as she must present that alleged reality of the symbol to the senses of the worshipper in form of fetishes and idols,—whereas she could only fulfil her true vocation when, by an ideal presentment of the allegoric figure, she led to apprehension of its inner kernel, the truth ineffably divine.

To see our way clear in this, we should have most carefully to test the origin of religions. These we must certainly deem the more divine, the simpler proves to be their inmost kernel. Now, the deepest basis of every true religion we find in recognition of the frailty of this world, and the consequent charge to free ourselves therefrom. It is manifest that at all times it needed a superhuman effort to disclose this knowledge to men in a raw state of nature, the Folk in fact, and accordingly the most successful work of the religious Founder consisted in the invention of mythic allegories, by which the people might be led along the path of faith to practical observance of the lessons flowing from that root-knowledge. In this respect we can but regard it as a sublime distinction of the Christian religion, that it expressly claims to bare the deepest truth to the "poor in spirit," for their comfort and salvation; whereas the doctrine of the Brahmins was the exclusive property of "those who know"—for which reason the "rich in spirit" viewed the nature-ridden multitude as shut from possibility of knowledge and only arriving at insight into the nullity of the world by means of numberless rebirths. That there was a shorter road to salvation, the most enlightened of the "Reborn" himself disclosed to the poor blind Folk: but the sublime example of renunciation and unruffled meekness, which the *Buddha* set, did not suffice his fervid followers; his last great doctrine, of the unity of all things living, was only to be made accessible to his disciples through a mythic explanation of the world whose wealth of imagery and allegoric comprehensiveness was taken bodily from the storehouse of Brahminic teachings, so astounding in their proofs of fertility and culture of mind. Here too, in all the course of time and progress of their transformation, true Art could never be invoked to paint and clarify these myths and allegories; Philosophy supplied her place, coming to the succour of the religious dogmas with the greatest refinements of intellectual exposition.

It was otherwise with the Christian religion. Its founder was not wise, but divine *; his teaching was the deed of free-willed suffering. To believe in him, meant to emulate him; to hope for redemption, to strive for union with him. To the "poor in spirit" no metaphysical explanation of the

* "Ihr Gründer war nicht weise, sondern göttlich"—evidently in answer to Nietzsche's "The founder of Christianity, as is self-evident, was not without the greatest defects and prejudices. . . . Socrates excels the founder of Christianity by his buoyant type of earnestness and that *wisdom full of roguish ruses* which constitutes the best state of mind for man. Moreover he had the greater intellect."—*Menschliches*, vol. ii. "Wanderer," aphor. 83 and 86.—Tr.

world was necessary; the knowledge of its suffering lay open to their feeling; and not to shut the doors of that, was the sole divine injunction to believers. Now we may assume that if the belief in Jesus had remained the possession of these "poor" alone, the Christian dogma would have passed to us as the simplest of religions. But it was too simple for the "rich in mind," and the unparalleled intricacies of the sectarian spirit in the first three centuries of Christianity shew us the ceaseless struggle of the intellectually rich to rob the poor in spirit of their faith, to twist and model it anew to suit their own abstractions. The Church proscribed all philosophical expounding of this creed, designed by her to instigate a blind obedience; only—whatever she needed to give her parentage a superhuman rank she appropriated from the leavings of the battles of the sects, thus gradually garnering that harvest of most complicated myths, belief in which as quite material verities she demanded with unbending rigour.

Our best guide to an estimate of the belief in miracles, will be the demand addressed to natural man that he should change his previous mode of viewing the world and its appearances as the most absolute of realities; for he now was to know this world as null, an optical delusion, and to seek the only Truth beyond it. If by a miracle we mean an incident that sets aside the laws of Nature; and if, after ripe deliberation, we recognise these laws as founded on our own power of perception, and bound inextricably with the functions of our brain: then belief in miracles must be comprehensible to us as an almost necessary consequence of the reversal of the "will to live," in defiance of all Nature. To the natural man this reversal of the Will is certainly itself the greatest miracle, for it implies an abrogation of the laws of Nature; that which has effected it must consequently be far above Nature, and of superhuman power, since he finds that union with It is longed for as the only object worth endeavour. It is this Other that *Jesus* told his poor of, as the "Kingdom of

God," in opposition to the "kingdom of the world;" He who called to Him the weary and heavy-laden, the suffering and persecuted, the patient and meek, the friends of their enemies and lovers of all, was their "Heavenly Father," as whose "Son" he himself was sent to these "his Brothers."

We here behold the greatest miracle of all, and call it "Revelation." How it became possible to turn it into a State-religion for Romish Cæsars and Inquisitors, we shall have to consider in later course of this essay; our present attention is claimed by the wellnigh consequential evolution of those myths whose ultimate exuberance defaced the dogma of the Church with artificiality, yet offered fresh ideals to Art.

What we understand in general by the artistic province, we might define as Evaluation of the Pictorial (*Ausbildung des Bildlichen*); that is to say, Art grasps the Figurative of an idea, that outer form in which it shews itself to the imagination, and by developing the likeness—before employed but allegorically—into a picture embracing in itself the whole idea, she lifts the latter high above itself into the realm of revelation. Speaking of the ideal shape of the Greek statue, our great philosopher finely says: It is as if the artist were shewing Nature what she would, but never completely could; wherefore the artistic Ideal surpasses Nature.* Of Greek theogony it may be said that, in touch with the artistic instinct of the nation, it always clung to anthropomorphism. Their gods were figures with distinctive names and plainest individuality; their names were used to mark specific groups of things (*Gattungsbegriffe*), just as the names of various coloured objects were used to denote the colours themselves, for which the Greeks employed no abstract terms like ours: "gods" were they called, to mark their nature as divine; but the Divine itself the Greeks called *God*, "ὁ θεός." Never did it occur to them to think of "God" as a Person, or give to him artistic shape as to their named gods; he remained

* Schopenhauer, *Welt als Wille und Vorstellung*, Book III. § 45.—Tr.

an idea, to be defined by their philosophers, though the Hellenic spirit strove in vain to clearly fix it — till the wondrous inspiration of poor people spread abroad the incredible tidings that the "Son of God" had offered himself on the cross to redeem the world from deceit and sin.

We have nothing here to do with the astoundingly varied attempts of speculative human reason to explain the nature of this Son of *the* God, who walked on earth and suffered shame: where the greater miracle had been revealed in train of that manifestation, the reversal of the will-to-live which all believers experienced in themselves, it already embraced that other marvel, the divinity of the herald of salvation. The very shape of the Divine had presented itself in anthropomorphic guise; it was the body of the quintessence of all pitying Love, stretched out upon the cross of pain and suffering. A—symbol?—beckoning to the highest pity, to worship of suffering, to imitation of this breaking of all self-seeking Will: nay, a picture, a very effigy! In this, and its effect upon the human heart, lies all the spell whereby the Church soon made the Græco-Roman world her own. But what was bound to prove her ruin, and lead at last to the ever louder "Atheism" of our day, was the tyrant-prompted thought of tracing back this Godliness upon the cross to the Jewish "Creator of heaven and earth," a wrathful God of Punishment who seemed to promise greater power than the self-offering, all-loving Saviour of the Poor. That god was doomed by Art: Jehova in the fiery bush, or even the reverend Father with the snow-white beard who looked down from out the clouds in blessing on his Son, could say but little to the believing soul, however masterly the artist's hand; whereas the suffering god upon the cross, "the Head with wounds all bleeding," still fills us with ecstatic throes, in the rudest reproduction.

As though impelled by an artistic need, leaving Jehova the "Father" to shift for himself, Belief devised the necessary miracle of the Saviour's birth by a *Mother* who, not herself a goddess, became divine through her virginal conception of a son without human contact, against the laws of Nature. A thought of infinite depth, expressed in form of miracle. In the history of Christianity we certainly meet repeated instances of miraculous powers conferred by pure virginity, where a metaphysical concurs very well with a physiologic explanation, in the sense of a *causa finalis* with a *causa efficiens*; but the mystery of motherhood without natural fecundation can only be traced to the greater miracle, the birth of the God himself: for in this the Denial-of-the-world is revealed by a life prefiguratively offered up for its redemption.* As the Saviour himself was recognised as sinless, nay, incapable of sin, it followed that in him the Will must have been completely broken ere ever he was born, so that he could no more suffer, but only feel for others' sufferings; and the root hereof was necessarily to be found in a birth that issued, not from the Will-to-live, but from the Will-to-redeem. But this mystery that seemed so plain to the illuminate, was exposed to the most glaring misinterpretations on the part of popular realism when demanded as an article of faith; the "immaculate conception" by the Virgin Mary might be phrased indeed, but never thought, still less imagined. The Church, which in the Middle Ages had her articles expounded by her handmaid, Scholastic philosophy, sought at last for means of visibly portraying

* In his *Welt als W. u. V.*, Book IV. § 70, Schopenhauer says: "The Christian doctrine symbolises *Nature*, the *Affirmation of the Will-to-live*, by Adam. . . . *Grace*, on the other hand, the *Denial of the Will*, *Redemption*, by the God become Man; who is free from all sin, i.e. from all life-willing, and neither can have issued from the Will's most positive act of affirmation, as we have, nor have, as we, a body through and through but concrete Will; born of a pure virgin, he has but a seeming body." And in his *Parerga*, § 167: "The woman's share in procreation is more guiltless than the man's; for he bestows upon the child its *will*, which is the first sin, and therefore the root of all evil; the woman, on the contrary, bestows its intellect, which is the pathway to redemption. . . . So that in conception the Will is given afresh the possibility of redemption." On this hypothesis the absence of a father, who bestows "Affirmation of the will," would be the "necessary miracle" conducting to birth of the true redeemer.—Tr.

them; above the porch of St. Kilian * at Wurzburg we may see a bas-relief of God the Father transmitting the embryo of the Saviour to the body of Mary by means of a blow-pipe. This instance may serve for thousands like it! Such appalling degradation of religious dogmas to artificiality we referred to in our opening paragraph, and this flagrant example will emphasise the redeeming effect of true idealistic art if we turn to their treatment by heaven-sent artists, such as Raphael in his so-called "Sistine Madonna." The Miraculous Conception still was handled in the Church's realistic spirit, to some extent, even when great artists painted its annunciation to the Virgin by an angel, albeit the spiritual beauty of the figures, removed from all materialism, here gives us a glimpse into the divine mysterium itself. But that picture of Raphael's shews us the final consummation of the miracle, the virgin mother transfigured and ascending with the new-born son: here we are taken by a beauty which the ancient world, for all its gifts, could not so much as dream of; for here is not the ice of chastity that made an Artemis seem unapproachable, but Love divine beyond all knowledge of unchastity, Love which of innermost denial of the world has born the affirmation of redemption. And this unspeakable wonder we see with our eyes, distinct and tangible, in sweetest concord with the noblest truths of our own inner being, yet lifted high above conceivable experience. If the Greek statue held to Nature her unattained ideal, the painter now unveiled the unseizable and therefore indefinable mystery of the religious dogmas, no longer to the plodding reason, but to enraptured sight.

Yet another dogma was to offer itself to the artist's phantasy, and one on which the Church at last seemed to set more store than on that of Redemption through Love. The World-overcomer was called to be World-judge. From the arm of his virgin mother the divine child had bent his searching gaze upon the world, and, piercing all its tempting show, had recognised its true estate as

* The Marienkapelle in the old Marktplatz.—Tr.

death-avoiding, death-accurst. Under the Redeemer's sway, this world of greed and hate durst not abide; to the downtrod poor, whom he called to free themselves through suffering and compassion, to meet him in his Father's kingdom, he must shew this world in the scales of justice, its own weight dragging it down to the slough of sin. From the sun-drenched heights of those fair hills on which he loved to preach salvation to the multitude in images and parables, whereby alone could he gain the understanding of his "poor," he pointed to the gruesome death-vale of "Gehenna"; thither, upon the day of judgment, should avarice and murder be condemned, to fleer at one another in despair. Tartarus, Inferno, Hela, all places of post-mortem punishment of wicked men and cowards, were found again in this "Gehenna"; and to our day the threat of "Hell" has remained the Church's vital hold upon men's souls, from whom the "Kingdom of Heaven" has moved farther and farther away. The Last Judgment: a prophecy here big with solace, there terrible! No element of ghastly hatefulness and loathly awe, but was pressed into the service of the Church with sickening artifice, to give the terrified imagination a foretaste of that place of everlasting doom where the myths of each religion besmirched with belief in the torments of Hell were assembled in most hideous parody. As though in commiseration of the horrible itself, a supremely lofty artist felt impelled to paint this nightmare too: the thought of Christ seemed incomplete without this picture of the final judgment. Whilst Raphael had shewn us God born from the womb of sublimest love, Michael Angelo's prodigious painting shews us the God fulfilling his terrible work, God hurling from the realm of the elect all those belonging to the world of ever-dying death: yet—by his side the Mother whence he sprang, who bore divinest suffering with and for him, and now rains down on those unsharing in redemption the eternal glance of sorrowing pity. There the fount, but here the full-fed stream of the Divine!

Though we have not been attempting an account of Art's historical development from the religious idea, but simply an outline of their mutual affinities, yet that historic career must be touched upon in dealing with the circumstance that it was almost solely plastic art, and that of Painting in particular, which could present the religious dogmas—originally themselves symbolical—in an ideally figurative form. *Poetry*, on the contrary, was constrained by their very symbolism to adhere to the form laid down by canon as a matter of realistic truth and implicit credence. As these dogmas themselves were figurative concepts, so the greatest poetic genius—whose only instruments are mental figures—could remodel or explain nothing without falling into heterodoxy, like all the philosopher-poets of the earliest centuries of the Church, who succumbed to the charge of heresy. Perhaps the poetic power bestowed on *Dante* was the greatest e'er within the reach of mortal; yet in his stupendous poem it is only where he can hold the visionary world aloof from dogma, that his true creative force is shewn, whereas he always handles the dogmatic concepts according to the Church's principle of literal credence; and thus these latter never leave that lowering artificiality to which we have already alluded, confronting us with horror, nay, absurdity, from the mouth of so great a poet.

Now, in respect of plastic art it is palpable that its ideally creative force diminished in exact proportion as it withdrew from contact with religion. Betwixt those sublimest revelations of religious art, in the godlike birth of the Redeemer and the last fulfilment of the work of the Judge of the world, the saddest of all pictures, that of the Saviour suffering on the cross, had likewise attained to its height of perfection; and this remained the archetype of the countless representations of martyred saints, their agonies illumined by the bliss of transport. Here the portrayal of bodily pain, with the instruments of torture and their wielders, already led the artists down to the common actual world, whose types of human wickedness and cruelty surrounded them beyond escape. And then came "Characteristique," with its multiple attraction for the artist; the consummate "portrait" of even the vulgarest criminal, such as might be found among the temporal and spiritual princes of that remarkable time, became the painter's most rewarding task; as on the other hand, he early enough had taken his motives for the Beautiful from the physical charms of the women in his voluptuous surroundings.

The last sunset flush of artistic idealising of the Christian dogma had been kissed by the morning glow of the reviving Grecian art-ideal: but what could now be borrowed from the ancient world, was no longer that unity of Greek art with Antique religion whereby alone had the former blossomed and attained fruition. We have only to compare an antique statue of the goddess Venus with an Italian painting of the women chosen to impersonate this Venus, to perceive the difference between religious ideal and worldly reality. Greek art could only teach its sense of form, not lend its ideal content; whilst the Christian ideal had passed out of range of this sense-of-form, to which the actual world alone seemed henceforth visible. What shape this actual world at last took on, and what types alone it offered to the plastic arts, we will still exclude from our inquiry; suffice it to say that that art which was destined to reach its apogee in its affinity with religion, completely severing itself from this communion—as no one can deny—has fallen into utter ruin.

Once more to touch the quick of that affinity, let us turn one glance to the *Art of Tone.*

While it was possible for Painting to reveal the ideal content of a dogma couched in allegoric terms, and, without throwing doubt on the figure's claim to absolute credence, to take that allegory itself as object of ideal portrayal, we have had to see that Poetry was forced to leave its kindred power of imagery unexercised upon the dogmas of the Christian Church; employing concepts as its vehicle (*durch Begriffe darstellend*), it must retain the conceptual form of the dogma inviolate in every point. It therefore was solely in the lyrical expression of rapturous worship that poetry could be approached, and as the religious concept must still be phrased in forms of words canonically fixed, the lyric necessarily poured itself into a purely musical expression, un-needing any mould of abstract terms. Through the art of Tone did the Christian Lyric thus first become itself an art: the music of the Church was sung to the words of the abstract dogma; in its effect however, it dissolved those words and the ideas they fixed, to the point of their vanishing out of sight; and hence it rendered nothing to the enraptured Feeling save their pure emotional content.

Speaking strictly, the only art that fully corresponds with the Christian belief is Music; even as the only music which, now at least, we can place on the same footing as the other arts, is an exclusive product of Christianity. In its development, alone among the fine arts, no share was borne by re-awaking Antique Art, whose tone-effects have almost passed beyond our ken: wherefore also we regard it as the youngest of the arts, and the most capable of endless evolution and appliance. With its past and future evolution, however, we here are not concerned, since our immediate object is to consider its affinity to Religion. In this sense, having seen the Lyric compelled to resolve the form of words to a shape of tones, we must recognise that Music reveals the inmost essence of the Christian religion with definition unapproached; wherefore we may figure it as bearing the same relation to Religion which that picture of Raphael's has shewn us borne by the Child-of-god to the virgin Mother: for, as pure Form of a divine Content freed from all abstractions, we may regard it as a world-redeeming incarnation of the divine dogma of the nullity of the phenomenal world itself. Even the painter's most ideal shape remains conditioned by the dogma's terms, and when we gaze upon her likeness, that sublimely virginal Mother of God lifts us up above the miracle's irrationality only by making it appear as wellnigh possible. Here we have: "That signifies." But Music says: "That is,"—for she stops all strife between reason and feeling, and that by a tone-shape completely removed from the world of appearances, not to be compared with anything physical, but usurping our heart as by act of Grace.

This lofty property of Music's enabled her at last to quite divorce herself from the reasoned word; and the noblest music completed this divorce in measure as religious Dogma became the toy of Jesuitic casuistry or rationalistic pettifogging. The total worldlifying of the Church dragged after it a worldly change in Music: where both still work in unison, as in modern Italy for instance, neither in the one's displays nor the other's accompaniment can we detect any difference from every other parade of pomp. Only her final severance from the decaying Church could enable the art of Tone to save the noblest heritage of the Christian idea in its purity of over-worldly reformation; and the object of the remainder of our essay shall be, to foreshadow the affinities of a Beethovenian Symphony with a purest of religions once to blossom from the Christian revelation.

To reach that possibility, however, we first must tread the stony path on which may be found the cause of downfall even of the most exalted religions, and therewith the ground of decadence of all the culture they called forth, above all of the arts they fructified. However terrible may be the scenes the journey must unfold to us, yet this alone can be the road conducting to the shore of a new hope for the human race.

II.

IF we follow up that phase in the evolution of the human race which we call the Historic, as based on sure tradition, it is easier to comprehend why the religions arising in course of this period fell deeper and deeper in their inward spirit, the longer was their outward rule. The two sublimest of religions, Brahminism with its offshoot Buddhism, and Christianity, teach alienation from the world and its passions, thus steering straight against the flow of the world-tide without being able in truth to stem it. Hence their outer continuance seems explicable only by their having brought to the world the knowledge of Sin on the one hand, and used that knowledge, on the other, to found beside the temporal dominion over man's body a spiritual dominion over his soul which fouled the purity of the religion in measure with the general deterioration of the human race.

This doctrine of man's sinfulness, which forms the starting-point of each of these sublime religions, is unintelligible to the so-called "Free-thinker," who will neither allow to existing Churches a right to the adjudgment of sin, nor to the State a warrant to declare certain actions as criminal. Though both rights may be open to question, it would none the less be wrong to extend that doubt to the core of Religion itself; since it surely must be admitted in general that, not the religions themselves are to be blamed for their fall, but rather the fall of mankind, as traceable in history, has brought their ruin in its train; for we see this Fall of Man proceeding with so marked a nature-necessity, that it could but carry with itself each effort to arrest it.

And precisely by that misappropriated doctrine of Sin itself, can this shocking progress of events be shewn most plainly; for proof whereof we think best to commence with the Brahminic doctrine of the sinfulness of killing living creatures, or feeding on the carcasses of murdered beasts.

Upon probing the sense of this doctrine, with its resultant dissuasion, we light at once on the root of all true religious conviction, and at like time the deepest outcome of all knowledge of the world, both in essence and manifestation. For that teaching had its origin in recognition of the unity of all that lives, and of the illusion of our physical senses which dress this unity in guise of infinitely complex multitude and absolute diversity. It was thus the result of a profound metaphysical insight, and when the Brahmin pointed to the manifold appearances of the animate world, and said "This is thyself!" there woke in us the consciousness that in sacrificing one of our fellow-creatures we mangled and devoured ourselves. That the beasts are only distinguished from man by the grade of their mental faculties; that what precedes all intellectual equipment, what desires and suffers, is the same Will-to-live in them as in the most reason-gifted man; that this one Will it is, which strives for peace and freedom amid our world of changing forms and transitory semblances; and finally, that this assuagement of tumultuous longing can only be won by the most scrupulous practice of gentleness and sympathy toward all that lives,—upon this the religious conscience of the Brahmin and Buddhist has stood firm as a rock till this day. We learn that about the middle of last century certain English speculators bought up the whole rice-harvest of India, and thus induced a famine in the land, which swept away three millions of the natives: yet not one of these starving wretches could be moved to slay and eat his household animals; only after their masters, did they famish too. A mighty testimony to the genuineness of a religious belief, with which, however, the confessors themselves have been expunged from "*History*."

If on the other hand we look a little closer at the human race in its stamp upon History, we can only ascribe its deplorable infirmity to the same mad *Wahn** that prompts the savage animal to fall upon its prey when no

* See footnote to page 13, Vol. IV.—Tr.

longer driven by hunger—sheer pleasure in its raging strength. Though physiologists are still divided as to whether Man was meant by Nature to feed exclusively on fruits, or also upon flesh-meat, from its first faint glimmerings History shews Man's constant progress as a beast of prey. As such he conquers every land, subdues the fruit-fed races, founds mighty realms by subjugating other subjugators, forms states and sets up civilisations, to enjoy his prey at rest.

Insufficient as are all our scientific data as to the first starting-point of this historic evolution, we may take it for granted that the birth and earliest dwelling-place of the human species may be set in countries warm and clad with ample vegetation. It seems more difficult to decide what violent changes drove a great portion of the human race from its natural birthplaces to rawer and inhospitable regions. At the first dawning of history we believe we find the aborigines of the present Indian peninsula in the cooler valleys of the Himalayan highlands, supporting themselves as graziers and tillers of the soil; from here, under guidance of a religion whose gentleness accorded with the herdsman's needs, we see them return to the lower valleys of the Indus, and thence again resume possession, as it were, of their ancient home, the delta of the Ganges. Great and deep must have been the impressions of this return from exodus upon the mind of races who had now gone through so much: a smiling Nature offered them with willing hand its varied products; fed without care, an earnest contemplation would lead them to profound reflection on that former world wherein they had learnt the stress of need and bitter toil, ay, of strife and warfare for possession. To the Brahmin, now feeling himself re-born, the warrior would appear a necessary guardian of exterior peace, and therefore worthy sympathy; but the hunter to him was an object of horror, and the slayer of man's friends, the domestic animals, unthinkable. No boar-tusks sprang from this people's gums, and yet it remained more courageous than any other race on earth, for it bore each agony and every form of death at the hands of its later torturers in staunchness to the purity of its gentle faith; from which, unlike the professors of all other religions, no Brahmin or Buddhist could be turned away for fear or gain.

But in the selfsame valleys of the Indus we think we see at work that cleavage which parted cognate races from those returning southwards to their ancient home, and drove them westwards to the broad expanse of hither-Asia, where in course of time we find them as conquerors and founders of mighty dynasties, erecting ever more explicit monuments to History. These peoples had wandered through the wastes that separate the outmost Asiatic confines from the land of Indus; ravenous beasts of prey had taught them here to seek their food no longer from the milk of herds, but from their flesh; till blood at last, and blood alone, seemed fitted to sustain the conqueror's courage. Stretching northwards from the Indian highlands, the wild steppes of Asia—whither the aborigines of milder climates once had fled from huge disturbances of Nature—had already nursed the human beast of prey. From there, throughout all earlier and later times, have poured the floods destroying every recommencement of a gentler manhood; the very oldest sagas of the Iranian race recount a constant warfare with the Turanian peoples of these steppes. Attack and defence, want and war, victory and defeat, lordship and thraldom, all sealed with the seal of blood: this from henceforth is the History of Man. The victory of the stronger is followed close by enervation through a culture taught them by their conquered thralls; whereon, uprooting of the degenerate by fresh raw forces, of blood-thirst still unslaked. Then, falling lower and yet lower, the only worthy food for the world-conqueror appears to be human blood and corpses: the Feast of Thyestes would have been impossible among the Indians; but with such ghastly pictures could the human fancy play, now that the murder of man and beast had nothing strange for it. And why should the imagination of civilised modern man recoil in horror from such pictures, when it has accustomed itself to the sight of a Parisian slaughter-house in its early-morning traffic, and perhaps of a field of carnage on the evening of some glorious victory? In truth we seem to have merely improved on the spirit of Thyestes' feast, developing a heartless blindness to things that lay before our oldest ancestors in all their naked horror. Even those nations which had thrust as conquerors into hither-Asia could still express their consternation at the depths to which they had sunk, and we find them evolving such earnest religious ideas as lie at root of the Parsee creed of Zoroaster. Good and Evil, Light and Darkness, Ormuszd and Ahriman, Strife and Work, Creation and Destruction:—"Sons of the Light, have fear of the Shadow, propitiate the Evil and follow the Good!"—We here perceive a spirit still akin to the old Indus-people, but caught in the toils of sin, and doubting as to the issue of a never quite decisive fight.

But yet another issue from the degradation of its innate nobleness was sought by the baffled will of the human race, becoming conscious of its sinfulness through pain and suffering; to highly-gifted stocks, though the Good fell hard, the *Beautiful* was easy. In full avowal of the Will-to-live, the Greek mind did not indeed avoid the awful side of life, but turned this very knowledge to a matter of artistic contemplation: it saw the terrible with wholest truth, but this truth itself became the spur to a re-presentment whose very truthfulness was beautiful. In the workings of the Grecian spirit we thus are made spectators of a kind of pastime, a play in whose vicissitudes the joy of Shaping seeks to counteract the awe of Knowing. Content with this, rejoicing in the semblance, since it has banned therein its truthfulness of knowledge, it asks not after the goal of Being, and like the Parsee creed it leaves the fight of Good and Evil undecided; willing to pay for a lovely life by death, it merely strives to beautify death also.

We have called this a pastime, in a higher sense, namely a play of the Intellect in its release from the Will, which it now only serves for self-mirroring,—the pastime of the over-rich in spirit. But the trouble of the constitution of the World is this: all steps in evolution of the utterances of Will, from the reaction of primary elements, through all the lower organisations, right up to the richest human intellect, stand side by side in space and time, and consequently the highest organism cannot but recognise itself and all its works as founded on the Will's most brutal of manifestations. Even the flower of the Grecian spirit was rooted to the conditions of this complex existence, which has for base a ball of earth revolving after laws immutable, with all its swarm of lives the rawer and more inexorable, the deeper the scale descends. As manhood's fairest dream that flower filled the world for long with its illusive fragrance, though to none but minds set free from the Will's sore want was it granted to bathe therein: and what but a mummery at last could such delight well be, when we find that blood and massacre, untamed and ever slipped afresh, still rage throughout the human race; that violence is master, and freedom of mind seems only buyable at price of serfdom of the world? But a heartless mummery must the concernment with Art ever be, and all enjoyment of the freedom thereby sought from the Will's distress, so long as nothing more was to be found in art: the Ideal was the aim of the single genius, and what survived its work was merely the trick of technical dexterity; and so we see Greek art without the Grecian genius pervading all the Roman Empire, without drying one tear of the poor, or drawing one sob from the withered heart of the rich. Though a broader patch of sunshine might deceive us, as spread in peace above the kingdom of the Antonines, we could only style it a short-lived triumph of the artistic-philosophic spirit over the brutal movement of the restless self-destroying forces of the Will of History. Yet even here 'tis but the surface that could cheat us, making us take a lethargy for healthy calm. On the other hand, it was folly to think that violence could be restrained by howsoever prudent steps of violence. Even that world-truce was based on the Right of the Stronger, and never, since the human race first fell a-hungering for bloody spoil, has it ceased to found its claim to tenure and enjoyment on that same "right" alone. To the art-creative Greek, no less than the rudest Barbarian, it was the one sole law that shaped the world. There's no blood-guiltiness which even this fair-fashioning race did not incur in rabid hate against its neighbour; till the Stronger came upon it too, that Stronger fell in turn before a yet more violent, and so the centuries have ever brought fresh grosser forces into play, and thrown ourselves at last to-day behind a fence of yearly waxing giant-guns and bastions.

From of old, amid the rage of robbery and blood-lust, it came to wise men's consciousness that the human race was suffering from a malady which necessarily kept it in progressive deterioration. Many a hint from observation of the natural man, as also dim half-legendary memories, had made them guess the primal *nature* of this man, and that his present state is therefore a degeneration. A mystery enwrapped Pythagoras, the preacher of vegetarianism; no philosopher since him has pondered on the essence of the world, without recurring to his teaching. Silent fellowships were founded, remote from turmoil of the world, to carry out this doctrine as a sanctification from sin and misery. Among the poorest and most distant from the world appeared the Saviour, no more to teach redemption's path by precept, but example; his own flesh and blood he gave as last and highest expiation for all the sin of outpoured blood and slaughtered flesh, and offered his disciples wine and blood for each day's meal:—"Taste such alone, in memory of me." This the unique sacrament of the Christian faith; with its observance all the teaching of the Redeemer is fulfilled. As if with haunting pangs of conscience the Christian Church pursues this teaching, without ever being able to get it followed in its purity, although it very seriously should form the most intelligible core of Christianity. She has transformed it to a symbolic office of her priests, while its proper meaning is only expressed in the ordinance of periodic fasts, and its strict observance is reserved for a few religious orders, more in the sense of an abstinence conducing to humility, than of a medicine for body alike and soul.

Perhaps the one impossibility, of getting all professors to continually observe this ordinance of the Redeemer's, and abstain entirely from animal food, may be taken for the essential cause of the early decay of the Christian religion as Christian Church. But to admit that impossibility, is as much as to confess the uncontrollable downfall of the human race itself. Called to upheave a State built-up on violence and rapine, the Church must deem her surest means the attainment of dominion over states and empires, in accordance with all the spirit of History. To subject decaying races to herself she needed the help of terror; and the singular circumstance that Christianity might be regarded as sprung from Judaism, placed the requisite bugbear in her hands. The tribal God of a petty nation had promised his people eventual rulership of the whole world and all that lives and moves therein, if only they adhered to laws whose strictest following would keep them barred against all other nations of the earth. Despised and hated equally by every race in answer to this segregation, without inherent productivity and only battening on the general downfall, in course of violent revolutions this folk would very probably have been extinguished as completely as the greatest and noblest stems before them; Islam in particular seemed called to carry out the work of total extirpation, for it took to itself the Jewish God, as Creator of heaven and earth, to raise him up by fire and sword as one and only god of all that breathes. But the Jews, so it seems, could fling away all share in this world-rulership of their Jehova, for they had won a share in a development of the Christian religion well fitted to deliver it itself into their hands in time, with all its increment of culture, sovereignty and civilisation. The departure-point of all this strange exploit lay ready in the historical fact—that Jesus of Nazareth was born in a corner of their little land, Judæa. Instead of seeing in so incomparably humble an origin a proof that among the ruling and highly-cultured nations of that historic period no birth-place could be found for the Redeemer of the *Poor*; that for very reason of its utmost lowliness this Galilee, distinguished by the contempt of the Jews themselves, could alone be chosen for cradle of the new belief,—to the first believers, poor shepherds and husbandmen in dull subjection to the Jewish law, it seemed imperative to trace the descent of their Saviour from the royal house of David, as if to exculpate his bold attack on all that Jewish law. Though it is more than doubtful if Jesus himself was of Jewish extraction, since the dwellers in Galilee were despised by the Jews on express account of their impure origin, we may gladly leave this point with all that concerns the history of the Redeemer to the Historian, who for his part declares that "he can make nothing of a sinless Jesus." For us it is sufficient to derive the ruin of the Christian religion from its drawing upon Judaism for the elaboration of its dogmas. As we before have suggested, however, it is precisely hence that the Church obtained her source of might and mastery; for wherever Christian hosts fared forth to robbery and bloodshed, even beneath the banner of the Cross it was not the All-Sufferer whose name was invoked, but *Moses*, *Joshua*, *Gideon*, and all the other captains of Jehova who fought for the people of Israel, were the names in request to fire the heart of slaughter; whereof the history of England at time of the Puritan wars supplies a plain example, throwing a light on the whole Old-Testament evolution of the English Church. Without this intrusion of the ancient Jewish spirit, and its raising to an equal rank with the purely Christian evangel, how were it possible to the Church till this day to claim for her own a "civilised world" whose peoples all stand armed to the teeth for mutual extermination, at the first summons of the Lord of War to squander every fruit of peace in methodically falling on each other's throats? Manifestly it is not Jesus Christ, the Redeemer, whose pattern our army-chaplains commend to their battalions ere going into action; though they call on him, they can but mean Jehova, Jahve, or one of the Elohim, who hated all other gods beside himself, and wished them subjugated by his faithful people.

Now if we probe to the bottom of our boasted Civilisation, we find that it really has been made to do duty for the never fully-flowered spirit of the Christian religion, the latter being merely used for hallowing a compromise between brutality and cowardice. We may regard it as characteristic of the onset of this civilisation, that the Church made over her condemned heretics to the Temporal power, with the recommendation that no blood be shed in the execution of her sentence, while she had nothing to advance against their burning at the stake. In this bloodless mode the strongest and noblest minds were rooted out, and, bereft of these, the nations were taken under tutelage of "civilising" powers who, borrowing a leaf from the Church, have substituted what modern philosophers term *abstract* destruction by bullet and cannon-ball for the *concrete* wounds of sword and spear. And as the sight of bullocks offered to the gods had become an abomination to us, in our neat water-swilled shambles a daily blood-bath is concealed from all who at their mid-day meal shall feast upon the limbs of murdered household animals dressed up beyond all recognition.

Though all our States are founded on conquest and the subjugation of the earlier inhabitants, and the latest conqueror has always taken the land and soil as hereditament,—whereof England still affords a well-preserved example,—yet debilitation of the ruling races has also opened the way to a gradual effacement of the barbaric look of so unequal a division of property: money at last could buy the land from its indebted owner and give its purchaser the selfsame right as the whilom conqueror, and the Jew now bargains with the Junior for possession of the world, while the Jurist tries to find a common platform with the Jesuit for the rights of man in general. But alas! this show of peace is shadowed by the fact that no man trusts another, for the right of might still reigns supreme in every mind, and all mutual commerce of the nations is only held possible under the thumb of politicians who wakefully observe the Machiavellian maxim: "What thou wouldst not he to thee should do, that let thy nearest neighbour rue!" And it is quite in keeping with this idea of maintenance of the State, that its embodiments, our sovereign masters, put on a military uniform when grand occasions call for royal attire, however ill its bare utilitarian cut becomes the frame of men more nobly clad throughout all time in robes of highest Justice.

If thus we see that even our complex Civilisation cannot succeed in veiling our utterly unchristian origin; and if the Gospel, to which we nevertheless are sworn in tenderest youth, cannot be summoned to explain, to say nothing of justifying it,—we can only recognise our present state as a triumph of the foes of the Christian faith.

Whoever has made this clear to himself, will have no difficulty in discovering why an equal and ever deeper decline is manifest in the sphere of mental culture: violence may civilise, but Culture must sprout from the soil of peace, as it draws its very name from tillage of the fields. From this soil alone, belonging only to the busily creative Folk, have sprung in every age all knowledge, sciences and arts, nursed by religions in harmony with the people's spirit for the time being. But the conqueror's brute force draws near these sciences and arts of peace, and tells them, "What of you may serve for war, shall prosper; what not, shall perish." Thus the law of Mahomet has become the fundamental law of all our civilisations, and we have but to glance at our sciences and arts, to see how it suits them. Let there anywhere arise a man of brains, whose heart means honestly, the sciences and arts of Civilisation soon shew him how the land lies. Their question is: "Art thou of use, or not, to a heartless and sordid civilisation?" With regard to the so-called Natural sciences, especially of Chemistry and Physics, our War-offices have been taught the possibility of their discovering any number of new destructive substances and forces, though alas! no means be yet forthcoming of stopping frost or hailstorms. These sciences are therefore petted. The dishonouring diseases of our culture invite our Physiologists to man-degrading experiments in speculative vivisection; the State and Reich protect them, on the "scientific standpoint." The ruin which a Latin renaissance of Grecian art once wrought on all sound evolution of a Christian culture for the people, is aggravated year by year by a lumbering Philology, which fawns upon the guardians of the ancient law of the Right of the Stronger. And every art is coaxed and pampered, so soon as it appears of service to blind us to our misery. Distraction! Dissipation! but no Collection—except at best a monetary one for sufferers by fire and flood, for whom our war-chests have nothing to spare.

And for *this* world men still paint and make their music! In the galleries Raphael is admired, admired and analysed again, and his "Sistine" remains a grandest masterpiece in the eyes of the connoisseur. In the concert-halls Beethoven also is heard; but if we ask what a Pastoral Symphony can possibly say to our public, the question brings us to most serious thoughts. More and more importunately have they pressed on the author of this essay, and he now will try to tell them to his kindly readers,—provided the hypothesis of a profound decline of Historic Man has not already scared them from all further journeying on the path just struck.

III.

THE theory of a degeneration of the human race, however much opposed it seem to Constant Progress, is yet the only one that, upon serious reflection, can afford us any solid hope. The so-called "Pessimistic" school of thought would thus be justified in nothing but its verdict on historic man; and that must needs be vastly modified, were the natural attributes of pre-historic man so clearly ascertained that we could argue to a later degeneration not unconditionally inherent in his nature. If, that is, we found proofs that this degeneration had been caused by overpowering *outward* influences, against which pre-historic man could not defend himself through inexperience, then the hitherto accepted history of the human race would rank for us as the painful period of evolution of its consciousness, in order that the knowledge thus acquired might be applied to combating those harmful influences.

Indefinite though be the results of our Scientific Research,—and often contradicted in so brief a time that they rather fog, than enlighten us,—yet one hypothesis of our geologists appears established past all cavil: namely that the youngest offspring of the animal population of this earth, the human race to which we still belong, has survived, or at least a great portion of it, a violent transformation of the surface of our planet. A careful survey of our earthly ball confirms this: it shews that at some epoch of its last development great stretches of the continent sank down and others rose, while floods immeasurable poured hither from the Southern Pole, only to be arrested by the jutting headlands of the Northern hemisphere, like monstrous ice-guards, after driving before them all the terrified survivors. The evidence of such a flight of the animal kingdom from the tropics to the rawest northern zones supplied by our geologists in the results of their excavations, such as skeletons of elephants in Siberia for instance, is now well-known. For our inquiry, on the other hand, it is important to form some notion of the changes which such violent displacements must necessarily have induced among the animal and human races of the earth, erewhile brought up in the mother-bosom of their primitive lands of birth.

The emergence of huge deserts, like the African Sahara, must certainly have cast the dwellers on the once luxuriant coasts of inland seas into such straits of hunger as we can only form an idea of by recalling stories of the awful sufferings of the shipwrecked, whereby completely civilised citizens of our modern states have been reduced to cannibalism. On the swampy margins of Canadian lakes animal species allied to the panther and tiger still live as fruit-eaters, whereas upon those desert fringes the historic tiger and lion have become the most bloodthirsty of all the beasts of prey. That it must have been hunger alone, which first drove man to slay the animals and feed upon their flesh and blood; and that this compulsion was no mere consequence of his removal into colder climes, as those assert who deem the consumption of animal-food in northern parts a duty of self-preservation,—is proved by the patent fact that great nations with ample supplies of grain suffer nothing in strength or endurance even in colder regions through an almost exclusively vegetable diet, as is shewn by the eminent length of life of Russian peasants; while the Japanese, who know no other food than vegetables, are further renowned for their warlike valour and keenness of intellect. We may therefore call it quite an abnormality when hunger bred the thirst for blood, as in the branches of the Malayan stock transplanted to the northern steppes of Asia; that thirst which history teaches us can never more be slaked, and fills its victims with a raging madness, not with courage. One can only account for it all by the human beast of prey having made itself monarch of the peaceful world, just as the ravening wild beast usurped dominion of the woods: a result of those preceding cataclysms which overtook primeval man while yet all unprepared for either. And little as the savage animals have prospered, we see the sovereign human beast of prey decaying too. Owing to a nutriment against his nature, he falls sick with maladies that claim but him, attains no more his natural span of life or gentle death, but, plagued by pains and cares of body and soul unknown to any other species, he shuffles through an empty life to its ever fearful cutting short.*

As we began with a general outline of the effects produced by the human beast of prey upon world-History, it now may be of service to return to the attempts to counteract them and find again the "long-lost Paradise"; attempts we meet in seemingly progressive impotence as History goes on, till finally their operation passes almost wholly out of ken.

Among these last attempts we find in our own day the societies of so-called Vegetarians: nevertheless from out these very unions, which seem to have aimed directly at the centre of the question of mankind's Regeneration, we hear certain prominent members complaining that their comrades for the most part practise abstinence from meat on purely personal dietetic grounds, but in nowise link their practice with the great regenerative thought which alone could make the unions powerful. Next to them we find a union with an already more practical and somewhat more extended scope, that of the *Prevention of Cruelty to Animals*: here again its members try to win the public's sympathy by mere utilitarian pleas, though a truly beneficial end could only be awaited from their pursuing their pity for animals to the point of an intelligent adoption of the deeper trend of Vegetarianism; founded on such a

* The author here refers expressly to a book by A. Gleizès, "Thalysia, or the Healing of Mankind," most admirably translated from the French and edited by Robert Springer (Berlin, 1873; publisher, Otto Jahnke). Without a close acquaintance with the results, embodied in this book, of the most diligent researches which seem to have occupied the whole lifetime of one of the most amiable and profound of Frenchmen, it will be hard to win the reader's assent to the conclusions I have attempted to draw from its contents as to the possibility of a regeneration of the human race.—R. WAGNER.

mutual understanding, an amalgamation of these two societies might gain a power by no means to be despised. No less important would be the result, were this amalgamation then to take in hand the so-called Temperance-unions, and elevate the only tendency betrayed by them as yet. The plague of drunkenness, that last destroyer to seize the modern victims of our civilised state of siege, brings revenue of all kinds to the State, to part with which it has never evinced the smallest inclination; yet the unions formed for its suppression look simply to the practical aim of cheaper insurance for ships and freights, and the better guarding of their warehouses by sober servants. With contempt and scorn does our Civilisation regard the efforts of these three unions, each wholly ineffectual in its severance; whilst amazement caps disdain, as at a mad presumption, when the apostles of Peace-societies submissively address their protests to our mighty lords of War. 'Twas but the other day we had an instance and the answer of our famous "Battle-planner" that the obstacle to peace, for the next two centuries or so, was the lack of "religiosity" among the nations. What may here be meant by "religiosity," or religion in general, is at anyrate not easy to clear up; above all, it would be hard to imagine the irreligiousness of the peoples and nations themselves as the real foe of a ceasing of war. Our General-Field-Marshal [Moltke] must surely have meant something other than this, and a glance at recent manifestoes of certain international Peace-societies might explain why one would not give much for their practical "religiosity."

On the other hand, an experiment has lately been made in providing religious instruction for those great Trade-unions which no philanthropist can any longer deem unjustified, but whose actual or alleged encroachments on the established social order could only seem unwarrantable in the eyes of its protectors. Every demand, even the apparently most proper, addressed by so-called *Socialism* to a Society the product of our civilisation, speaking strictly, sets the rights of that Society itself at once in question. Because of this, and since it can but seem infeasible to lawfully propose a lawful dissolution of what exists by law, the postulates of the Socialists must needs appear confused and therefore leading to false reckonings, whose mistakes the ready reckoners of our Civilisation have no difficulty in laying bare. Yet upon strong and inner grounds one might regard even present-day Socialism as well worth consideration by our established Society, if once it entered into true and hearty fellowship with the three associations named above, of the vegetarians, the protectors of animals, and the friends of temperance. Were it possible to expect of men directed by our Civilisation to nothing but a correct enforcement of the most calculating Egoism, that this last-suggested fellowship could strike firm root among them—with full understanding of the deeper tendency of each of the mentioned groups, so powerless in their present separation—then were the hope of regaining a true Religion, also, no less legitimate. What would seem to have dawned on the founders of all those unions as a mere counsel of prudence, has really flowed, though no doubt in part unconsciously to themselves, from a root which we are not afraid to call the religious sense: at bottom of even the mutterings of the workman, who makes each object of utility without drawing the smallest particle of use from it himself, there lies a knowledge of the profound immorality of our civilisation, whose champions can in truth reply by naught but shameful sophisms; for, granted that it can be easily proved that wealth in itself cannot make men happy, yet none but the most heartless wretch would think of denying that poverty makes them wretched. To explain this sorry constitution of all human things our Old-testament Christian Church reverts to the fall of the earliest pair, which Jewish tradition derives—most strange to say—by no means from a forbidden taste of animal flesh, but from that of the fruit of a tree; wherewith we may couple the no less striking fact that the Jewish God found Abel's fatted lamb more savoury than Cain's offering of the produce of the field. From such suspicious evidences of the character of the Jewish tribal god we see a religion arise against whose direct employment for regeneration of the human race we fancy that a convinced vegetarian of nowadays might have serious complaints to lodge. But if an earnest communion with the Vegetarian must necessarily teach the Protector of Animals the true meaning of that pity which inspires himself; and if both then turned to the spirit-sodden pariah of our civilisation with tidings of new life through abstinence from that poison taken to benumb despair,—then results might be anticipated such as have followed the experiments already tried in certain American prisons, where the greatest criminals have been transformed by a wisely-planned botanic regimen into the mildest and most upright of men. Whose memory would the groups of this community in truth be celebrating when they gathered, after each day's work, to refresh themselves with Bread and Wine?

If this be a dream whose realisation is forbidden by no rational hypothesis save that of absolute Pessimism, it perhaps may be no less profitable to pursue in thought the acts of such a union, starting from the religious conviction that the degeneration of the human race has been brought about by its departure from its natural food, the only basis of a possible regeneration. The easily ascertainable fact that merely a portion—supposed to be a third—of mankind is involved in this departure, and the example of physical health displayed by the larger half that has stayed true to its natural diet, might fitly teach us the path to strike for regeneration of the depraved but ruling portion. Should the assumption prove correct that animal food is indispensable in Northern climates, what is to prevent our carrying out a sensibly conducted transmigration to those quarters of our globe whose rich fertility is sufficient to sustain the present population of every country in the world, as has been asserted of the South American peninsula in itself? Our rulers leave the luxuriant reaches of South Africa to the policy of English traders, and do no better for the healthiest of their subjects than to let them move away from death-by-starving—at best unhindered, but always left without a helping hand to foreign exploitation. Since this is thus, our unions would have to devote their greatest care and energy to Emigration, perchance with some success: and according to recent experiences it seems not improbable that these Northern lands, now said to positively call for flesh-food, would soon be abandoned to the undivided possession of hunters of boars and big game, who could give a very good account of themselves as destroyers of the somewhat too prolific beasts of prey in the deserted districts, untroubled any longer by a lower populace all clamorous for bread. For ourselves, there surely could be no moral harm in our acting on the words of Christ: "Render unto Cæsar the things that are Cæsar's, and to God the things that are God's," and leaving the huntsman his preserves while we cultivate our acres; but the grabbing, grasping money-bags of our Civilisation, swelled by the sweat of our brow—should *they* cry Fie, we'd lay them on their backs and bring them, like the swine, to wondering silence at the sight of heaven, ne'er seen by them before.

In this by no means timid picture of an attempt at regeneration of the human race we may neglect, for the present, all objections which friends of our Civilisation are likely to raise. On this side our assumption of most fruitful possibilities rests on the results of honest scientific studies, a clear insight into which has been facilitated for us by the devoted toil of noble minds—whereof we have already mentioned one of the foremost. Waiving all such conceivable objections, we therefore have only to confirm ourselves in one radical persuasion: namely that all real bent, and all effective power to bring about the great Regeneration, can spring from nothing save the deep soil of a true Religion. And now that our general survey has repeatedly brought us within range of vivid hints in its regard, we must turn in especial to this main head of our inquiry; for it is from it, as premised in our title, that we first shall gain a certain outlook upon Art.

We started with the theory of a corruption of pre-historic man; by the latter, however, we in nowise mean primeval man, of whom we can have no definite knowledge, but those races of whom we know no deeds, though their works we do know. These works are each invention of that culture which Historic Man has only trimmed to suit his civilising ends, by no means renovated or increased; above all Speech, which shews a progressive degeneration from Sanskrit to the newest European amalgam. Whoever rightly weighs these aptitudes of the human race,—so astounding to us in our present decline,—must come to the conclusion that the giant force which shaped this world by testing every means of self-appeasement, from destruction to re-fashioning, had reached its goal in bringing forth this Man; for in him it became conscious of itself as *Will*, and, with that knowledge, could thenceforth rule its destiny. To feel that horror at himself so needful for his last redemption, this Man was qualified by just that knowledge, to wit the recognition of himself in every manifestment of the one great Will; and the guide to evolution of this faculty was given him by Suffering, since he alone can feel it in the requisite degree. If we involuntarily conceive of the Divine as a sphere where Suffering is impossible, that conception ever rests on the desire of something for which we can find no positive, but merely a negative expression. So long as we have to fulfil the work of the Will, that Will which is ourselves, there in truth is nothing for us but the spirit of Negation, the spirit of our own will that, blind and hungering, can only plainly see itself in its un-will toward whatsoever crosses it as obstacle or disappointment. Yet that which crosses it, is but itself again; so that its rage expresses nothing save its self-negation: and this self-knowledge can be gained at last by Pity born of suffering—which, cancelling the Will, expresses the negation of a negative; and that, by every rule of logic, amounts to Affirmation.

If we take this great thought of our philosopher [Schopenhauer] as guide to the inexorable metaphysical problem of the purpose of the human race, we shall have to acknowledge that what we have termed the decline of the race, as known to us by its historic deeds, is really the stern school of Suffering which the Will imposed on its blind self for sake of gaining sight,—somewhat in the sense of the power "that ever willeth ill, and ever doeth good." According to what we have learnt of the gradual formation of our globe, it has once already brought forth races like to man, and, by a fresh upheaval of its crust, destroyed them; as regards their successor, the present human race, we know that at least a great portion thereof was driven from its primal birthplace by some mighty transformation of the surface of the Earth, the last till now. No paradisiac ease can therefore be the final answer to the riddle of this violent stress, whose every utterance remains a source of fear and horror to our minds. Before us still will lie the same old possibilities of havoc and destruction, whereby it manifests its actual essence; our own descent from the germs of life we see the ocean's depth bring forth anew in hideous shapes, can never more be hidden from our awe-struck thought. And this human race, endowed with faculty of knowledge and of meditation, and thus of laying the Will's tumultuous storm,—is it not founded still, itself, on all the lower grades where incomplete attempts to gain a higher step, obstructed by mad hindrances in their own will, have stayed immutable for us to see, abhorrent or with pity?

If this outlook filled with sorrow and dismay the noblest races of mankind, brought up to gentleness and lapped in a tender Nature's mother-bosom, what grief must seize them at the dreaded sight of their own fall, their degeneration to the lowest foregoers of the human race, with no defence but patience? The history of this falling off—already broadly outlined—should teach us, when regarded as the human race's school of suffering, in consciousness to remedy an evil springing from the headstrong blindness of the world-creative Will, and ruinous to all attainment of its own unconscious goal; to rebuild, as it were, the storm-wrecked house, and ensure against its fresh destruction.

That all our machines are of no avail for this, might soon be brought home to the present race; for those alone can master Nature, who understand and place themselves in line with her; and this would first be effected by a more reasonable distribution of the people of the earth upon its surface. Our bungling Civilisation, on the contrary, with its puny mechanical and chemical appliances, its sacrifice of the best of human forces for their installation, delights in waging almost childish war with the impossible. But we, supposing even that a cataclysm should shatter our earthly dwelling-place, for all time should we be secure against the possibility of the human race's falling back from its attained development of higher morals, had the experience of the history of that former fall established in our minds a true religious sense—akin to that of those three-million Hindus of whom we spoke before.

And to guard against all re-subjection to the blindfold Will, must a new religion first be founded? Already in our daily meal should we not be celebrating the Redeemer? Could we need the huge array of allegories wherewith all religions hitherto, and in particular the deep Brahminical, have been distorted to a mummery? Have we not the actual documents of life set down for us, in our history that marks each lesson by a true example? Let us read it aright, this history, in spirit and in truth; not by the lie and letter of our university-historians, who know but actions, sing their pæans to the widest conqueror, and shut their ears to manhood's suffering. With the Redeemer in heart, let us recognise that not their actions, but their sufferings bring near to us the men of bygone days, and make them worth our memory; that our sympathy belongs not to the victor, but the vanquished hero. However great may be the peace of mind resulting from regeneration of the human race, yet in the Nature that surrounds us, the violence of ure-elements, the unchanged emanations of the Will beneath us and on either hand in sea or desert, —ay, even in the insect, in the worm we tread upon unheeding, shall we ever feel the awful tragedy of this World-being, and daily have to lift our eyes to the Redeemer on the cross as last and loftiest refuge.

Well for us if then, in conscience of pure living, we keep our senses open to the mediator of the crushingly Sublime, and let ourselves be gently led to reconcilement with this mortal life by the *artistic teller* of the great World-tragedy. This Poet priest, the only one who never lied, was ever sent to humankind at epochs of its direst error, as mediating friend : us, too, will he lead over to that reborn life, to set before us there in ideal truth the "likeness" of this passing show, when the Historian's realistic lie shall have long since been interred beneath the mouldering archives of our Civilisation. Those allegorical accessories which hitherto have overlaid the noblest kernel of Religion to such a point that, now that their literal credibility is conclusively refuted, this kernel itself is found corroded ; that theatrical hocus-pocus by which the so easily gullible fancy of the poor, especially in southern lands, is turned from true religiousness to a frivolous playing with things divine, —no more shall we need these proved debasers of religious cults. We began by shewing how Art's greatest genius had been able to save for us the old exalted meaning of those allegories themselves, by moulding them to the Ideal ; and how the selfsame art, then turning to the material side of life as if sated with fulfilment of that ideal mission, had been dragged to its own downfall by the worthlessness of this reality. But now we have a new reality before us, a race imbued with deep religious consciousness of the reason of its fall, and raising up itself therefrom to new development ; and in that race's hand the truthful book of a true history, from which to draw its knowledge of itself without all self-deception. What their great Tragedians shewed the decadent Athenians once in sublimely shaped examples, without being able tó arrest the frenzied downfall of their nation; what Shakespeare held before a world that vainly thought itself the renaissance of art and man's free intellect,—its heartless blindness striving for a beauty all unfelt,—the wondrous mirror of those dramatic improvisations in which he shewed that world its utter emptiness, its violence and horror, without the bitter undeception being even heeded in his time: these *works* of the Sufferers shall now be ever present with us, whilst the deeds of the "makers of history" shall in them alone live on. So would the hour of redemption of the great Cassandra of world-history have sounded, of redemption from the curse of finding no one to believe her prophecies. To us shall all these poet-sages once have spoken; to us will they speak afresh.

It hitherto has been a commonplace of heartless and thoughtless minds alike, that so soon as the human race were freed from the common sufferings of a sinful life, its state would be one of dull indifference,*—whereon it is to be remarked that they consider a mere freedom from the very lowest troubles of the Will as lending life its varied charm, whilst the labours of great thinkers, poets and seers, they have always densely set aside. We, on the contrary, have learnt that the life essential to us in the future can only be freed from those cares and sufferings by a conscious impulse, whereto the fearful riddle of the world is ever present. That which, as simplest and most touching of religious symbols, unites us in the common practising of our belief; that which, ever newly living in the tragic teachings of great spirits, uplifts us to the altitudes of pity,—is the knowledge, given in infinite

* Another allusion to Nietzsche's *Menschliches*, where Aphorism 235 begins as follows: "The Socialists want to bring about the Well-living of the Greatest Number. If the lasting home of this Well-living, the perfect State, were actually attained, then this Well-living would have destroyed the soil whence grows the powerful intellect, the mighty individual in general: I mean, the force of Energy. Mankind would have grown too torpid, when this State arrived, to be able to beget a genius. Ought one not, therefore, to wish that life may retain its violent character, and that savage forces and energies may ever be called forth afresh?"—Tr.

variety of forms, of the Need of Redemption. In solemn hours when all the world's appearances dissolve away as in a prophet's dream, we seem already to partake of this redemption in advance: no more then tortures us the memory of that yawning gulf, the gruesome monsters of the deep, the reeking litter of the self-devouring Will, which Day—alas! the history of mankind, had forced upon us: then pure and peace-desiring sounds to us the cry of Nature, fearless, hopeful, all-assuaging, world-redeeming. United in this cry, by it made conscious of its own high office of Redemption of the whole like-suffering Nature, the soul of Manhood soars from the abyss of semblances, and, loosed from all that awful chain of rise and fall, the restless Will feels fettered by itself alone, but from itself set free.

The children of a parish-priest in new-converted Sweden once heard a Nixie singing to her harp upon the shore: "Sing as you will," they cried to her, "you'll never get to heaven." Sadly the fairy sank her head and harp: the children heard her weep, and ran to tell their father. He counselled them, and sent them back to greet the Nixie with good tidings. "Come, Nixie, dry your tears," they cried: "Father bids say, you yet may hope for heaven." Then all night through they heard the waters echoing with songs so sweet, that never man heard sweeter.—The Redeemer himself has bidden us sound and sing our longing, faith and hope. Its noblest legacy the Christian Church has left us in the all-uttering, all-expressing soul of the Christian religion: wafted beyond the temple-walls, the holy strains of Music fill each sphere of Nature with new life, teaching redemption-starved mankind a second speech in which the Infinite can voice itself with clearest definition.

But what have even the divinest works of music said to our modern world? What can these sounding revelations from the redeeming dream-world of purest knowledge tell to a concert-public of to-day? To whom the unspeakable bliss has been vouchsafed of taking one of the last four Symphonies of Beethoven into his heart and soul without alloy, let him conceive the constitution of a whole great audience prepared to receive an effect from any of these works in perfect correspondence with their nature: perhaps he might be assisted by an analogy from the remarkable devotions of the Shakers in America, who, after solemn attestation of their heartfelt vow of abstinence, all join in song and dance within the temple. If this is but expression of a childlike joy at innocence regained, for our part, after celebrating in our daily meal the Will's sure triumph over itself through knowledge wrung from manhood's fall, we might view the plunge into the waves of those symphonic revelations as a religious act of hallowed cleansing. Glad shouts ascending to divinest rapture. "Divin'st thou thy Creator, World?"—so cries the Poet, obliged to hazard an anthropomorphic metaphor for That which words can ne'er convey. But, above all possibility of concrete thought, the Tone-poet Seer reveals to us the Inexpressible: we divine, nay, feel and see that this insistent World of Will is also but a state that vanishes before the One: "I know that my Redeemer liveth!"

"Have you ever had to rule a State?" asked Mendelssohn Bartholdy once of Berthold Auerbach, who had been indulging in reflections on the Prussian Government, apparently distasteful to the famed composer. "Do you want to found a new religion?"—the author of the present essay might be asked. As that person, I should freely admit that it would be just as impossible as that Herr Auerbach could have deftly ruled a State, if Mendelssohn had managed to procure one for him. My thoughts have come to me as to a working artist in his intercourse with public life: in that contact it must seem to me that I should light upon the proper road if I weighed the reasons why even considerable and envied successes have left me uncontented with the public. Upon this road I grew convinced that Art can only prosper on the basis of true Morals, and thus could but ascribe to it a mission all the higher when I found it altogether one with true Religion. Any judgment of the history and future of the human race must remain beyond the artist's reach while he approached it in the sense of Mendelssohn's question, and had to view the State as something like a mill in which the human grain, already bolted on the threshing-floor of War, must be ground before it could be relished. As on my path I had felt a wholesome shudder at this drilling of mankind to barren aims, at last it dawned on me that another, better state of future man—conceived by others as a hideous chaos — might well arise in comely order, if Religion and Art not only were retained therein, but for the first time gained their right acceptance. From this path all violence is quite shut out, for it merely needs the strengthening of those seeds of Peace which all around have taken root, though scant as yet and feeble.

But things may turn out otherwise, should Wisdom more and more recede from rampant Violence. What this last can do, we note with the same astonishment once humorously expressed by Frederick the Great when a royal guest, after witnessing a field-manœuvre, declared his wonder at the soldiers' matchless discipline: "Not that's the greatest marvel," he replied, "but that the knaves don't shoot us dead." Considering the elaborate springs which are set in motion for military Honour, it fortunately is not to be anticipated that the war-machine will consume its own vitals, and collapse in such a way as to leave the great Frederick with no more marvels of his kind. Nevertheless it can but rouse our apprehension, to see the progress of the art-of-war departing from the springs of moral force, and turning more and more to the mechanical: here the rawest forces of the lower Nature-powers are brought into an artificial play, in which, for all arithmetic and mathematics, the blind Will might one day break its leash and take an elemental share. Already a grim and ghostly sight is offered by the armoured Monitors, against which the stately sailing-ship avails no more: dumb serving-men, no longer with the looks of men, attend these monsters, nor even from their awful furnace-holds will they desert: but just as in Nature everything has its destroying foe, so Art invents torpedoes for the sea, and dynamite cartouches, or the like, for everywhere else. 'Twere thinkable that all of this, with art and science, valour, point-of-honour, life and chattels, should one day fly into the air through some incalculable accident. When every pledge of peace was thus exploded in the grandest style, it would only need the outbreak of a general famine—already slowly, but infallibly prepared: then should we stand once more where world-Historical development began, and it really might look "as if God had made the world that the Devil might take it," as our great philosopher found stated in the Judæo-Christian dogma.

So reign the Will there in its full brutality. Happy we, if we have turned us to *the Fields of hoary eld*!

"WHAT BOOTS THIS KNOWLEDGE?"

A SUPPLEMENT TO "RELIGION AND ART." *

SHOULD ye ask, "Of what use is the knowledge of man's historic fall, since it is just through his historic evolution that we all have become what we are?" one first might waive your question somewhat thus: "Ask those who from all time have made that knowledge wholly theirs, and learn from them to inwardly digest it. 'Tis no new thing, for all great spirits have been led by it alone. Ask the real great poets of every age; ask the founders of true religions." Willingly would we refer you also to the mighty chiefs of States, if among the very greatest of them we could presuppose a full acquaintance with it; that is impossible, however, because their trade has ever pointed them to mere experiments with given historic conditions, but never allowed a free glance past those conditions to their primal state. It therefore is the helmsman of the State himself, by whose miscarriages we may the plainest prove the ill results of non-obtainal of that knowledge. Even a Marcus Aurelius could only attain to knowledge of the world's nullity, but never to the idea of an actual downfall of a world that might have been so different,—to say nothing of the cause of this fall. That worthlessness has ever been the base of absolute Pessimism; by which despotic statesmen, and rulers in general, have but too gladly let themselves be led, were it only for convenience. On the contrary, a more thorough-going knowledge of the cause of our decline leads forthwith to the possibility of a just as radical regeneration; again without all reference to

* "*Was nützt diese Erkenntniss?*" *Ein Nachtrag zu: Religion und Kunst* originally appeared in the *Bayreuther Blätter* for December, 1880.—Tr.

Statesmen, since such a knowledge passes far beyond the sphere of their violent, but always fruitless action.

Accordingly, to discover of whom we need *not* ask for vital knowledge of the world, we have only to take a general survey of the present so-called "political situation." This latter characterises itself, if we pick up the nearest newspaper and read it in the sense that nothing there concerns us personally: at once we light upon Shalt without Have, Will without Notion, and all with such a boundless greed of Might that even the mightiest thinks he owns none, until he has still more. What he dreams of doing with this Might, one seeks in vain to fathom. Everywhere we see the image of Robespierre,* who, when the guillotine had brushed away each hindrance to the revelation of his nostrums, had nothing left to recommend but Virtuousness in general,—a doctrine far more simply gained before him in Masonic lodges. As far as looks go, all our Statesmen now are striving after Robespierre's prize. Even last century this look was less affected; then men fought frankly for dynastic interests—carefully supervised, to be sure, by the interest of the Jesuits, who recently again alas! misled the last brute-force ruler of France. He deemed needful for insurance of his dynasty, and in the interest of civilisation, to deal Prussia a slap in the face; and as Prussia had no mind to calmly take it, things came to a war for German Unity. That Unity was won in course, and duly fixed by contract; but what it after all might mean, again was hard to answer. They tell us we shall hear some day, when much more Might has been procured: German Unity must first be primed to shew her teeth in every quarter, even if it leaves her with nothing to chew. One thinks one sees Robespierre presiding over his Committee of *Salut Public*, when one conjures up the picture

* A striking repetition of the thought expressed (to some extent in the selfsame words) in Wagner's letter to August Roeckel of January 25, 1854. The parallelism is easily accounted for, however, as these *Letters to Roeckel* only returned to their author after the death of their recipient (June 18, 1876), and apparently but a little while before the present article was written.—Tr.

of the strong man armed behind locked doors, in ceaseless search for means of increase to his garnered Might. What there was to do and tell to the world with the Might once proved, might have dawned on that strong man armed in the nick of time, had this *knowledge* but enlightened him. We gladly believe in his love of peace ; though 'tis a sorry proof, to be forced into war, and though we sincerely hope that true Peace will some day be won on a peaceful path, it should have occurred to the beater-down of peace's last disturber that the wantonly-provoked and fearful war would be fitly crowned by an other peace than this treaty of Frankfort-on-Main, which points direct to constant readiness for further war. Here a knowledge of the need and possibility of true regeneration of the human race, now crushed by an embattled Civilisation, could well have inspired a pact conducting to peace of the world itself: then would have been no forts to seize, but to demolish, no warrants of surer war to take, but pledges of sound peace to give; whereas historic rights alone were weighed against historic claims, and settled by the one established right of Conquest. With the best will in the world, it would seem that the pilot-of-State can see no farther. They all must prate of universal peace; even Napoleon III. had his mind on it,—but a peace of profit to his dynasty and France: for in no other way can these strong men armed conceive of peace, than under the wide-respected guardianship of countless cannons.

At anyrate we may conclude that, if *our* knowledge is to be treated as useless, the world-knowledge of our great Statesmen works us positive and serious harm.—

In the past I have found that my exposures of the downfall of our Public Art met little contradiction, but my ideas on its regeneration were violently opposed. If we leave out of count the flat Optimists proper, the hopeful babes of Abraham's bosom, we may take it that the sight of a degenerate world, of the perversion and badness of men in general, does not especially repel: what all think in secret of each other, they know right well; but Science herself does not confess it, for she has learnt to find her reckoning in "constant progress." And Religion? Luther's main revolt was against the Roman Church's shameless Absolution, which went so far as to accept deliberate prepayment for sins not yet committed: his anger came too late; the world soon managed to abolish Sin entirely, and believers now look for redemption from evil to Physics and Chemistry.

We will admit that it is no easy task, to persuade the world of the use of this our knowledge, even though it leave the uselessness of its mean knowledge ungainsaid. But let us not therefore refrain from a closer search into that use. For this we must turn, not to the dull-brained throng, but to those better minds whose own prevailing cloudiness as yet prevents the freedom-bearing rays of rightful knowledge from piercing to that multitude. This cloud is still so dense, that it is truly astounding to see the highest minds of every age since the rise of the Bible enveloped in it, and thereby led to shallowness of judgment. Take Goethe, who held Christ for problematical, but the good God for wholly proven, albeit retaining the liberty to discover the latter in Nature after his own fashion; which led to all manner of physical assays and experiments, whose continued pursuit was bound, in turn, to lead the present reigning human intellect to the result that there's no God whatever, but only "Force and Matter." It was reserved for a master-mind—how late alas!—to light this more than thousand-years' confusion in which the Jewish God-idea had plunged the whole of Christendom: that the unsatisfied thinker at last can set firm foot again on a soil of genuine Ethics, we owe to Kant's continuator, large-hearted *Arthur Schopenhauer*.

Who would gain an idea of the confusion of modern thought, the maiming of the intellect of to-day, let him consider the untold difficulty that impedes a proper understanding of the most lucid of all philosophical systems—that of Schopenhauer. The reason is simple enough, when we recognise that the perfect understanding of this philosophy would effect as radical a revolution in our hitherto established modes of thought, as that demanded of the heathen by their conversion to Christianity. Nevertheless it is quite appalling to find this philosophy, based as it is on the most perfect of ethics, described as shorn of hope; from which it follows, that we wish to be of good hope without the consciousness of true morality. That upon this very depravation of men's hearts rests Schopenhauer's relentless condemnation of the world—in its only aspect shewn to us by history,—affrights all those who take no pains to track the paths so plainly traced by Schopenhauer for turning the misguided Will. Yet these paths, which well may lead to hope, are clearly and distinctly pointed out by our philosopher, and it is not his fault if he was so fully occupied with the correct portrayal of the only world that lay before him, that he was compelled to leave their actual exploration to our own selves; for they brook no journeying save on foot.

In this sense, and as guide to an independent treading of the path of surest hope, nothing better can be recommended in our present state than to make Schopenhauer's philosophy, in its every bearing, the basis of all further mental and moral culture; and at nothing else have we to labour, than to get the necessity of this acknowledged in every walk of life. Should that succeed, the beneficial, the truly regenerative result were then immeasurable; for on the contrary we see to what mental and moral unfitness the lack of a right, all-permeating knowledge of the world's root-essence has now debased us.

The Popes knew well what they were doing, when they withdrew the Bible from the Folk; for the Old Testament in particular, so bound up with the New, might distort the pure idea of Christ to such a point that any nonsense and every deed of violence could claim its sanction; and such a use they deemed more prudent to reserve for the Church herself. Wellnigh we must view it as a grave misfortune, that Luther had no other weapon of authority against the degenerate Roman Church, than just this Bible; from whose full text he durst drop nothing, without disarming. It even had to serve him for the drafting of a catechism for the poor neglected Folk; and with what despair he clutched at it, we may see from the heart-rending preface to that little book. If we hear aright the true deep note of pity for his people, that lent the soulful Reformer the sublime precipitance of the rescuer of a drowning man *; that haste wherewith he brought the people in extremis the only spiritual food and covering that came to hand,—if we follow this, we may take example by himself for the provisional repairing of that food and clothing, now found no longer adequate, to last for stouter service. To denote the starting-point of such an undertaking, let us cite a fine passage from one of Schiller's letters to Goethe:—

> "If one would lay hand on the characteristic mark of Christianity, distinguishing it from all mono-theistic religions, it lies in nothing less than the *upheaval of Law*, of Kant's 'Imperative,' in whose place it sets free Inclination. In its own pure form it therefore is the presentation of a beautiful morality, or of the humanising of the Holy; and in this sense it is the only *æsthetic* religion."—

From this fair picture let us cast one glance upon the Ten Commandments of the Mosaic tables of the Law—which even Luther found needful to take as first instruction to a people both mentally and morally brutalised under rule of the Roman Church and Germanic fist-right—and we there shall discover no faintest trace of a truly Christian thought; taken strictly, they are mere *forbiddals*, to most of which the character of *commands* was first assigned by Luther's running commentary. We have no idea of entering upon a criticism of those Commandments, for we should only encounter our police and criminal legislation, to which their supervision has been committed in the interest of civic order, even to the point of punishment for Atheism—wherefrom, perchance, the "other gods" alone would pass scot-free.

* Cf. Nietzsche's perversion of the idea of Pity: "One springs to the rescue of a man, who has fallen into the water, just twice as fast when witnesses are present who do not dare."—*Menschliches*, Aph. 325.—Tr.

If we leave these edicts on one side, as fairly well safeguarded, we come at once to the Christian command—if so we may term it—in the setting-up of the three so-called Theologic Virtues. These are commonly arranged in an order that appears to us not quite the right one for development of the Christian spirit; we should like to see "Faith, Hope, and Charity" transposed into "Love, Faith, and Hope." It may seem a contradiction to uphold this sole redeeming and engladdening trinity as the essence of all *virtue*, and its exercise as a *commandment*, seeing that its units, on the other hand, are claimed as grants of Grace. What a merit lies in their attainment, however, we soon shall see if first we weigh the almost exorbitant demand on the natural man conveyed by the injunction of "Love," in its exalted Christian sense. Through what is it, that our whole civilisation is going to ground, if not through lack of Love? The heart of youth, to which the world of nowadays unveils itself with waxing plainness, how can it love this world when it is recommended naught save caution and suspicion in its dealings with it? Surely there can be but one right way of guidance for that heart, the path whereon the world's great lovelessness should be accounted as its *suffering*: then would the young man's roused compassion incite him to withdraw himself from the causes of that Suffering of the world's, to flee with knowledge from the greed of passions, to lessen and avert the woes of others. But how to wake this needful knowledge in the natural man, since the first and most un-understandable to him is his fellow-man himself? Impossible, that commandments here should bring about a knowledge only to be woken in the natural man by proper guidance to an understanding of the natural descent of all that lives.—The surest, nay, in our opinion almost the only thing to lead to this, would be a wise employment of the Schopenhauerian philosophy, whose outcome, to the shame of every earlier philosophic system, is the recognition of a *moral meaning of the world*; which crown of all Knowledge might then be practically realised through Schopenhauer's Ethics. Only the love that springs from pity, and carries its compassion to the utmost breaking of self-will, is the redeeming Christian Love, in which Faith and Hope are both included of themselves,—*Faith* as the unwavering consciousness of that moral meaning of the world, confirmed by the most divine exemplar; *Hope* as the blessed sense of the impossibility of any cheating of this consciousness.

And whence could we derive a clearer guidance for the heart afflicted by the cheat of this world's material semblance, than from our philosopher, if only we could bring that understanding within the natural powers of unlearned men? In such a sense we fain would see an attempt to draft a popular version of his matchless treatise "On apparent Design in the Fate of the Individual": how surely were the term "eternal Providence"—so frequently employed for very sake of its equivocation—then justified in its true sense; whereas the contradiction thus expressed now drives despairing souls to flattest atheism. To people harassed by the arrogance of our chemists and physicists, and who begin to hold themselves for weak of brain if they shrink from accepting a resolution of the world into "force and matter,"—to them it were no less an act of charity, could we shew them from the works of our philosopher what clumsy things are those same "molecules and atoms." But what an untold boon could we bring to men affrighted on the one hand by the thunders of the Church, and driven to desperation by our physicists on the other, could we fit into the lofty edifice of "Love, Faith, and Hope" a vivid knowledge of the *ideality* of that world our only present mode of apperception maps out by laws of Time and Space; then would each question of the troubled spirit after the "when" and "where" of the "other world" be recognised as answerable by nothing but a blissful smile. For if there be an answer to these so infinitely weighty-seeming questions, our philosopher has given it with insurpassable beauty and precision in that phrase which he merely meant, in a measure, to define the ideality of Space and Time: "Peace, rest and happiness dwell there alone where is *no When, no Where.*"

Yet the Folk—from whom we stand so lamentably far, alas!—demands a realistic notion of divine eternity in the affirmative sense, such as Theology herself can only give it in the negative "world without end." Religion, too, could ease this craving by naught but allegoric myths and images, from which the Church then built that storeyed dogma whose collapse has become notorious. How these crumbling blocks were turned to the foundation of an art unknown to the ancient world, I have endeavoured to shew in my preceding article on "Religion and Art"; of what import to the "Folk" itself this art might become through its full emancipation from unseemly service, and upon the soil of a new moral order, we should set ourselves in earnest to discover. Here again our philosopher would lead us to a boundless outlook on the realm of possibilities, if we sought out all the wealth contained in the following pregnant sentences:—"Complete contentment, the truly acceptable state, never present themselves to us but in an image, in the *Artwork*, the Poem, in Music. From which one surely might derive the confidence that somewhere they exist in sooth." What here was hardly utterable without an almost sceptic smile, through its intrusion on a strictly philosophic system, for us might well become the starting-point of very serious inferences. The perfect "likeness" of the noblest artwork would so transport our heart that we should plainly find the archetype, whose "somewhere" must perforce reside within our inner self,* filled full with time-less, space-less Love and Faith and Hope.

But not even the highest art can gain the force for such a revelation while it lacks the support of a religious symbol of the most perfect moral ordering of the world, through which alone can it be truly understanded of the people:

* Cf. *Luke*, xvii. 21: "Neither shall they say, Lo here! or, lo there! for behold, the kingdom of God is within you."—Tr.

only by borrowing from life's exercise itself the likeness of the Divine, can the artwork hold this up to life, and holding, lead us out beyond this life to pure contentment and redemption.

A great, nay, an immeasurable field of search were thus defined in outlines sharp enough, perhaps, yet not so easily discernible through their remoteness from the common life; and its closer survey might well repay the trouble. That the Politician cannot guide us here, we have felt necessary to state quite plainly; and it further seems to us of weight to pursue our searches quite apart from the unfruitful field of Politics. On the other hand we must follow with the utmost diligence, and to its farthest bifurcation, each path whereon man's mental culture may lead to the establishment of true morality. Our heart's desire must be no less, than to win comrades and helpers on every one of these domains. Already we have gained some; our sympathy with the movement against Vivisection, for instance, has made us acquainted with kindred spirits in the realm of Physiology, who, armed with special scientific knowledge, have stood by our side against the impudent assertions of legalised defilers of Science,—though unresultfully alas!, as at present is unavoidable. Those peaceable associations to whom the practical fulfilment of our thoughts seems allotted by their very nature, we have mentioned elsewhere; we now have only to express the hope that their useful workers will turn to us, and combine their separate interests in that one great interest which might be expressed somewhat as follows:—

We recognise the cause of the fall of Historic Man, and the necessity of his regeneration; we believe in the possibility of such Regeneration, and devote ourselves to its carrying-through in every sense.

It may be open to question, whether the work of such a fellowship would not by far transcend the immediate scope of addresses to a Patronate of Stage-festivals. We will hope, however, that the honoured members of this Verein have hitherto lent a not unwilling ear to kindred subjects. As far as the author of the present lines is concerned, he must in any case declare that henceforth nothing but advices from the aforesaid field may be expected of him.

CONTINUATIONS OF "RELIGION AND ART."

I.*

"KNOW THYSELF."

REAT KANT taught us to postpone the wish for knowledge of the world to criticism of man's power of knowledge; if we thus arrived at the most complete uncertainty about the reality of the world, *Schopenhauer* next taught us to draw the most infallible conclusions as to the world's In-itself from a farther-reaching criticism, no longer of our mental faculties, but of that Will in us which goes before all knowledge. "Know thyself, and thou hast read the world" —the Pythia said; "look round thee, all of this art thou" —the Brahmin.

How totally these lessons of ancestral wisdom had been lost to us, we may judge by their having to be re-discovered after tens of centuries by Schopenhauer treading in the shining wake of Kant. For if we view the present state of all our Sciences and Statecraft, we find them void of any true religious core, and simply wed to a barbaric babbling, to which two thousand years of practice have given a well-nigh venerable aspect in the people's purblind eye.

Who ever finds that "Know thyself" applied to any rating of the world? Not one Historic action do we know, that betrays this doctrine's influence on the transactors. We strike away at what we know not, and should we haply hit ourselves, we think another struck us. Who has not witnessed this once more in the present stir against the Jews, let us say, when looked at in light of that doctrine? What has given the Jews their now so dreaded power

* "*Erkenne dich selbst*" appeared in the *Bayreuther Blätter* for February-March (double no.) 1881.—Tr.

among and over us, not one man seems to stop and ponder; or if he goes into the question, he seeks no farther than the facts and phases of the last ten years, or at most a few years earlier: nowhere can we trace as yet an inclination to a deeper search into ourselves, in this case to a thorough criticism of the will and spirit of all that conglomerate of nature and civilisation which we, for instance, call the "German."

Yet the movement here alluded to perhaps is more adapted than any other to set us marvelling at ourselves: in it we seem to see the late rewakening of an instinct that appeared extinct. A man who some thirty years ago drew notice to the Jews' inaptitude for taking a productive share in our Art, and felt impelled to renew that attempt just eighteen years thereafter,* was met by the utmost indignation of Jews alike and Germans; it became quite dangerous to breathe the word "Jew" with a doubtful accent. But what once roused the bitterest ill-will when spoken on the field of ethical Æsthetics, we suddenly hear cried in vulgar brutal tones upon the field of civic intercourse and party politics. The fact that lies between these two expressions, is the bestowal of full right upon the Jews to regard themselves in all conceivable respects as Germans †—much as a blanket authorised the blacks in Mexico to hold themselves for whites. Whoever weighs this matter well, even if its real absurdity escapes him, must at least be highly astonished at the levity—nay, the frivolity of our State-authorities, who could decree so vast, so incomputable a transformation of our national system without the smallest sense of what they were doing.

The formula ran as "Equalisation of the rights of all German citizens, without regard to difference of 'Confession.'"

How was it possible for there to be Germans, at any time, who could conceive of all that keeps the Jewish stem so wide apart from us under the idea of a religious

* See *Judaism in Music*, Vol. III. of the present series.—Tr.

† Decreed by the Reichstag in 1871.—Tr.

"confession," seeing it was first and solely in German history that divisions arose in the *Christian* Church which led to the State-acknowledgment of various confessions? However, if only we will turn that "Know thyself" with ruthless energy upon ourselves, this curiously perverted formula may afford us one of the principal clues to explanation of the seemingly inexplicable. The first thing then to strike us, will be the recent experience that our clerics feel lamed at once in their agitation against the Jews when Judaism itself is seized by the root, and the patriarchs for instance, great Abraham in particular, are submitted to a criticism involving the actual text of the Mosaic books.* At once the groundwork of the Christian Church, its "positive" religion, seems to reel beneath their feet; a "Mosaic Confession" is recognised; and its adherents are accorded the right to take their place beside us, to examine the credentials of a second revelation through Jesus Christ—whom even in the opinion of the late English Prime Minister they regard as one of their countless minor prophets, of whom we have made by far too much ado. To tell the truth, it will fall hard to prove by the aspect of the Christian world, and the character of the Culture shed upon it by a Church so soon decayed, the superiority of the revelation through Jesus Christ to that through Abraham and Moses: in spite of its dispersion, the Jewish stock has remained one whole with the Mosaic laws to this very day, whereas our culture and civilisation stand in the most crying contradiction to Christ's teaching. To the Jew who works the sum out, the outcome of this culture is simply the necessity of waging wars, together with the still greater one, of having money for them. Accordingly he sees our State society divided into a military and a civil class: as it is a couple of thousand years since he did anything in the military line, he devotes his knowledge and experience with great gusto to the civil class, for he observes that this must find

* It was not very long before this was written, that biblical critics began to turn their attention from the New to the Old Testament.—Tr.

the money for the military, and in that affair his talents have been trained to highest virtuosity.

Now the astounding success of our resident Jews in the gaining and amassing of huge stores of money has always filled our Military State authorities with nothing but respect and joyful admiration: so that the present campaign against the Jews seems to point to a wish to draw the attention of those authorities to the question, Where do the Jews get it from? The bottom of the whole dispute, as it appears to us, is Property, Ownership, which we suddenly perceive to be in jeopardy, notwithstanding that each outlay of the State has the look of aiming more at the insurance of possession than anything else.

If the application of "Know thyself" to our Church's religious descent would turn out poorly for our case against the Jews, the result will be no less unfavourable if we investigate the nature of the only thing our State systems understand by *possession*, before endeavouring to secure it from the Jews' encroachments.

"Property" has acquired an almost greater sacredness in our social conscience than religion: for offence against the latter there is lenience, for damage to the former no forgiveness. Since Property is deemed the base of all stability, the more's the pity that not all are owners, that in fact the greater proportion of Society comes disinherited into the world. Society is manifestly thus reduced by its own principle to such a perilous inquietude, that it is compelled to reckon all its laws for an impossible adjustment of this conflict; and protection of property—for which in its widest international sense the weaponed host is specially maintained—can truly mean no else than a defence of the possessors against the non-possessors. Many as are the earnest and sagacious brains that have applied themselves to this problem, its solution, such as that at last suggested of an equal division of all possessions, has not as yet been found amenable; and it seems as if the State's disposal of the apparently so simple idea of Property had driven a beam into the body of mankind that dooms it to a lingering death of agony.

As the historic origin and evolution of our States seems worth a close examination in any verdict on their character, since thence alone do rights and conditions of right appear deducible, so the inequality of Possession, nay, its total absence in one great section of the State's constituents as result of the latest conquest of a country —e.g. of England by the Normans, or of Ireland in turn by the English—should be matter for explanation and, if need be, for vindication also. Far from embarking on inquiries of such difficulty ourselves, we have merely to point out the patent metamorphosis of the original idea of Property by the legal hallowing of usurpation, and to say that right by purchase nowadays has taken the place of right by earning, between which two came right by violence of seizure.

Clever though be the many thoughts expressed by mouth or pen about the invention of *money* and its enormous value as a civiliser, against such praises should be set the curse to which it has always been doomed in song and legend. If *gold* here figures as the demon strangling manhood's innocence, our greatest poet shews at last the goblin's game of *paper money*. The Nibelung's fateful ring become a pocket-book, might well complete the eerie picture of the spectral world-controller. By the advocates of our Progressive Civilisation this rulership is indeed regarded as a spiritual, nay, a moral power; for vanished Faith is now replaced by "Credit," that fiction of our mutual honesty kept upright by the most elaborate safeguards against loss and trickery. What comes to pass beneath the benedictions of this Credit we now are witnessing, and seem inclined to lay all blame upon the Jews. They certainly are virtuosi in an art which we but bungle: only, the coinage of money out of nil was invented by our Civilisation itself; or if the Jews are blamable for that, it is because our entire civilisation is a barbaro-judaic medley, in nowise a Christian creation.

A little self-knowledge on this point, methinks, would not come amiss to the representatives of the Church themselves, particularly when combating the seed of Abraham, in whose name they still go on to claim fulfilment of certain promises of his Jehova. A Christianity which has accommodated itself to the brute violence of every ruling power in the world might find itself, when turning from the raging to the reckoning beast of prey, outmatched in cleverness and cunning by its foe; wherefore there is little present hope of special welfare from the support of either our Church or our State authorities.

However, an inner motive plainly lies at bottom of the present movement, little as it may be evinced by the behaviour of its leaders so far. We expressed our belief, above, that this motive was the re-awakening of an instinct lost to the German nation. People speak of an antagonism of *races*. In this sense we should have fresh cause for self-inspection, as it would necessitate our defining the relation of certain given breeds of man to one another. Here it would probably have to be recognised at the outset that, in talking of a German "race," it would be very difficult, nay, wellnigh impossible to compare it with a race so strongly pronounced, and still unaltered, as the Jewish. When learned men debate the relative value of mixed or pure-bred races, for the evolution of mankind, the decision must surely hinge on what we mean by man's developmental progress. The so-called Romanic nations, and the English too, are praised as hybrid stocks that obviously surpass in Culture-progress the peoples of a haply pure Germanic breed. On the other hand, if one declines to be blinded by the glamour of this culture and civilisation, and seeks the welfare of mankind in its bringing-to-birth of great characters, one finds that these far rather come to light—nay, almost solely—in pure-bred races; where it seems that the still unbroken nature-force of Race at first makes up for every higher human virtue yet unformed, and only to be won through life's sore trials, by that of *pride*. This peculiar pride of race, that still gave us in the

Middle Ages such towering characters as Princes, Kings and Kaisers, may be met even to-day in the old nobility of German origin, although in unmistakable degeneration; and that degeneration we should have to take seriously into account if we wished to explain the fall of the German Folk, now exposed defenceless to the inroads of the Jews. For this, the proper course might be to first recall the unexampled devastation which Germany suffered through the Thirty Years War: after by far the greatest part of the male population had been rooted out of town and country, while the female had been violated to no less a degree by Walloons, Croats, Spaniards, French and Swedes, the relatively little-injured nobles may scarcely have felt themselves one racial body with the remnant of this decimated people. That feeling of community we still find markedly expressed in many a preceding epoch; and then it was the true patrician families, that contrived to re-illume the proper spirit after serious diminutions of the nation's substance. This we may see in the revival of Germanic races by new offshoots from the parent stock, when tribal migration had robbed the home-stayers of their first heroic clans; we see it in the resuscitation of the German language by patrician poets of the Hohenstaufen era, after monkish Latin had become the only medium of gentility, whereas the spirit of their poetry thrust down to the peasant's hut and shaped one wholly equal speech for Folk alike and Noble; and once again we see it in the stand against the outrage foisted on the Germans by the Church of Rome, when the example of its lords and princes led the Folk to stout defence. 'Twas otherwise after the Thirty Years War: the nobles found no nation left, to which to feel their kinship; the great monarchic powers shifted from the stricter seat of Germany towards the Slavic east: degenerate Slavs, decadent Germans, form the soil of the eighteenth century's history, a soil to which the Jew might confidently migrate from a Poland and a Hungary sucked dry, since even prince and noble durst no longer be ashamed of doing business with him; for—Pride itself had just been pledged already, exchanged for vanity and greed.

Though in recent days we see these last two traits of character adopted by the Folk itself—our ancient relatives the Swiss can think of us no otherwise!—and though the title "German" has thus been almost coined anew, yet this new-birth still lacks too much, to constitute a real rebirth of racial feeling, a thing that always finds its first expression in a settled instinct. Our nation, one may say, has not the natural instinct for that which suits it, for what becomes it, helps and furthers it; estranged from itself, it dabbles in foreign manners. On none other have great and original spirits been bestowed, as on it, without its having known in time to treasure them: yet if the silliest news-writer or political cheap-jack but brazens out his lying phrases, it chooses him to represent its weightiest interests; whilst if the Jew comes tinkling with his bell of paper, it throws its savings at his feet, and makes him in one night a millionaire.

The Jew, on the contrary, is the most astounding instance of racial congruence ever offered by world-history. Without a fatherland, a mother-tongue, midst every people's land and tongue he finds himself again, in virtue of the unfailing instinct of his absolute and indelible idiosyncrasy: even commixture of blood does not hurt him; let Jew or Jewess intermarry with the most distinct of races, a Jew will always come to birth. Not into the remotest contact is he brought with the religion of any of the civilised (*gesittete*) nations; for in truth he has no religion at all—merely the belief in certain promises of his god which in nowise extend to a life beyond this temporal life of his, as in every true religion, but simply to this present life on earth, whereon his race is certainly ensured dominion over all that lives and lives not. Thus the Jew has need to neither think nor chatter, not even to calculate, for the hardest calculation lies all cut and dried for him in an instinct shut against all ideality. A wonderful, unparalleled phenomenon: the plastic dæmon of man's downfall in triumphant surety; and German citizen of State, to boot, with a Mosaic confession; the darling of Liberal princes, and warrant of our national unity!—

Despite the enormous disadvantage at which the German race (if so we still may call it) appears to stand against the Jewish, we yet have ventured to suggest the re-awakening of a German instinct as one factor in the present agitation. As, however, we have been obliged to discard all idea of its being a purely racial instinct, we perhaps might search for something higher: a bent that, merely vaguely (*wahnvoll*) felt by the Folk of to-day, would at first appear indeed as instinct, though really of far nobler origin and loftier aim, and which might haply be defined as the spirit of the purely-Human.

From the Cosmopolitan proper, if such a man exists in fact, we probably should have little to expect for the solution of our problem. 'Tis no small thing, to run through the history of the world and yet preserve love for the human species. Here nothing but a rooted feeling of kinship with the immediate nation whence we sprang, can serve to re-knit the strand dissevered by a survey of the whole: here operates the thing we feel ourselves to be; we pity, and strive our best to hope, as for the future of our nearer family. Fatherland, mother-tongue: woe to the man bereft of these! But what unmeasured happiness, to recognise in one's mother-tongue the speech of one's ure-fathers! Through such a tongue our feelings and beholdings stretch right back to early Man himself; no fence and pale there hedge our nobles in, and far beyond the fatherland at last assigned us, beyond the landmarks of historic knowledge and all our outer trappings thence derived, we feel ourselves one kin with pristine Man's creative beauty. Such is our German language, the only heritage retained intact from our forefathers. Do we feel our breath fast quitting us, beneath the pressure of an alien civilisation; do we fall into uncertainty about ourselves: we have only to dig to the roots in the true father-soil of our language, to reap at once a reassuring answer on ourselves, nay, on the truly Human. And this possibility, of always drawing from the pristine fount of our own nature, that makes us feel ourselves no more a race, no mere variety of man, but one of Manhood's primal branches,—'tis this that ever has bestowed on us great men and spiritual heroes, as to whom we have no need to trouble whether fashioners of foreign fatherless civilisations are able to understand and prize them; whilst we again, inspired by the deeds and gifts of our forefathers, and gazing with unclouded eye, are able to rightly estimate those foreigners, and value them according to the spirit of pure Humanity indwelling in their work. For the sterling German instinct asks and seeks for nothing but this Purely-Human, and through that search alone can it be helpful—not merely to itself, but to all that shews the pure and genuine under never so great disguise.

Whom could it escape, that, suffering from the inability to truly manifest itself in either national or church-religious life, this noble instinct could but lead a feeble, indistinct, misunderstandable and scamped existence hitherto? In not one of those parties which aspire to guide the movements of our political or our intellectual national life, especially at the present day, does it seem to us, alas! to find a voice; even the names they take proclaim them not of German origin, still less inspired by German instinct. What "Conservatives," "Liberals" and "Conservative-liberals," and finally "Democrats," "Socialists," or even "Social-democrats" etc., have lately uttered on the Jewish Question, must seem to us a trifle foolish; for none of these parties would think of testing that "Know thyself" upon themselves, not even the most indefinite and therefore the only one that styles itself in German, the "Progress"-party. There we see nothing but a clash of interests, whose object is common to all the disputants, common and ignoble: plainly the side most strongly organised, i.e. the most unscrupulous, will bear away the prize. With all our comprehensive State- and National-Economy, it would seem that we are victims to a dream now flattering, now terrifying, and finally asphyxiating: all are panting to awake therefrom; but it is the dream's peculiarity that, so long as it enmeshes us, we take it for real life, and fight against our wakening as though we fought with death. At last one crowning horror gives the tortured wretch the needful strength: he wakes, and what he held most real was but a figment of the dæmon of distraught mankind.

We who belong to none of all those parties, but seek our welfare solely in man's wakening to his simple hallowed dignity; we who are excluded from these parties as useless persons, and yet are sympathetically troubled for them,—we can only stand and watch the spasms of the dreamer, since no cry of ours can pierce to him. So let us save and tend and brace our best of forces, to bear a noble cordial to the sleeper when he wakes, as of himself he must at last. But only when the fiend, who keeps those ravers in the mania of their party-strife, no more can find a where or when to lurk among us, will there also be no longer—any Jews.

And the very stimulus of the present movement—conceivable among ourselves alone—might bring this great solution within reach of us Germans, rather than of any other nation, if only we would boldly take that "Know thyself" and apply it to the inmost quick of our existence. That we have naught to fear from ultimate knowledge, if but we conquer all false shame and quarry deep enough, we hope the anxious may have culled from the above.

2.

HERO-DOM AND CHRISTENDOM.*

FTER recognising the necessity of a regeneration of the human race, if we follow up the possibilities of its ennoblement we light on little else than obstacles. In our attempt to explain its downfall by a physical perversion we had the support of the noblest sages of all time, who believed they found the cause of degeneration in the substituting of animal for vegetable food; thus we necessarily were led to the assumption of a change in the fundamental substance of our body, and to a corrupted blood we traced the depravation of temperaments and of moral qualities proceeding from them.

Quite apart from such an explanation, one of the cleverest men of our day has also proved this fall to have been caused by a corruption of blood, though, leaving that change of diet wholly out of sight, he has derived it solely from the crossing of races, whereby the noblest lost more than the less noble of them gained. The uncommonly circumstantial picture of this process supplied us by Count Gobineau in his "*Essai sur l'inégalité des races humaines*" † appeals to us with most terrible force of conviction. We cannot withhold our acknowledgment that the human family consists of irremediably disparate races,‡ whereof the noblest well might rule the more ignoble, yet never raise them to their level by commixture, but simply sink

* *Heldenthum und Christenthum* originally appeared in the Bayreuther Blätter for September 1881.—Tr.

† Vide p. 39 antea.—Tr.

‡ Cf. "Alles ist nach seiner Art: an ihr wirst du nichts ändern"—*Siegfried*, act ii—which even Schopenhauer, so unappreciative of the literary *Ring des Nibelungen*, marked strongly with approval.—Tr.

to theirs. Indeed this one relation might suffice to explain our fall; even its cheerlessness should not blind us to it: if it is reasonable to assume that the dissolution of our earthly globe is purely a question of time, we probably shall have to accustom ourselves to the idea of the human species dying out. On the other hand there is such a matter as life beyond all time and space, and the question whether the world has a moral meaning we here will try to answer by asking ourselves if we mean to go to ground as beasts or gods.

The first point will be, to examine the special attributes of those noblest races, through whose enfeeblement they lost themselves among ignoble races. The more definitely has recent science inclined us to accept the natural descent of man's lower races from the animal species most resembling them, the harder is it to assent to a derivation of the so-called white race from those black and yellow: as to the explanation of the white tint itself our physiologists are still at variance. Whilst yellow races have viewed themselves as sprung from monkeys, the white traced back their origin to gods, and deemed themselves marked out for rulership. It has been made quite clear that we should have no History of Man at all, had there been no movements, creations and achievements of the white men; and we may fitly take world-history as the consequence of these white men mixing with the black and yellow, and bringing them in so far into history as that mixture altered them and made them less unlike the white. Incomparably fewer in individual numbers than the lower races, the ruin of the white races may be referred to their having been obliged to mix with them; whereby, as remarked already, they suffered more from the loss of their purity than the others could gain by the ennobling of their blood.

Without touching on the endless varieties produced by ever fresh inarchings of scions from the old root-stocks, our object merely bids us linger with the purest and noblest, to realise its overwhelming difference from the less. If a review of all the races makes it impossible to deny the oneness of the human *species*; and if that common factor may be defined, in its noblest sense, as the capacity for conscious suffering,—we shall have to seek for what distinguishes the white race, if we are actually to rank it high above the others. With fine acumen Gobineau discovers it, not in an exceptional development of moral qualities, but in a larger store of the temperamental attributes from which those morals flow.* These we should have to look for in that keener and withal more delicate sensibility of Will which shews itself in a complex organism, united with the requisite intensity of Intellect: the point being that, in answer to the cravings of the will, the intellect shall rise to that clear-sightedness which casts its own light back upon the will, and, taming it, becomes a moral prompting; whereas the overpowering of the intellect by the blindly craving will denotes the lower nature, since here we cannot class the stimuli as motives lit as yet by light of intellect, but simply as common promptings of the senses. However passionate may be the signs of Suffering in these lower natures, its conscious record in the downtrod intellect will be comparatively feeble; on the contrary it is just the strength of consciousness of Suffering, that can raise the intellect of higher natures to knowledge of the meaning of the world. Those natures in which the completion of this lofty process is evidenced by a corresponding deed, we call Heroic.—

The plainest type of heroism is that evolved by the Hellenic sagas in their *Herakles*. Labours put upon him to destroy him, he executes in proud obedience, and frees the world thereby from direst plagues. Seldom, in fact scarcely ever, do we find the hero otherwise than in a state of suffering prepared for him by fate: Herakles is persecuted by Hera out of jealousy of his divine begetter, and kept in menial subjection. In this main trait we surely should not do wrong to recognise an allusion to

* "Mit schöner Sicherheit erkennt ihn *Gobineau* nicht in einer ausnahmsweisen Entwicklung ihrer moralischen Eigenschaften selbst, sondern in einem grösseren Vorrathe der Grundeigenthümlichkeiten, welchen jene entfliessen."

that school of arduous labours in which the noblest Aryan stems and races throve to grandeur of demigods: the by no means mildest climates whence they enter history at last, as men matured, supply us with a clue to the fortunes of their ancestry. Here we find the fruit of suffering and deprivations vanquished by heroic toil, that proud self-consciousness whereby these stocks are once for all distinguished from the others throughout our whole world-history. Like Herakles and Siegfried, they were conscious of divine descent: a lie to them was inconceivable, and a free man meant a truthful man. Nowhere in history do these root-qualities of the Aryan race shew forth more plainly than in the contact of the last pure-bred Germanic branches with the falling Roman world. Here history repeats the one great feature of their mythic heroes: with bloody hands they serve the Romans, and—rate them infinitely lower than themselves, much as Herakles despised Eurystheus. The accident of their becoming masters of the great Latino-Semite realm was fatal to them. Pride is a delicate virtue and brooks no compromise, such as crossing of breed: but the Germanic race without this virtue has—naught to tell us. For this Pride is the soul of the truthful, of the free though serving. He knows no fear (*Furcht*), but respect (*Ehrfurcht*)—a virtue whose very name, in its proper sense, is known to none save those oldest Aryan peoples; whilst honour (*Ehre*) itself is the sum of all personal worth, and therefore can neither be given nor received, as is our practice to-day, but, a witness of divine descent, it keeps the hero unashamed even in his most shameful of sufferings. From Pride and Honour sprang the rule that, not property ennobles man, but man this property; which, again, was expressed in the custom that excessive possessions were speedily shared out, for very shame, by him to whom they haply fell.

Upon looking back to these characteristics and the inviolably noble code that flowed therefrom we certainly are justified in seeking the cause of their loss and its decay in a depravation of those races' blood, since we see the fall undoubtedly accompany their hybridising. This fact has been so completely established by the talented and energetic author named above, that we need only refer our friends to his work on the Disparity of the Races of Man, to rest assured that what we now propose to link thereto will not be viewed as superficial guess-work. For we now must seek the Hero where he turns against the ruin of his race, the downfall of its code of honour, and girds his erring will to horror: the hero wondrously become divine—the *Saint.*

It was a weighty feature of the Christian Church, that none but sound and healthy persons were admitted to the vow of total world-renunciation; any bodily defect, not to say mutilation, unfitted them.* Manifestly this vow was to be regarded as issuing from the most heroic of all possible resolves, and he who sees in it a "cowardly self-surrender"—as someone recently suggested,†—may bravely exult in his own self-retention, but had best not meddle any further with things that don't concern him. Granted that different causes moved different men to so completely turn their will from life, yet the act itself is always characterised by utmost energy of will; was it the look, the likeness or the mental picture of the Saviour suffering upon the cross, the influence of a pity overcoming all self-will was invariably united with the deepest horror at the attributes of this world-shaping Will, and to such a point that the will exerted all its strength in revolt against itself. From that moment we see the saint outvie the hero in his endurance of suffering, his self-offering for others; almost more unshakable than the hero's pride is

* Cf. "Doch büssen wollt' er [Klingsor] nun, ja heilig werden. Ohnmächtig in sich selbst die Sünde zu ertödten, an sich legt er die Frevlerhand, die nun, dem Grale zugewandt, verachtungsvoll dess' Hüter von sich stiess"—*Parsifal*, act i.—Tr.

† Cf. Nietzsche's *Morgenröthe* (pubd. July 1881), Aph. 38:—"The same impulse that becomes a painful feeling of *cowardice* under the reproaches cast on it by custom, becomes an agreeable feeling of *humility* if a code such as the Christian commends it to man's heart and calls it *good.*"—Tr.

the saint's humility, and his truthfulness becomes the martyr's joy.

Now what part can "Blood," the quality of Race, have played in fitting for the exercise of so holy a heroism? The last, the Christian dispensation had its origin in that intensely complex blend of races white and black which, dating from the rise of the Chaldæo-Assyrian empire, supplied the basic character of the nations of the later Roman empire. The author of the great work now before us calls this character the Semitic, after one of those main stocks transplanted from North-eastern parts to the Assyrian plains; he proves to demonstration its transforming influence on Hellenism and Romanism, and finds its essential features still preserved in the self-styled "Latin" race despite all fresh cross-breeding. This race's property is the Roman Catholic Church; its patron-spirits are the saints that Church has canonised, nor should their value be diminished in our eyes by their now being upheld to the people's veneration in nothing but un-Christian pomp. But after centuries of huge perversion of the Semite-Latin Church we see no longer any genuine Saints, no Hero-martyrs of the Truth, arise therefrom; and if the falsehood of our whole Civilisation bears witness to corrupted blood in its supporters, 'twould be no stretch for us to say that the blood of Christendom itself is curdled. And what a blood? None other than the blood of the Redeemer's self, which erewhile poured its hallowing stream into the veins of his true heroes.

The blood of the Saviour, the issue from his head, his wounds upon the cross,—who impiously would ask its race, if white or other? Divine we call it, and its source might dimly be approached in what we termed the human species' bond of union, its aptitude for Conscious Suffering. This faculty we can only regard as the last step reached by Nature in the ascending series of her fashionings; thenceforth she brings no new, no higher species to light, for in it she herself attains her unique freedom, the annulling of the internecine warfare of the Will. The hidden background of this Will, inscrutable in Time and Space, is nowhere manifest to us but in that abrogation; and there it shews itself divine, the Willing of Redemption. Thus, if we found the faculty of conscious suffering peculiarly developed in the so-called white race, in the Saviour's blood we now must recognise the quintessence of free-willed suffering itself (*des bewusst wollenden Leidens selbst*), that godlike Pity which streams through all the human species, its fount and origin.

What we here can only touch in terms most hard to understand, and easily misconstrued, may take a more familiar aspect in the light of history. How high the most advanced white race could raise itself in weightiest matters of the world through keenness of that faculty which we have called the human species' bond of union, we see in its religions. The Brahminic religion we surely must rank as the most astounding evidence of the breadth of view and faultless mental accuracy of those earliest Aryan branches; on a groundwork of profoundest knowledge of the world they built a religious structure that has weathered all these thousand years unshaken, a dogma still obeyed by many million men as habit of all life and thought, high arbiter of death and suffering. It had one only fault: it was a race-religion. The deepest explanations of the world, the loftiest injunctions for redemption from it, to-day are taught, believed and followed by a vastly hybrid populace wherein no trace of true morality can be detected. Without tarrying by this sight, or even seeking out the grounds of this phenomenon, let us merely remember that a race of conquerors and subjugators, appraising the enormous gulf between themselves and inferior races, founded at once a religion and a civilisation, whose mutual support and interaction were to ensure the permanence of a dominion based on careful calculation of existing natural factors. A masterpiece without its equal: binding the cruelly oppressed to their oppressors by so firm a metaphysical concordat, that any mutiny was made unthinkable; for even the Buddha's broad endeavour for the human species must break against the stubborn racial veto of the white dictators, and become a superstition freshly palsying the yellow race.

From what blood, then, could the ever more consciously suffering genius of mankind bring forth a saviour, seeing that the blood of the white race was manifestly paling and congealing?—For the origin of natural Man our *Schopenhauer* propounds an hypothesis of wellnigh convincing power*: going back to the physical law [Mariotti's] of increase of force under compression, he explains the unusual frequency of births of twins after abnormal periods of mortality as if the vital force were doubling its exertions under pressure of a pestilence that threatened to exterminate the species; which leads him to the theory that the procreative force in a given type of animals, threatened with extinction by opposing forces through some inherent defect in its organism, may have become so abnormally augmented in one mated pair that not merely does a more highly organised individual issue from the mother's womb, but in that individual a quite new *species*. The blood in the Redeemer's veins might thus have flowed, as divine sublimate of the species itself, from the redemptive Will's supreme endeavour to save mankind at death-throes in its noblest races.

Though we must regard this as the extreme limit of a speculation hovering between Physics and Metaphysics, and eschew all further pursuit of a path that has betrayed so many of our able minds into the most nonsensical farragos—especially under guidance of the Old Testament—yet from this hypothesis concerning the Redeemer's blood we may derive a second and the weightiest distinction of his work, namely the simplicity of his teaching, which consisted almost solely in Example. The blood

* *Parerga* II., § 93.—In the succeeding chapter, § 94, Schopenhauer also lays stress on the impossibility of Man's three chief races having sprung from one and the same pair, though he rejects their loose division into "white, yellow and black" (adopted by our author apparently for sake of common parlance) and adopts the modern designations of "Caucasian, Mongolian and Æthiopic."—Tr.

of suffering Mankind, as sublimated in that wondrous birth, could never flow in the interest of howsoever favoured a single race; no, it shed itself on all the human family, for noblest cleansing of Man's blood from every stain. Hence the sublime simplicity of the pure Christian religion, whereas the Brahminic, for instance, applying its knowledge of the world to the ensurance of supremacy for one advantaged race, became lost in artificiality and sank to the extreme of the absurd. Thus, notwithstanding that we have seen the blood of noblest races vitiated by admixture, the partaking of the blood of Jesus, as symbolised in the only genuine sacrament of the Christian religion, might raise the very lowest races to the purity of gods. This would have been the antidote to the decline of races through commingling, and perhaps our earth-ball brought forth breathing life for no other purpose than that ministrance of healing.*

Let us not mistake, however, the enormity of the assumption that the human species is destined to attain a uniform equality; and let us admit that such equality is unimaginable in any but a horrifying picture, like that which Gobineau feels bound to hold before us in his closing words. Yet it is only through our being obliged to look at it through the reek of our Civilisation and Culture, that this picture gains its full repellence: and to recognise these as themselves the lying offspring of the human race's misdirection, is the task of that spirit which left us when we lost our nobleness of blood and at like time found the Christian martyrs' antidote employed for binding us to all the lies and humbug of Church-rule.

* "Während wir somit das Blut edelster Racen durch Vermischung sich verderben sehen, dürfte den niedrigsten Racen der Genuss des Blutes Jesu, wie er in dem einzigen ächten Sakramente der christlichen Religion symbolisch vor sich geht, zu göttlichster Reinigung gedeihen. Dieses Antidot wäre demnach dem Verfalle der Racen durch ihre Vermischung entgegen gestellt, und vielleicht brachte dieser Erdball athmendes Leben nur hervor, um jener Heilsordnung zu dienen." I have thought it best to quote the German of these last two sentences, as their construction presents peculiar difficulties to the translator; a remark that applies, in fact, to almost all the remainder of this article.—Tr.

Assuredly no task can be more cheerless, than to review the human races journeyed westward from their central-Asiatic home, and find that all their civilisation and religion has never yet enabled them to take concerted steps for so distributing themselves over the kindliest regions of the earth that by far the largest portion of the obstacles to a free and healthy evolution of pacific polities (*friedfertiger Gemeinde-Zustände*) should disappear through mere abandonment of the forbidding wastes which now so long have lodged their greatest numbers. It certainly may be right to charge this purblind dulness of our public spirit to a vitiation of our blood—not only by departure from the natural food of man, but above all by the tainting of the hero-blood of noblest races with that of former cannibals now trained to be the business-agents of Society,—provided one does not overlook the further fact, that no blaze of orders can hide the withered heart whose halting beat bewrays its issue from a union pledged without the seal of love, be it never so consanguineous.

However, if we mean to seek a gladdening outlook on the future of the human race past all these horrors, nothing can be of greater urgence than to follow up each vestige of surviving qualities, and count the possibilities of their enhancement. Here we shall have to bear in mind that, if the noblest race's rulership and exploitation of the lower races—quite justified in a natural sense—has founded a sheer immoral system throughout the world, any equalising of them all by flat commixture decidedly would not conduct to an æsthetic state of things. To us Equality is only thinkable as based upon a universal moral concord, such as we can but deem true Christianity elect to bring about; and that only on the subsoil of a true, but no mere "rational" Morality (as I lately saw desired by a philologist), can a true æsthetic Art bear fruit, the life and sufferings of all great seers and artists of the past proclaim aloud.—

And now that we have reached our own domain [viz. Art.—Tr.], we will take breath for further dealings with the problem broached.

END OF THE PATRONAT-VEREIN.

Brief an H. v. Wolzogen.

The following "Letter to Hans von Wolzogen," editor of the Bayreuther Blätter, *appeared in the issue of that journal for April 1882, a little over three months before the first performance of* Parsifal.

TRANSLATOR'S NOTE.

My dear Friend.

EXT autumn it will be five years since you sacrificed yourself in my behalf, and took your stand beside me in a fresh attempt to found a Patronate for the practical execution of my idea. And now, though not indeed in sight of our ultimate goal, we have got so far that we should close one chapter of our labours.

Owing chiefly to your share in these labours, a wider knowledge of that idea of mine has now been spread, than I had managed to disseminate even by the Festivals of six years back. Yet the very recognition of this progress has convinced us that we could never arrive at our nearest practical goal, the renewing of Stage-festivals, on the path we had struck, that of enrolling Patrons. To satisfy my friends' impatience for a performance of "Parsifal," and to enable it to take place in this year 1882, I at last decided on offering my work to the general public under the usual conditions of admittance to a theatre. Looked at practically, then, I have to thank the existing Patronatverein for providing the means to embark on an enterprise in which, confiding in the support of the larger public, I can now engage without alarm. According to my latest information, all danger of financial failure appears already set aside; so that it is to be hoped that after redeeming my pledges to the Patronatverein * I shall find myself in a position to carry on the undertaking at my own risk, and annually repeat the Bayreuth Bühnenfestspiels in the manner now dictated by necessity, namely as thoroughly public performances.

For the immediate future these repetitions will be re-

* Namely the two private performances, on July 26 and 28, that preceded the public performances of July 30 to August 29, 1882.—Tr.

stricted to the Bühnenweihfestspiel * "Parsifal," and that for both an inner and an outer reason. The outer concerns the revenue from such performances, providing they are nowhere offered to the public save at Bayreuth, under my own supervision; the inner reason (the only virtual motive for that outer) concerns the altogether distinctive character of this my work, that character which has prompted me to name it a Bühnenweih-Festspiel. As to this, my friend, you have already expressed yourself so admirably in these Blätter of ours, that I have nothing to add beyond a reference to the removal of the "Ring des Nibelungen" from the Bayreuth Festival-house by causes which I believe I have rendered powerless to influence me with "Parsifal," for simple reason of its poem having taken me into a sphere which must properly remain defended from our Opera-houses.

In what manner the exclusive performances of "Parsifal" at Bayreuth may serve the hopes I once aroused in kindly friends, and which they still may cherish, of the founding of a "School,"—will soon transpire from the character of these performances and of the circumstances under which they take place. The very frequency of the performances to be given in course of one month suggested to me a multiple casting of the parts, especially the more exacting ones, to obviate all possibility of interruption by physical ailments: and this was easy, for I received the prompt and willing promise of every one of the talented artists whose assistance I invited. This friendly circumstance has incited me to throw open the Bayreuth Festivals to every gifted singer I become acquainted with, both now and in the future, as a school for practising the style by me inaugurated; which again, regarded practically, ensures me the advantage of avoiding the disturbing influence of those hot disputes about the artists' precedence so readily

* Though "*Bühnenfestspiel*" may be conveniently rendered as "Stage-festival," it is impossible to find a portable English expression for "a festival that consecrates the stage,"—which is the meaning conveyed by Wagner's last neologism, "*Bühnenweihfestspiel.*" I must therefore retain the German term.—Tr.

explainable under existing stage conditions. For the most eminent will tell himself that, if he stands aside to-day, he is giving his comrade and substitute a helpful and improving example in every respect; from the most-expert the less-experienced will learn, ay, discover what may still be lacking toward the artistic perfection of the general performance. In this sense I should annually be calling the best singers together for exercises chiefly helpful to them through their mutual observation and instruction of each other; and this of itself would exclude all those who see in every confrontation an insult to their pride of rank, that "honour" which has come to be a not entirely unconceited maxim in the face of Theatre-Intendants.

Now, I consider that yearly repetitions of "Parsifal" are peculiarly adapted to serve the present generation of artists as a school for the style I have founded, were it only for reason that in its study we have virgin soil unspoilt by evil habits such as have ruined my older works, whose mode of representation has already been subjected to the needs of our common Operatic routine. Not without a shudder could I face just yet the task of preparing my older works for model performance at our festivals in the fashion I intend with "Parsifal," since it would inflict on me a toil proved fruitless by experience: in similar attempts before, the excuse I have received from our best singers themselves for the most unimaginable misunderstandings, nay transgressions, has always been the answer of my simpleton, "I knew it not." To ground this knowledge, would be the office of our "school," and *then* alone could it successfully take up my older works. May the right persons be found: in any case I can offer them no other guidance than our Bühnenweihfestspiel.

Now, though I am most thankfully appreciative of all the help so kindly tendered us in furtherance of these festivals, on the other hand I see the time arrived for writing off the mutual obligations of our union. You, my friend, have lately expressed yourself in our Blätter with profound understanding of the very earnest matters here involved. If we have been compelled to renounce all hope of the continuance of our Bühnenfestspiels being guaranteed by the funds of a Patronate-capital; and if we have found ourselves obliged to look for assistance to the general public, whose contributions are no longer given for the realisation of an idea, but paid for a place in the theatre: then, as you have most rightly said, the former bond of union of our friends has come to have a purely theoretic meaning. To such an end our "Bayreuther Blätter" themselves have conducted, though at first we merely meant them for a chronicle of the progress of our undertakings, as also for a possible aid to understanding of the latter. However, two things are needful to all knowledge, namely subject and object; and as our Art-work was the object, we could not well avoid a criticism of the Public, as the subject before which the artwork was to be set. Nay, we were led at last to deem a thorough inquiry into the qualities of this Public no less expedient than a criticism of man's power of judgment appeared to *Kant*, when he made that criticism the preliminary to all right conclusions on the reality or ideality of the world as object. The necessity of criticising the Public—without whom the existence of a dramatic artwork is particularly inconceivable—took us seemingly so far away from our immediate goal, that I myself have of late been troubled by a certain fear lest we no longer are keeping our proper place towards our Patrons. But all incongruence will cease at once, if the "Bayreuther Blätter" are openly translated from their first and narrower office to the broader mission now accrued. As publisher of this widened monthly, whose tendence you recently most aptly defined, you will enter much the same relation with the public as my Festivals will place myself in after the redeeming of my pledges to the Patronat-Verein.* Perhaps we both shall therewith do

* In 1883, accordingly, the sub-title of the Bayreuther Blätter was changed from "Monthly paper of the Bayreuth Patronat-Verein" to "Journal for discussion of the possibilities of a German Culture." The Patronat-Verein (the

the right, because the only possible, thing under prevailing conditions. Whatever communications I still may owe from my chosen field of criticism of the "subject," I shall gladly hand to you alone for friendly publication in the "New Bayreuther Blätter"; and that perhaps with less constraint than now, when I probably have often digressed a little too far for some of our gracious patrons. Nevertheless I can but think that in any criticism of the Public the widest digression would have a more distinct and stimulant effect than—what we cannot be too much on our guard against—a too narrow restraint within the limits of the customary and, through too near acquaintance with it, the soporific. We must take our stand upon the mountain-top, to gain clear outlook and deep insight. Above all, let us shun complacency, even with a vegetarian diet!

With heartiest greetings,

Your

RICHARD WAGNER.

Palermo, 13th March, 1882.

second) had meanwhile come to a voluntary end, but Richard Wagner had made provision for its former members receiving both the new Blätter and a seat for *Parsifal* in return for an annual subscription of 20 marks (=£1) to that journal. The first quarterly number (published by Freiherr Hans von Wolzogen) did not appear, however, until just after the master's death, and within another couple of months a new association, the Allgemeiner Richard Wagner Verein (largely consisting of the older "local" Vereins) was formed to support the Bayreuth work in general; by the end of the year this new Verein adopted the Blätter as its official organ, with Freiherr von Wolzogen for its editor as before.—Tr.

THE STIPENDIARY FUND.

Offenes Schreiben

an

Herrn Friedrich Schön in Worms.

Prior to the publication of this "Open Letter to Herr Friedrich Schön of Worms" (B. Blätter, July 1882) Richard Wagner had written Herr Schön a private letter on the same subject (of May 28, 1882, since published in the first number of the B. Bl. for the present year, 1897). From that private letter it appears that its recipient had asked the master in what further manner he could help the Bayreuth work; Wagner replies, "By starting a fund for enabling the needy to attend the performances."—The idea of free admission to the Theatre had been entertained by Wagner for fully half his lifetime (see Vol. I. p. 64) and had already taken more definite form shortly after the first Bayreuth Festivals (see page 18 antea*). Now, however, it shapes itself into a provision not only for admittance to the theatre, but also for the expenses of travelling etc. which the poorer class of students and art-lovers cannot so well afford.*

No nobler work in connection with Bayreuth has ever been carried out, than this.

Started at once by Herr Schön with a handsome donation, the "Stipendien-Fonds" had by April 1883 attained the sum of 3,120 marks (£156). A "Stipendien-Stiftung" (Stipend-foundation) was then established, under the special superintendence of Herr Schön himself, in relation with the Festival-management. To shew how this branch has prospered, I may refer to the latest balance-sheet, where it appears that on Oct. 1, 1896, the funded capital of the Stipendienstiftung amounted to 28,000 marks (£1,400), and the income for the past two years to close on £500, of which over £450 was spent on the purchase of tickets for distribution to, and the provision of money for the travelling and incidental expenses of nearly a hundred people who otherwise would not have been able to attain their heart's-desire, a visit to the great revival of the Ring des Nibelungen *in 1896.*

TRANSLATOR'S NOTE.

MOST HONOURED SIR AND FRIEND!

TO you, above all the generous benefactors of the Bayreuth idea, I hold myself bound to explain my views and feeling as regards the *school* you so wish to promote, somewhat more minutely than in my recent open letter to our friend Hans von Wolzogen.

I will begin by referring you to the report with which I opened the first number of the Bayreuther Blätter.* At that time it was a positive relief to my conscience, over-burdened with a duty self-imposed, that I had to attest the outward impossibility of the projected School, though I myself had offered something like it. Let me here confess that in the five years since elapsed I have made up my mind that, were the means I then desired now placed at my command in amplest measure, I should have to decline point-blank all founding of a school. I no longer believe in our music, and avoid it on principle wherever it confronts me; in the event of a fulfilment of our friend Count Gobineau's prophecy that Europe will be submerged by Asiatic hordes in ten years' time, and our whole civilisation and culture destroyed, I should not blink an eyelid, for it is to be presumed that our music-plying would be the first thing to go by the board.

I have often declared my belief that Music is the saving genius of the German people, and I have been able to prove it by the revival of the German spirit from the days of Bach to Beethoven †: on no other field did the German's mission, the influence of his character upon the world without, evince itself more surely than on this; German Music was a hallowed emanation of the human

* See page 23 *antea*.—Tr.

† See Vol. IV. pp. 162-163; Vol. V. p. 95, etc., etc.—Tr.

spirit, and dæmonically-suffering godlike natures were her priests. But as the Evangel faded when the Redeemer's cross was hawked at every street-stall, so the genius of German music has grown mute since she was dragged round the world-mart as métier, with professional gutter-wags to celebrate her progress.

To you, my honoured friend, this will be nothing new, as for thirty years I have fairly exhausted the theme in articles and essays. The only thing I perhaps have outlived, is my allowing myself to try so many ways of linking on to the Existing my high opinion of the destiny of German Music, and above all, my projects for the fostering of her works. At the close of my memorial on a Royal Music-school to be founded in Munich * I permitted myself to enumerate my previous drafts of organisation and other writings bearing on the subject. That none of this was heeded or approved for execution [by the committee of 1865], shews plainly that people thought me out of my element.

And they were right. I am no musician, and I am sure of it when anybody brings me a famous composition by one of our celebrated masters of the day and for the life of me I cannot see its music. Obviously I am afflicted with an infirmity which unfits me to participate in our musical progress. Perchance I might have been made use of as a Conservator, for it had to be allowed that I understood how to conduct a few of Beethoven's Symphonies. Even now (I tell you this sincerely) had anyone set up a school for me, most probably I should have confined myself to these my favourite works ; and that in the stricter sense of a conserver, or a preacher who, when all is said, can give his congregation no more urgent message than the Gospels. Only, these obstinately conservative efforts would have booted nothing, with that Asiatic hurricane soon sweeping over us : for things would then fare as with those who came after the great folk-migration—to whom but few of Sophocles' and Æschylus' tragedies were saved,

* See Vol. IV. p. 223.—Tr.

but most of the works of Euripides—and our posterity would be left with about nine Symphonies by Brahms to two at most of Beethoven's; for the copyists always have marched with the times.

However, even such a Beethoven-Conservancy would tire me now too much. Liszt has gone before me to the seventies, and already I have followed him into the seventieth; with neither of us have folk known what to do, though I have been more fortunate than my great friend, who plays the pianoforte too well not to be plagued to the end of his life for lessons,—a right naïve expression of one of the most popular misunderstandings of our musical "now-time." You too, my honoured friend, will surely reduce your magnanimous wishes to my superintendence of the Bayreuth Bühnenfestspiels for as long as I may; and believe me, that is no such sinecure for my old age. You know how I propose to employ the series of public performances of "Parsifal" for consolidating the style of delivery and portrayal demanded by my works, through giving all the better talents known to me the opportunity of sharing by turns in the cast. The idea of making myself useful in this way was suggested to me by the extraordinary willingness with which I was met by our most gifted artists in particular. So many of them bemoaned their never having been able to get me to teach them the proper rendering of my "parts," and pressed me for the opportunity of such a study. Consequently I am provided with so multiplex a troop of artists for the coming performances of "Parsifal," that all fear of alteration of the dates announced * is obviated in advance; though I am aware of the new difficulties which might accrue, not only from the redoubling of my labours in the solo-practice, but particularly from the moral distraction of possible rivalries. Especially since we have heard so much of the "creation" of rôles and parts at French and Italian theatres, the distinction of such a creative act is not gladly forgone by

* As happened with the first performance of *Siegfried* in 1876 owing to the illness of Herr Betz, the impersonator of "Wotan."—Tr.

ourselves. The notion is, that one has fixed the character of a rôle for good and all, if one has been the first to appear in it before the public. Unfortunately the aim has often been less to arrive at real correctness in one's own conception, than to have it accepted as correct by those who follow after; for the fact of their regarding it as a model to be imitated, confirms the "creator" in his faith in its superior worth. Much mischief has resulted, especially when the creating was done behind the author's back.

It appears, however, that all the kind artists who are now about to gather round me, with a zeal most honouring to myself, are chiefly concerned with ensuring the authentic conception and execution of their tasks through my personal guidance; so that on this occasion I at anyrate may hope to exert a not unprofitable influence on both the mind and the morality of an artist-class made somewhat uncertain about the status of its services not only by our Stage-Intendants, but above all by our theatre-goers. Little support from outside shall I be able to count upon, and I heartily wish my else so trusty friend, the German public, not to leave me this time without its aid.*

This Public, which now once more will have to pass its verdict, I commend to the special regard of my quondam Patrons. My last and larger undertakings have always had to face the difficulty of a notable disbursement: if none but the contributors to the covering of these costs were to be entitled to enjoy and educate themselves at our Bühnenfestspiels, then—we must openly admit it—our work was foredoomed to barrenness. But now that the pinch (*Noth*) of our latest experiences again has driven us to attempt the continuance of our festivals by opening our auditorium to the high-paying public;

* Certainly in 1882 there was infinitely less of that "taking sides" for this or that singer, which unfortunately has since been fostered by the increasing presence of the newspaper-critic and the diminishing novelty of the work itself.—Tr.

and although it is easier for a camel to go through the eye of a needle than a rich man through the gate of heaven, yet few but the rich will gain entrance to our theatre,—to me the first and weightiest office of a newly-formed Patronate would appear to be the furnishing of those on whom poverty has imposed the lot of so many of Germania's ablest sons with an absolutely free admittance, nay, if need be, with their travelling-expenses and temporary cost of maintenance.

We have already been in correspondence about this weighty matter, and here I merely offer it as a suggestion to the new Patronate; for the organisation of any such body should be wholly independent from the first, a moral act of the public for the public, without any stricter connection with the Management of the Festivals (*Verwaltungsrath*) than that the latter would at all times do its utmost to assist the Patronate by a gift of seats. Leaving the formation of this new Verein to you, dear Sir, so proved a friend and well-wisher, to-day I need only lay stress on the great and good results which I anticipate from its endeavours. If the Verein has been the patron of the art-work hitherto, it will now become the patron of that public which desires to cheer and cultivate itself thereby. Here is the best conceivable School for our purpose; and if we still must go on teaching—that is, explaining and interpreting the broad relation with farthest-reaching realms of culture into which we believe our art-work brings us—then a plentifully-tended journal,* an enlargement of our existing Bayreuther Blätter, would keep the freest channel open. But no one should be debarred by lack of means from the possibility of taking a most effectual share in our efforts and achievements: what ridiculously paltry scholarships, for prize-compositions and the like, now foolishly attempt by the stipulation

* "Eine reichlichst gepflegte Zeitschrift"—owing to the ambiguity of the verb "pflegen," it is difficult to determine whether our author means "a handsomely endowed" or "with a large staff of contributors," so that I am obliged to employ a vague and rather clumsy epithet.—Tr.

of finishing lessons in Paris or Rome, we shall far more sensibly effect by throwing open to every competent person a vital interest in the cultivation of our own Art. And finally, we thus shall be conforming to the spirit of my own illustrious benefactor, who once again, as Protector of our Festivals, has placed me in the position through his most gracious and bountiful assistance to produce my work this year, and moreover, to keep the Bühnen-*Weih*-Festspiel wholly free from any possible jarring contact, has magnanimously renounced the wish to see it repeated at his own Court-theatre.

Filled with the blessing of this thought, I bear you my respectful thanks, dear Sir and Friend, above all our present Patrons; and in particular for having been the very one to supply the earnest cause of my addressing you this open letter.

Most sincerely:

RICHARD WAGNER.

Bayreuth, 16th June, 1882.

"PARSIFAL" AT BAYREUTH, 1882.

Das Bühnenweihfestspiel in Bayreuth. 1882.

The following article appeared in the double number of the Bayreuther Blätter for November-December, 1882.

TRANSLATOR'S NOTE.

S our Dedication-feasts of nowadays retain their popularity chiefly through the attendant so-called "church-wake" ("*Kirmes-Schmaus*"), I believed that my only course, in setting the symbolic (*mystich bedeutsame*) Love-feast of my Grail-Knights before a modern opera-public, would be to think of the Bühnenfestspielhaus as this time hallowed for the picturing of so sublime a rite. And though converted Jews—who make the most intolerant Catholics, as Christians tell me—have taken umbrage at the thought, I had no need to dilate on it with those who gathered round me in this bygone summer for the representation of my work. Whoever had the mind and eye to seize the character of all that passed within the walls of that house during those two months, both the productive and the receptive, could not describe it otherwise than as governed by a consecration that shed itself on everything without the smallest prompting. Experienced managers asked me after the authority presiding over this so amazingly accurate execution of every scenic, musical and dramatic detail upon, above, below, behind and before the stage; I cheerfully replied that it was Anarchy, for all did what they *would*, to wit, the right. And so it was: each understood the whole, and the object aimed at by the whole. No one thought too much expected of him, no one too little offered him. Success was to each of greater moment than applause, to receive which from the audience in the wonted evil manner was deemed obnoxious; whilst the lasting interest of our visitors rejoiced us as a testimony to the correctness of our estimate of our own efforts. Fatigue we knew not; though the influence of wellnigh continuously dull and rainy weather was most depressing, everyone declared himself relieved at once when he set

to work in the theatre. If the author of all the labours transferred to his artistic friends and comrades was often haunted by the presage of a scarcely avoidable lassitude, each nightmare was swiftly dispelled by a hearty assurance of the highest spirits from all concerned.

Disputes about rank were impossible where six singers of so-called "first rôles" had undertaken the un-named leadership of Klingsor's Flower-maidens, while their followers were played with the greatest alacrity by representatives of every branch. Had there really been need of an example for the actors of the principal parts—it could have been given them by the artistic unanimity of those magic-flower-maids. They were foremost in fulfilling one of the weightiest requirements, which I had to make the pivot of a proper rendering: that passionate accent which modern stage-singers have acquired from the operatic music of our day, breaking every melodic line without distinction, was to be interdicted here. I was understood at once by our fair friends, and soon their coaxing strains took on an air of childlike naïvety that, touching through a matchless intonation, was utterly opposed to that idea of sensual seduction which certain people had presupposed as the composer's aim. I do not believe that so magical a maiden grace has ever been displayed by song and gesture, as our lady artists gave us in this scene of "Parsifal."

To turn this Magic to a *Consecration* imbuing the whole stage-festival, soon became the earnest care of all engaged in the rehearsals and performances; and what unwonted demands were thus made upon Style, will be evident if we reflect that the strongly passionate, the fierce, nay savage, had to be expressed according to its natural character in single portions of the drama. The difficulty of the task thereby imposed on the leading actors was ever more apparent to us. Before all else we had to adhere to the greatest distinctness, especially of speech: a passionate phrase must have a confusing, and may have a forbidding effect, if its logical tenour remains unseized; but to seize it without effort, we must be enabled to plainly understand the smallest link in the chain of words at once: an elided prefix, a swallowed suffix, or a slurred connecting syllable, destroys that due intelligibleness forthwith. And this self-same negligence directly extends to the melody, reducing it through disappearance of the musical particles to a mere trail of isolated accents, which, the more passionate the phrase, at last become sheer interjections; the weird, nay the ridiculous effect whereof we feel at once when they strike on our ear from some distance, without a vestige left of the connecting links. If in our study of the Nibelungen-pieces six years back the singers already were urged to give precedence to the "little" notes, before the "big," it was solely for sake of that distinctness; without which both drama and music, speech and melody, remain equally un-understandable, and are sacrificed to that trivial Operatic effect whose employment on my own dramatic melody has called forth such confusion in our musical so-called "public opinion" that nothing but this indispensable distinctness can clear it up. But that involves complete abandonment of the false pathos fostered by the mode of rendering condemned.

Violent outbursts of poignant passion, the natural vents of a deeply tragical subject, can only produce their harrowing effect when the standard of emotional expression which they exceed is observed in general. Now we deemed this moderation best ensured by a wise economy in the use of breath and plastic movement. In our practices we became aware of the clumsy waste of breath, in the first place, committed in most of our opera-singing; for we soon discovered what a single well-placed breath could do toward giving a whole sequence of tones its proper sense, both melodic and logical. Simply by a wise restraint and distribution of force we—naturally—found it so much easier to render justice to what I have termed the "little" notes, which, lying lower for the most part, yet form important links in speech and melody; and just because the advantage of rounding off the entire phrase in one respiration forbade us to squander too much breath on the higher notes, which stand forth of themselves. So we were able to keep long lines of melody unbroken, however great the play of colour in their feeling accents,—eloquent instances whereof I may recall to our hearers with *Kundry's* lengthy narration of Herzeleide's fate, in the second act, and Gurnemanz' description of Good Friday's magic in the third.

In close connection with the advantage of a wise economy in the expenditure of breath, for the effectual understanding of the dramatic melody, we recognised the need of ennobling the plastic movements by a most conscientious moderation. Those screams, which are almost the only thing heard of the tune in our common operatic style, have always been accompanied by violent movements of the arms, employed at last so uniformly that they have lost all meaning and can but give the innocent spectator the absurd impression of a marionette. By all means, the conventional deportment of our well-bred classes would be out of place in a dramatic portrayal, especially when it is raised by music to the sphere of ideal pathos: here we no longer want etiquette, but the natural grace of sublimity. With the great distance often unavoidable in our theatres, the modern actor is precluded from depending on a mere play of features for his desired effect, and the mask of paint with which he combats the bleaching glare of the footlights allows him little but an indication of the general character, not of the hidden movements of the inner soul. In Musical Drama, however, the all-explaining eloquence of the harmonic tone-play affords an incomparably surer and more convincing means of effect than possibly can stand at service of the mere mimic; and dramatic melody intelligibly delivered, as set forth above, makes a nobler and more distinct impression than the most studied discourse of the best-skilled physiognomist, when it is least impeded by those artifices which alone can help the latter.

On the other hand the singer seems more directed, than

the mime, to plastic movements of the body itself, and particularly of those vehicles of feeling, the arms: yet in the use of these we had to abide by the selfsame law that kept the stronger accents of the melody in union with its particles. Whereas in operatic pathos we had accustomed ourselves to throw wide our arms as if calling for help, we found that a half-uplifting of one arm, nay, a characteristic movement of the hand, the head, was quite enough to emphasise a somewhat heightened feeling, since a powerful gesture can only have a truly staggering effect when emotion bursts at last its barriers like a nature-force full long held back.

The singer's law for shifting place is commonly an inconsiderate routine, as his most strenuous attention is claimed by the frequently serious difficulties of his purely-musical task; but we soon discovered how much was accomplished toward raising our dramatic performance above the operatic level by a careful ordering of his paces and his standing still. As the main affair of older Opera was the monologic aria, which the singer was almost compelled to fire into the face of the audience, so to say, the notion arose that even in duets, trios, nay, whole general musters, the so-called ensembles, everyone must discharge his part into the auditorium from a similar position. As walking was thus altogether precluded, the arms were set in that almost continuous motion of whose impropriety, nay absurdity, we had already grown aware. Now, if in genuine Musical Drama the *dialogue*, with all its amplifications, becomes the unique basis of dramatic life; and therefore if the singer no longer has aught to address to the audience, but all to his interlocutor,—we could but see that the usual alignment of a pair of Duettists robbed their impassioned talk of all dramatic truth: for they either had to tell the audience at large what was meant for one another, or to shew it nothing but their profile, with the resulting indistinctness both of speech and acting. To vary the monotony, one generally had made the two singers cross each other and change places, during an orchestral interlude. But the alertness of the dialogue itself supplied us with the aptest change of posture; for we had found that the sharper accents at close of a phrase or speech occasioned a movement of the singer, which had only to take him about one step forward and he was placed with his back half-turned to the audience but his face shewn full to his partner, as if in expectation of an answer; whilst the other need merely take about one step back, to begin his reply, and he was in the position to address his colleague—who now stood diagonally in front of him—without being turned from the audience.

By this and similar devices we were able to save the stage-picture from ever standing stock-still, and to win from all the changeful motives, offered alike by solemn earnestness and graceful mirth, that animation which alone can give a drama its due import of an action true to life.

Yet, for all our technical provisions and agreements, and all the special talent of the artists, which alone could give them real effect, such fair success could never have been compassed if the musical and scenic elements had not contributed their own full share from every side. As regards the scenery in its widest sense, the first thing to claim our solicitude was a fitness in the costumes and decorations. Here much had to be invented, needless as it might seem to those accustomed to cater for the love of pomp and entertainment by a skilful combination of all the tried effects of Opera. As soon as it came to the question of a costume for Klingsor's magic Flower-maidens, we found nothing but models from ballet or masquerade: the now so favourite Court-carnivals, in particular, had betrayed our most talented artists into a certain conventional lavishness of ornament that proved quite futile for our object, which was only to be attained on lines of ideal naturalness. These costumes must completely harmonise with Klingsor's magic garden itself, and we had to be quite sure that, after many attempts, we had found the right motive for this floral majesty, unknown to physical experience, before we could introduce into it living female forms that seemed to spring quite naturally from out its wizard wealth. Then with two of those giant flower-bells, that decked the garden in their rich profusion, we had the costume for our magic-maiden; to give the last touch to her attire, she had only to snatch up one of the glowing flower-cups all strewn around, to tilt it child-like on her head—and, forgetting each convention of the opera-ballet, we might take the thing as done.

Though our utmost diligence was spent on giving the height of solemn dignity to the ideal temple of the Grail, whose model could only be taken from the noblest monuments of Christian architecture, yet the splendour of this sanctuary of a divinest halidom was by no means to be extended to the costume of its knights themselves: a noble templar-like (*klosterritterliche*) simplicity arrayed their figures with a picturesque severity, yet human grace. The significance of the kingship of this brotherhood we sought in the original meaning of the word "King" itself, as head of the race, a race here chosen to protect the Grail: nothing was to distinguish him from the other knights, save the mystic import of the lofty office reserved for him alone, and his sufferings understood by none.

For the funeral of the first king, Titurel, a pompous catafalque had been suggested, with black velvet drapery suspended from on high, whilst the corpse itself was to be laid out in costly robes of state with crown and sceptre, somewhat as the King of Thule had often been depicted to us at his farewell drink. We resigned this grandiose effect to a future opera, and abode by our undeviating principle of reverent simplicity.

Only on one point had we to make a tiresome compromise, on this occasion. By a still inexplicable misreckoning, the highly-gifted man to whom I owe the whole stage-mounting of the "Parsifal," as formerly of the Nibelungen-pieces—and who was torn from us by sudden death before the full completion of his work,*—had

* Karl Brandt.—Tr.

calculated the speed of the so-called *Wandeldekoration* (moving-scenery) in the first and third acts at more than twice as fast as was dictated in the interest of the dramatic action. In this interest I had never meant the passing of a changing scene to act as a decorative effect, however artistically carried out; but, at hand of the accompanying music, we were to be led quite imperceptibly, as if in dream, along the "pathless" adits to the Gralsburg; whose legendary inaccessibility to the non-elect was thus, withal, to be brought within the bounds of dramatic portrayal. When we discovered the mistake, it was too late to so alter the unusually complicated mechanism as to reduce the scenes to half their length; for this time I had to decide not only on repeating the orchestral interlude [Act i.] in full, but also upon introducing tedious retardations in its tempo: the painful effect was felt by us all, yet the mounting itself was so admirably executed that the entranced spectator was compelled to shut one eye to criticism. For the third act, however—though the moving scene had been carried out by the artists in an almost more delightful, and quite a different manner from the first,—we all agreed that the danger of an ill effect must be obviated by complete omission; and thus we had a fine occasion to marvel at that spirit which possessed all sharers in our artwork: the amiable and talented artists who had painted these sets *—which would have formed the principal attraction in any other stage-performance—themselves consented, without the faintest umbrage, to this second so-called *Wandeldekoration* being entirely discarded this time, and the stage concealed for a while by the curtain. Moreover they gladly undertook to reduce the first *Wandeldekoration* by one half for the performances of next year, and to alter the second so that we should neither be fatigued and distracted by a lengthy change, nor need to have the scene cut short by closure of the curtain.

To have had my hints and wishes so intimately under-

* The Brothers Brückner, of Coburg; see page 103.—Tr.

stood in this last department, which I might call that of "scenic dramaturgy," was the great good fortune of my association with the excellent son of that lamented friend to whom,* almost exclusively, I owe the construction of our festival-house and its stage-apparatus. This young man evinced so plain a consciousness of the ideal aim in all the technical knowledge and practical skill acquired through his father's vast experience, that I only wish I could find his like in the stricter sphere of musical dramaturgy, on whom to devolve one day my burdensome and lonely office. On this latter field, alas! all is still so new, and hidden by the dust of bad routine, that experiences such as those we lately reaped in common through our study of "Parsifal" can only be compared with a breath of fresh air to the choking, or a flash of light in darkness. Here indeed no Experience could help us as yet to a swift understanding, but Inspiration—that *Weihe!*—creatively supplied the place of years of conscious practice of the right. This was shewn by the progress of the repetitions; their excellence did not succumb to any chilling of the first day's warmth, as usual at our theatres, but markedly increased. As with the scenic-musical work on the stage, this might have been especially observed in the so decisive purely-musical work of the orchestra. If I there was helped to fair success by intelligent and devoted friends who self-sacrificingly took duties given to none but inferiors elsewhere, we here were taught how much the German bandsman's sense of beauty and fine feeling is susceptible of, when he knows himself released for a time from incompatible demands upon his faculties, to give his whole mind to the solving of higher tasks, imposed elsewhere in haste. Brought into thorough concord with the singers by the proved acoustics of its installation, our orchestra attained a beauty and spirituality of expression already sadly missed by every hearer who returns to the gorgeous opera-houses of our great cities and has to suffer from their primitive arrangements for the band.

* See page 309.—Tr.

Thus even the influence of our surrounding optic and acoustic atmosphere bore our souls away from the wonted world; and the consciousness of this was evident in our dread at the thought of going back into that world. Yes, "Parsifal" itself had owed its origin and evolution to escape therefrom! Who can look, his lifetime long, with open eyes and unpent heart upon this world of robbery and murder organised and legalised by lying, deceit and hypocrisy, without being forced to flee from it at times in shuddering disgust? Whither turns his gaze? Too often to the pit of death. But him whose calling and his fate have fenced from that, to him the truest likeness of the world itself may well appear the herald of redemption sent us by its inmost soul. To be able to forget the actual world of fraud in this true-dream image, will seem to him the guerdon of the sorrowful sincerity with which he recognised its wretchedness. Was he to help himself with lies and cheating, in the evaluation of that picture? [*To the artists*] You all, my friends, found that impossible; and it was the very truthfulness of the exemplar which he offered you to work upon, that gave you too the blessed sense of world-escape; for you could but seek your own contentment in that higher truth alone. And that you found it, was proved me by the hallowed grief of our farewell, when after all those noble days the parting came. To us all it gave the surety of another joyful meeting.

My salutations now for that!—

Venice, 1. November 1882.

A YOUTHFUL SYMPHONY.

Bericht

über die

Wiederaufführung eines Jugendwerkes.

An den

Herausgeber des "Musikalischen Wochenblattes."

The "Report on the re-performance of an early work" appeared in the Musikalisches Wochenblatt *at the beginning of the year 1883.*

Richard Wagner's Symphony in C, the subject of this "Report," was performed in England, for the first time, at the London Symphony Concert of November 29th, 1887, under the bâton of Mr Henschel. It had been leased by Frau Wagner to the concert-agent, Herr Wolf, for the period of one year only. A considerable sum had been paid by Herr Wolf for the right of performance, which sum was devoted by Frau Wagner to the "Stipendiary Fund" already discussed on pages 294 et seq. *At the expiration of the twelvemonth the work was withdrawn, as originally intended.*

TRANSLATOR'S NOTE.

Dear Herr Fritzsch!

O explanation is needed, of your getting a piece of news from myself once again for your paper. You had the courage to publish my Gesammelte Schriften und Dichtungen in nine volumes—and a very big edition, which has proved somewhat a burden to you as time ran on—and also to pay me a fee for them. No one else would undertake it, twelve years back; even my essay on Beethoven had been returned to me by one of your predecessors, shortly before, because the Franco-German war upset him. Since then, not only have you published most helpful accounts of my works in your paper, but in all communications regarding myself you have insisted on an accentuated decency of tone, of whose value your colleagues elsewhere betray no very keen appreciation. The only mistake you have made, now and then, is in thinking to punish the impolitenesses of others by their reproduction in full, thereby acquainting the polished reader with the very things he would rather ignore. In the phenomenal world, however, every item may add to the interest!—

In reward for all the kindness shewn to me, you shall hear some absolutely private news to-day. Last Christmas eve, here in Venice, I kept a family jubilee of the first performance, exactly fifty years ago, of a Symphony composed by my own hand in my nineteenth year; from a non-autograph score it was played by the orchestra of professors and pupils of the local lyceum, S. Marcello, under my own direction, in honour of the birthday of my wife. I have stressed the "non-autograph"; and thereby hangs a singular tale that draws the thing into the realm of mystery, —my reason for confiding it to you.

Let us take it in historic order.

In Leipzig's pre-Judaic age, beyond the memory of more than a handful of my fellow-townsmen, the so-called Gewandhaus Concerts were accessible even to beginners of my "line"; the ultimate decision as to the admittance of new compositions lying in the hands of the Principal, a worthy old gentleman, Privy Councillor Rochlitz by name, who took things seriously and with a method. My Symphony had been laid before him, and I had to follow it up by a visit: when I introduced myself in person, the stately gentleman thrust up his spectacles and cried: "What's this? You are quite a young man: I had expected someone much older, a more experienced composer."—That promised well: the Symphony was accepted; though with the request that it first be played by the "Euterpe," if possible, as a sort of trial. Nothing was easier to accomplish: I was in the good books of this minor orchestral union, which had already performed a fairly fugal Concert-overture of mine in the "altes Schützenhaus" outside the Peter's-gate. At this time, about Christmas 1832, we had moved to the "Schneiderherberge" ("Tailor's house of call") by the Thomas-gate—a detail which I make a present to our witlings, for improvement. I remember that we were very much incommoded by the bad lighting there; after a rehearsal in which a whole concert-programme was attacked, however, we saw quite well enough to struggle through my Symphony: not that it gave myself much pleasure, for to me it seemed to scout all thought of sounding well. But what is faith for? Heinrich Laube, who at that time was making a name by his writings at Leipzig, not troubling his head how things sounded, had taken me under his protection; he praised my Symphony in the "Zeitung für die elegante Welt" with great warmth,*

* Glasenapp rightly observes that, as the performance in the Gewandhaus took place on January 10th, 1833, and the notice in the *Z. f. d. e. W.* did not appear until April 27th of that year, it cannot have been H. Laube's praise that assisted the work to a hearing. It is interesting to remark that at this concert Frl. Clara Wieck, afterwards Frau Schumann, appeared as a débutante. The

and eight days afterwards my good mother saw my work transplanted from the Tailors' inn to the Drapers' hall (*Gewandhaus*), where it suffered its performance under circumstances somewhat similar to the first. People were good to me in Leipzig then: a little admiration, and good-will enough, resigned me to the future.

But that future greatly changed. I had thrown myself on the operatic branch, and homeliness had reached its end in the Gewandhaus when *Mendelssohn* took up the reins a year or two thereafter [October 1835—Tr.]. Astounded at the ability of this still young master, I approached him during a subsequent stay in Leipzig (1834 or 1835), and, yielding to a curious inner need, I handed him, or rather, pressed on him the manuscript of my Symphony, with the petition—not even to look at it, but just to keep it by him. Of course I hoped he would peep into it nevertheless, and some day say a word to me about it. But this never happened. In course of years our paths brought us often in contact; we met, ate, and even music-ed together once in Leipzig; he attended a first performance of my "Flying Dutchman" in Berlin, and said that, as the opera had not quite absolutely failed there, I might rest satisfied with its success; on the occasion of a performance of "Tannhäuser" in Dresden, too, he declared that a canon in the Adagio of the second finale had pleased him much. Only about my Symphony, and its manuscript, never a word fell from his lips; sufficient cause for me never to ask about its fate.

The years slipped by: my famous and mysterious well-wisher was long since dead; when it occurred to certain friends of mine to ask about that Symphony. One of them was acquainted with Mendelssohn's son, and undertook to inquire of him, as the master's heir; other researches stayed as fruitless as this first one: the manu-

Symphony had already been played in private, under Dionys Weber, by the orchestra of the Conservatorium at Prague, where young Richard Wagner spent part of the summer and autumn of 1832.—In the preceding sentence a little play on words may be pointed out: Glaube (faith) and Laube.—Tr.

script was no longer in existence, or at least, it nowhere came to light. Then, a year or two back, an old Dresden friend informed me that a box of music had been found there, left ownerless by myself in time of stress: in it were discovered the orchestral parts of my Symphony, as written out for me in bygone days by a copyist at Prague. From these parts, at last restored to my possession, my young friend A. Seidl put a new score together for me, and, comfortably glancing over it after almost half a century, I fell a-pondering the import of that old manuscript's disappearance. Quite innocent, of course. For, conscious that its rediscovery could have no significance whatever, beyond a family-experience, I decided on letting my work sound out once more as a simple family-secret.

This happened in the friendliest fashion here in Venice, a few days back, and our experiences may now be told to you in brief. First of all, I must avow that the performance of the orchestra of the lyceum was highly gratifying to me, owing in part, no doubt, to a large number of rehearsals, which could not be accorded me at Leipzig long ago. The Italian musician's good qualities of tone and rendering might be made of excellent use, if German instrumental music were only to the taste of the Italian people. My Symphony really seemed to please. As for myself, this occupation with an early work taught me much about the characteristic course in the development of a musically productive gift to genuine independence. With great poets, like Goethe and Schiller, their youthful works at once proclaim the whole main theme of their productive life: Werther, Götz, Egmont, Faust, all were composed, or plainly sketched, by Goethe in his earliest spring-time. We find it otherwise with the musician: who would expect to recognise in their youthful works the true Mozart, the sterling Beethoven, with the same distinctness as he there detects the total Goethe, and in his striking works of youth the veritable Schiller? Without here going deeper into the enormous difference between the world-beholding of the Poet and the world-feeling of the Musician, to one thing we can point at once: namely that music is a truly artificial art, whose formal system must be learnt, and wherein conscious mastership, i.e. capacity of clear conveyance of one's own emotion, can only be attained through full acquirement of a second speech; whereas, whatever he beholds in truth, the poet can distinctly voice it in his mother-tongue forthwith. When the musician has dallied for a sufficient length of time with what he supposes to be the production of Melody, at last it frets and shames him to discover that he has merely been stammering out his favourite models: he longs for self-dependence; and this he can only win through gaining mastery of Form.* So the precocious Melodist turns Contrapuntist; now he has no more to do with melodies, but with themes and their working-out; it becomes his joy to sport with them, to revel in strettos (*Engführungen*), the overlapping of two, or three themes, till he has exhausted every possibility imaginable. How far I had brought it at that time, without losing sight or consciousness of the drastic firmness of the sense-of-form in my great Symphonic prototypes, Mozart and notably Beethoven,—it was this that astonished the worthy Hofrath Rochlitz when he beheld in the nineteen-summered youth before him the author of that symphony.

But my abandonment of symphony-writing had a valid reason, like enough; about which I took the opportunity, afforded by the re-discovery of this work, to clear my mind up. As its performance was to be a little surprise to my wife, I felt obliged to rob her in advance of all hope of meeting in my Symphony one trace of passion (*Sentimentalität*); if anything of Richard Wagner was to be detected therein, it would be at most the boundless confidence with which he stuck at nothing even then, and which saved him from that priggishness which soon became so irresistible to the Germans. Beyond my certainty in counterpoint—which Court-musician Strauss of Munich

* See Vol. I. page 7.—Tr.

would not allow me later on,—this confidence reposed at that time on a great advantage which I enjoyed over Beethoven: for when I took somewhere about the standpoint of his Second Symphony, I already knew the Eroica, the C minor and the A major Symphonies, which were still unknown to the master at the time he wrote the Second, or at most could only have been floating before him in dimmest outline. How much this lucky circumstance helped on my symphony, escaped neither myself nor my dear Franz Liszt, who attended the performance at the Liceo as one of the family, in the capacity of my father-in-law. In spite of principal themes like

which lend themselves quite well to counterpoint, but have little to say, my work passed muster as a "juvenile effort"; though I felt bound to add the epithet "old-fashioned." A secret Anti-semite of my acquaintance capped the "old-fashioned youthful work" (*Jugendwerk*) by the "new-fashioned Jew-work" (*Judenwerk*); but happily it came to no further controversy. However, just to give you a notion how far I had got with the Elegiac over fifty years ago, I present you with the theme—no! let us say, the melody of the second movement (Andante); although it probably would never have seen the light of the world without the Andante of the C minor, and the Allegretto of the A major Symphony, it pleased me so much in its day that I used it again for a melodramatic accompaniment to the Old Year's mournful leave-taking at a New Year's festival arranged in Magdeburg. With that meaning let it figure this time as my farewell to yourself.

RICHARD WAGNER.

Venice, New Year's Eve, 1882.

LETTER TO H. v. STEIN.

Brief an H. v. Stein.

The " Letter to H. v. Stein" appeared in the first quarterly number of the Bayreuther Blätter *for 1883, issued soon after Richard Wagner's death (February 13). Heinrich von Stein († June 20, 1887) was one of those young men of great promise whom a natural attraction gathered round the master; in 1879 he became the private tutor of Siegfried Wagner for a year or two, and thereafter a teacher at the universities of Halle and Berlin, but is best known to the world in general as the collaborator with C. F. Glasenapp in the compilation of the " Wagner-Lexikon." The collection of dramatic scenes, to which the master here refers, consisted of 12 sketches in dialogue, published shortly thereafter by E. Schmeitzner, of Chemnitz, under the title of " Helden und Welt." The book was prefaced by a letter from Stein to Wagner, of December 1882, together with the following answer; both were published in the aforesaid number of the* B. B. *with the first of the dramatic dialogues, " Solon and Crœsus."*

TRANSLATOR'S NOTE.

Dear Herr von Stein!

HEN I begged you to go on with your series of dramatic sketches of significant historic episodes, begun two years ago, I undertook to introduce to our friends any smaller or larger collection of such scenes, you meant to publish, with a few words explaining the importance I attach to similar works. Almost over-ripe for appearing in print, your booklet only waits for execution of my promise, to be laid before the reader. But while delays of every kind have hindered me, you yourself forestall me with a most delightful letter, in which you state the character you wish ascribed to this collection; and what you have said and suggested to me seems so adaptable for my remarks, that I can hardly do better than place your words before my own, and thus submit the matter interesting us to our friends in the form of an exchange of letters.

You have said that, brought into so close a contact with myself, you yielded to a longing to take your share in figure-work when you drafted these dramatic scenes. A stimulus to the selection of this particular form of artistic presentment you gained from the ingenious works of A. Rémusat, especially his Abelard, and probably still more pronouncedly from our Gobineau's brilliant handling of the chief characteristic moments of the Renaissance. Assuredly you could have made no happier advance, than this from the philosophic ruminator to the dramatic clairvoyant. Sight, sight, real *sight* — is what all lack. "Where are your eyes? Your eyes?"—one might forever cry to this eternally gossiping and eavesdropping world, where staring takes the place of sight. Who once has truly seen, knows what to think of it.

More than all Philosophy, Ethnology and History, one hour of genuine sight once taught me. It was the closing day of the Paris Universal Exhibition of 1867. The schools had free admittance on that day. Arrested in my egress from the building by the entry of thousands of male and female pupils of the Paris schools, for a whole hour I remained lost in inspection of almost every unit in this population of a future. The experience of that passing hour took such portentous shape at last, that I fell into a fit of tears and sobbing: this was remarked by a spiritual Sister who was conducting one of the troops of girls with utmost heed and scarcely dared to lift her eyes at the gate of entrance; her glance met mine too fleetingly to possibly awake in her an understanding of my state; yet I had just been practising my sight so keenly, that in that glance I read an inexpressibly beautiful solicitude as soul of all her life. This seized me all the more impressively, as in not one of the countless rows of led and leaders had I met its fellow, or anything alike. On the contrary, each face had filled me with dismay and sorrow: I saw all vices of the world-metropolis in embryo; by side of sickliness and stuntedness came coarseness and bad passions, hebetude and smothering of natural animation, fear and shrinking hand in hand with brazenness and cunning. And all this led by cleric teachers, for the most part, dressed in the hideous elegance of the new-fangled priesthood; themselves quite will-less, strict and harsh, yet more obeying than obeyed. All without soul—except that one poor sister.

A long deep silence rested me from the impression of that monstrous sight. Sight and silence: these after all may prove the elements of worthy rescue from this world. Only who lifts his voice from such a silence, may claim at length a hearing. You, my still so youthful friend, have won that right, at least in my eyes; and what I mean thereby, I now would state more plainly.—

To speak of the things of this world seems mighty easy, since all the world can talk of nothing else: but so to shew them that themselves they speak, is lent to few. To the world one can only speak when one shuts it completely out of one's sight. Who could address a Reichstag meeting, for instance, if he literally *saw* it? The parliamentary orator declaims to an abstractum, to parties, opinions, which style themselves in their turn "views" ("*Anschauungen*"); for all the people sitting there have changed to Views, and it is so hard to call them to account for insults because they say they never meant a person, but merely a view. I fancy that anyone who had mustered such an assembly man for man with seeing eyes, as fell to my lot with that Paris school-treat, would never say a word to it again in all his life. How indeed could he go on speaking to people to whom everything is shadow, mere view without perceptibility? Shew them the portraits of Gustavus Adolphus and Wallenstein, side by side, and ask them which of these two was the free hero, which the designing intriguer; they point to Wallenstein as the hero, and Gustavus as the plotter, because it is their "view."—

But these uninteresting nobodies, how different they seem at once when a Shakespeare bids them speak to us again: we hang upon their silliest words, those words the poet in his lifetime met by lofty silence. His silence here has turned to revelation; and the world from which we are transported, that world to which we now have nothing more to say, appears redeemed in the great poet's smile.

And this is of the essence of *Drama*, that is no form of poetry, but the likeness of the world reflected by our silent soul. Let those gentry of "views" go on writing their plays by the hundred, to mirror back their views; they cannot mislead us if we seek our own way to the Drama by mastering the art, not of talking about men and things, but of letting them speak for themselves. The success of your very first attempts in this art, dear friend, is explained at once by your having made that see-ing silence yours; for only thence can spring the force to re-present the seen. You had looked on History and its events, and could summon them to speech because you shewed us neither altogether History nor its events, which will always be obscure to us, but let historic persons speak, the persons witnessed in their deeds and sufferings. That History, in which no century, no decad e'er goes by without its tale of wellnigh nothing but the human race's shame,—we will leave it to the views of our Professors, to confirm their faith in constant progress; we have to do with men whom, the greater their pre-eminence, the less has History at any time known what to make of: their overstepping of the common bounds of Will, impelled by stern necessity, alone can give us such a comprehensive survey of the world that we forget at last its history,—the see-er's only possible reconcilement to it.

And so your scenes, instead of being simply treatises in form of dialogue, have won that true dramatic life which fascinates at once with the delight of seeing. They treat of no abstractions: your figures and their surroundings step before us full of life, quite individual and unexchangeable,—here Catherine of Sienna, there Luther,—all clad in flesh and palpitant as these.

Yet it is unmistakable that your desire to dramatise arose from the over-fulness of your heart. That *about which* we are more and more averse to talk, must speak out of and for itself. True, that we *have* views, and real views too; whereas those Reichs-professors use the term in pure confusion, as they find they cannot even speak of notions of their own, but at the most opinions, and opinions borrowed from the ruling public ones. Our beholdings of the world, however, have become our great and intimate concern. We ask ourselves the fate of this acknowledged world; and as in it we suffer and see others suffer, we seek a cure, or haply an ennoblement of Suffering. If we with all existing things are doomed to founder, —in that, too, will we see a goal, and shape our course to founder nobly.

The course to which we thus devote our lives you have

defined with such perfect plainness, simplicity and conclusive eloquence in your *Solon's* answer to a question of *Crœsus'*,* that I fain would stamp those words as fundamental theme of our further converse, and hence persuaded you to make them salient to the eye in type. Only in the light of that saying of your sage's, can the world seem worth our spending on it the sorest efforts of our lives, for only in such efforts can its meaning come to light. And even if the plan of your succeeding dramatic sketches was not dictated by a train of thoughts dependent on that fundamental theme, it yet was natural that each of them should stand in some relation to it. Thus you reach at last the picture "Homeless," with which you close your pregnant series for the present. As this displays an incident from modern life, it points us all directly back to life itself. Here we stand once more at brink of the abyss we dare not shun in coward dread, if we mean to prove our genuine saturation by that basic thought. Eh! it appears that deeds are wanted more than ever; though you yourself have truly shewn the curse that weighs on every action of the noblest, a curse which seems begotten of the world's dim consciousness that it is past all rescue. So, if our heart bids fair to sink, we'll call to mind your Solon. If we cannot redeem the world from its curse, yet active examples of most serious recognition of the possibility of future rescue may be given. We have to seek the paths which Nature herself may have prepared for us with tender care and forethought. These *Goethe* sought, and thus became so inspiriting a model to us. That the Devil himself must help the greybeard "Faust" to found a home for man's free action,† may prove indeed that this foundation was

* "Think'st thou, because I call myself philosopher, that I rate love and life as nothing worth? Nay, I know no surer truth than this: *whatever be the mighty secret at the back of things, the approach to it stands open to us in this poor life of ours alone, and thus our perishable actions bear withal such earnest, deep, and ineluctable significance.*"—Tr.

† Referring to Faust's last speech (Part II.), "Broad lands I open to earth's many millions, to dwell, if not secure, yet free of action." By aid of

yet no lasting refuge of the Pure: but it robbed the Devil of his mortgaged soul, for an angel of heaven loved the tireless one. In your comments on his "Wanderjahre" you have admirably shewn, my friend, how earnestly the poet tried to trace the preservative and evolutionary work of Nature in these social instincts of mankind:* he was filled, beyond dispute, with the idea of a re-foundation of Society upon a new domain of earth. But with his usual perspicacity he saw that little could be awaited from mere emigration, if it had not been preceded by a new-birth oi mind and spirit in the mother-home; and it was this he sought to set before us in inspiring emblems.

Carlyle has plainly proved to us the natural relation ot all Colonies to their mother-land:† as boughs lopped off

Mephistopheles, Faust has reclaimed a mighty region from the sea, and peopled it with colonists. In the poem the idea of "not secure" is shewn by the succeeding lines, "But he alone may claim his due in life and freedom, who battles for it day by day."—Tr.

* "Wie ernst der Dichter den im Schaffen der Natur aufgefundenen erhaltenden Bildungstrieb auch in diesen Instinkten der menschlichen Gesellschaft aufzusuchen sich angelegen sein liess, haben Sie, mein Freund, in den Zusammenstellungen seiner 'Wanderjahre' so vorsichtig als ersichtlich nachgewiesen."—H. v. Stein's article on the Third Part of *Wilhelm Meister* appeared in the *Bayreuther Blätter* for August 1881.—Tr.

† In *Latter-day Pamphlets*, No. IV. (1850): "England looking on her Colonies can say: 'Here are lands and seas, spice-lands, corn-lands, timber-lands, overarched by zodiacs and stars, clasped by many-sounding seas; wide spaces of the Maker's building, fit for the cradle yet of mighty Nations and their Sciences and Heroisms. Fertile continents still inhabited by wild beasts are mine, into which all the distressed populations of Europe might pour themselves, and make at once an Old World and a New World human. . . . Unspeakable deliverance, and new destiny of thousandfold expanded manfulness for all men, dawns out of the Future here. To me has fallen the godlike task of initiating all that: of me and of my Colonies, the abstruse Future asks, Are you wise enough for so sublime a destiny? Are you too foolish?' . . . Choose well your Governor. By him and his Collective Wisdom all manner of *true* relations, mutual interests and duties such as they do exist in fact between Mother Country and Colony, can be gradually developed into practical methods and results; and all manner of true and noble successes, and veracities in the way of governing, be won. . . . And surely were the Colonies once enfranchised from redtape, and the poor Mother Country once enfranchised from it . . . poor Britain and her poor Colonies might find that they had *true* relations to each other: that the Imperial *Mother* and her constitutionally

a tree and rooted bear none but its own life within them, grow old and die with it, so the farthest transplantations of a people's branches remain directly bound up with its life; they may wear the illusive look of youth, but rest upon the selfsame root on which the trunk has thriven, aged, turned sere, and dies. History teaches us that new stocks alone can start new life upon the soil of older and decaying peoples, but fall into a like decay when crossed with these. And should there be a possibility of the *German* stocks returning to a vitality quite lost to the so-called Latin world through its total Semitising, it could only be because their natural development had been arrested by their grafting on that world, and, led by their historic sufferings to knowledge of their imminent degeneration, they now were driven to save their purer remnant by transplanting it anew to virgin soil. To recognise this remnant, to prove it still alive in us and sound of seed, might then become our weightiest task: and, cheered by such a demonstration, could we but frame our measures on the laws of Nature—who offers us in visible mould the only proper guidance to all fashioning of both the individual and the species—we then might feel more justified in asking what may be the goal of this so enigmatic being of the world.

A difficult task indeed; all hurry must imperil the attempt at its solution: the sharper we thought to draw the outlines of the future, the less surely would they represent the natural course of things. Above all, our wisdom won in service of the modern State would have to hold its peace entirely, since State and Church could have no lesson for us save the warning of their dire example. None too far from the desired attainment could we begin, to keep the purely-Human in harmonious concord with the ever-Natural. If soberly we march ahead with

obedient Daughters was not a redtape fiction, provoking bitter mockery as at present, but a blessed God's-fact destined to fill half the world with its fruits one day!"—Tr.

measured steps, we shall know that we are continuing the life-work of our great poet, and feel ourselves conducted on the "rightful path" by his propitious footprints.

I have no need, my friend, to challenge you to take your share in such a work: in the best of senses you are engaged therein already.

RICHARD WAGNER.

Venice, 31. January 1883.

THE HUMAN WOMANLY.

Ueber das Weibliche im Menschlichen.

Although this fragment is not included in the Gesammelte Schriften, *but was published in the posthumous collection of* "Entwürfe" etc. *(1885), it demands a place in the present volume as concluding the series of articles on Religion and Art. Destined for the* Bayreuther Blätter, *to complete that series, it was commenced two days before the master's death in Venice. The marginal notes are the author's, and appear to represent the scheme on which he worked.*

TRANSLATOR'S NOTE.

Vendramin, 11. Feb. 1883.

ON THE WOMANLY IN THE HUMAN RACE.

(AS CONCLUSION OF "RELIGION AND ART.")

N all the treatises on the fall of human races, with which I am acquainted, I find but incidental notice given to the character of the marriage-bond and its influence upon the attributes of the species. It was with the intention of resuming this subject at greater length, that I added to my article on "Hero-dom and Christendom" the following remark: "no blaze of orders can hide the withered heart whose halting beat bewrays its issue from a union pledged without the seal of love, be it never so consanguineous."

If we pause for a moment's deep reflection, we might easily be terrified by the boundless vista opened out by such a thought. Yet, as I lately advocated our searching for the purely-Human in its agreement with the ever-Natural, mature consideration will shew us the only reasonable and luminous departure-point in the relation between man and woman, or rather, the male and female.

Whereas the fall of human races lies before us plain as day, we see the other animal species preserved in greatest purity, except where man has meddled in their crossing: manifestly, because they know no 'marriage of convenience' with a view to goods and property. In fact they know no marriage at all; and if it is Marriage that raises man so far above the animal world, to highest evolution of his moral faculties, it is the abuse of marriage, for quite other ends, that is the ground of our decline below the beasts.

Having thus been brought with almost startling swiftness face to face with the sin that has dogged the progress of our civilisation, excluding us from those advantages which the beasts retain still undisfigured in their propagation, we may consider ourselves as having also reached the moral gist of our problem.

It is disclosed at once in the difference between the relation of the male to the female in animal, and in human life. However strongly the lust of the male in the highest types of beasts may be already directed to the individuality of the female, yet it only protects its mate until she is in the position to teach the young to help themselves, which she does till they can finally be left to go their way and forget the mother also: here Nature's sole concern is with the species, and she keeps it all the purer by permitting no sexual intercourse save under influence of mutual 'heat.' Man's severance from the animal kingdom, on the other hand, might be said to have been completed by the conversion of his 'heat' into passionate affection for the Individual, where the instinct of Species, so paramount among the beasts, almost fades away before the ideal satisfaction of the being-loved by this one individual: in the woman alone, the mother, does that instinct seem to retain its sovereignty; and thus, although transfigured by his ideal love towards her individuality, she preserves a greater kinship to that nature-force than the man, whose passion now mates the fettered mother-love by turning to fidelity. Love's loyalty: marriage; here dwells Man's power over Nature, and divine we call it. 'Tis the fashioner of all noble races.

Only by such marriages could the races ennoble themselves in procreation.

Their emergence from the backward lower races might easily be explained by the prevalence of monogamy over polygamy; it is certain that the noblest white race is monogamic at its first appearance in saga and history, but marches toward its downfall through polygamy with the races which it conquers.

Polygamy (possession) at once among conquerors.

This question of Polygamy versus Monogamy thus brings us to the contact of the purely-human with the ever-natural. Superior minds have called Polygamy the more natural state, and the monogamic union a perpetual defiance of Nature. Undoubtedly, polygamous tribes stand nearer to the state of Nature, and, provided no disturbing mixtures intervene, thereby preserve their purity of type with the same success as Nature keeps her breeds of beasts unchanged. Only, a remarkable individuality the polygamous can not beget, save under influence of the ideal canon of Monogamy; a force which sometimes exerts its power, through passionate affection and love's loyalty, in the very harems of the Orientals. It is here that the Woman herself is raised above the natural law of sex (*das natürliche Gattungsgesetz*), to which, in the belief of even the wisest lawgivers, she remained so bound that the Buddha himself thought needful to exclude her from the possibility of saint-hood. It is a beautiful feature in the legend, that shews the Perfect Overcomer prompted to admit the Woman.

Ideality of the Man—Naturality of the Woman——(Buddha)—now—degeneration of the man—etc.

However, the process of emancipation of the Woman takes place amid ecstatic throes. Love—Tragedy.

SUMMARY.

SPOHR'S "JESSONDA" AT LEIPZIG.

Musical journals: who reads them, and what can one write for them? Philosophical treatises out of place, and reviews of new music a dead letter; perhaps the style of W. Tappert the fittest; had I his wit, and lived in a capital, I might write you oftener. The power of the accepted Critic: did I miss my vocation? (5). Present attempt at a report on an operatic performance at Leipzig an attempt to retrieve lost ground. Delight at hearing a band once again makes one lenient to minor faults: but what a medley is the whole genre of "German" Opera! It depends almost solely on music, not drama: Germans fail when striving for élégance; no self-reliance, and no encouragement thereto; Spohr's *à la polacca* and violin-passages for voice (8). German declamation moulded on foreign accent—result our Recitative. Yet our singers have much good stuff in them, were it rightly handled: Gura's impersonation an embodiment of tragic dignity and artistic simplicity. Let us, Kapellmeisters and all, acquire self-confidence (11).

TO THE WAGNER-VEREINS.

Pronounced success of latter performances in Festival of '76 might have warranted its prolongation, had the artists been able to stay; but we were drifting into a false position towards the public. Object of present appeal, to found a new Patronat-Verein for ensurance of continuation of our Festivals on the original lines; besides the seats to be devoted to our members, the State might be petitioned to provide a thousand seats, in every year, for needy artists and students; thus would the institution gain a national stamp throughout (18).

PROPOSED BAYREUTH "SCHOOL."

Offer to personally conduct "exercises and practices" in dramatic singing etc. at Bayreuth from Jan. '78 to summer of '83, with stage-performances of *Flying Dutchman* to *Parsifal* from summer '80 onwards (21).

INTRODUCTION TO BAYREUTHER BLÄTTER.

The first journal I have ever conducted. Of all the plans sketched out last autumn, this alone has proved feasible. Miracles of to-day take place on other fields than German Art: only result of my appeal has been the extension of Berlin High School of Music to affiliated provincial centres! Who taught these "higher" teachers? Our concert-institutes a chaos of false tempo and wrong expression (24). As we are denied all opportunity of practical instruction by examples, we must resign ourselves to theoretic instruction of one another by these *Blätter*. A hole-and-corner sheet, perhaps; but in Germany the "nook" alone has been productive, not the great city with its copies of the foreigner. Association the German's force; let us rest on that till 1880 and *Parsifal among ourselves* (27).

INTRODUCTION TO A WORK OF H. v. WOLZOGEN'S.

Object of our Verein should be more than a subscription for seats at performances; though articles from musicians would be very welcome, we can get none as yet; meanwhile the writers on our broader culture-principles have the field to themselves (29).

ANNOUNCEMENT TO THE PATRONAT-VEREIN.

Postponement of *Parsifal*, and offer to refund all subscriptions (30).

INTRODUCTION TO THE YEAR 1880.

As circular of July sifted out the few "seat-buying" subscribers, we may consider ourselves now all united in pursuit of same tendence. Our Public Art and its practitioners our greatest foes; we should do better to address ourselves to men in trade or politics. Yet, with our land and goods all pledged to the Jews, the State has nothing to spare for higher culture; and even if a millionaire endowed our institute, the Reich would place his treasure under lock and key (33). Another Hope: though God be robbed of his heavenly seat by science, there is a god within the human breast, and in us Germans he implanted music. Let us hold our German music holy, and ward off all profaning hands; then haply we may find an exit from the misery that hedges us to-day (35).

ANNOUNCEMENT OF "PARSIFAL" PERFORMANCES.

Though Patronate funds alone would not warrant it, by throwing performances open to paying public the Bayreuth Festivals will be resumed in '82, and, it is hoped, continued thereafter. But "Parsifal" is *nowhere* else to be performed (37).

INTRODUCTION TO A WORK OF COUNT GOBINEAU'S.

Relation of Art to Life: the world itself must supply the soil for Art; but what a world! Our truly lofty minds stand lonelier every day, and rarer; we can imagine the greatest poets etc. surrounded by a world to which they have nothing to say. A sigh of deepest pity for the human race might teach us once again to seek out paths of higher hope (40).

MODERN.

"An important Jewish voice" on the Jews' conquest of the modern world: I had thought our Jewish fellow-citizens preferred to keep such matters dark. What is the "modern world"? The same old world *plus* the Jews; their ruin of the German language and usurpation of our Press; literary "orthodoxy" sneered at,—yet they were not the first to invent "modernism" (45). Will the Jews make a "mode" of their own, and deliver us from Paris? But they have no originality; even their exquisite surnames now are borrowed; fine feathers and the "power of the pen." What "orthodoxy" is it, that they are fighting? And "popularity the shibboleth"; a fatal "*mot d'ordre*" for us Germans (49).

PUBLIC AND POPULARITY.

I.—Bad, good and middling: the Middling is the worst; a public reared thereon must raise itself, to appreciate the Good. *Gartenlaube* and its public; what a misnomer for a conglomerate of readers without judgment or initiative! The theatre *has* a public, whose judgment often confounds Directors; but no good thing can ever be created with an eye to the public's demands, and when surrendered to it notwithstanding, it is produced in style of the Middling, which alone is given well at our theatres (56). The mediocre, in a good sense, the product of Talent; Genius attains a goal we others do not even see. Virtuosity the mark of talent: French literature=phrase, but no novelty of thought; ridiculous for Germans to ape this style, for the mark of German Spirit is to *see* a thing before writing about it. Each of our poets and thinkers had to form a language for himself; history of German Literature the fall from Goethe and Schiller to the feuilletonist street-arab (58). Freedom of the Press, but has it ever dragged to light some unknown genius? Schopenhauer left for the English to discover, and now decried as preaching suicide! Yet it is the Public's own fault that it is so badly served (61).

II.—What is Criticism? The critics we may dismiss with the reading public for whom they write; but the *vox populi*? The evil is, that the German audience, unlike the Parisian, is so miscellaneous, especially at the Opera; various grades of receptivity assembled side by side, so that every reporter can take his own cue from some spectator near him (64). No *style* at our opera-houses to cultivate the public's sense of Form; psychologic impressions at mercy of chance, no discrimination between good and bad performances—e.g. mangling of *Ring* at outside theatres. German public still a naïve one; therefore one must seize it by its true element of Soul: the creative artist must imagine for himself an Ideal Public (66). The Good in art, like the Morally good, has no ulterior object; the Bad makes for pleasure and profit. How shall the Good gain *popularity*? Only the highest purity in the commerce of an artwork with its public can form the basis of a noble popularity (69).

III.—Now for the Academic public, which haughtily looks down on artists as the belated offspring of an obsolete world-view. Our Universities our Princes' pride, next to their armies; but all the statesman wants from them is good tough Civil Servants—the toughening done on the school-bench, the letting-off-steam at the university. These are the men who would have to vote in parliament on any artistic proposal; their favourite plays (72). Next the Professors: all claim their share in "constant progress"; even Philology expects salvation through Chemistry, which the new "historic school" of Philosophy wants to combine with Logic as substitute for Metaphysics and demolisher of "genius"; poor Darwin would be surprised to find his theory made do duty for each mystery of Being (75). The comprehending Subject left with sole right to existence! It is scarcely a man among men, and the State expends too much on its support, for the last thing the Professor would dream of, would be an address to the Folk. Theology? It has turned the God of Jesus to Jehova, casting in its lot with Judaism (78). Voltaire and Schiller's different treatment of Joan of Arc; Raphael's Sistine Madonna with the babe whose eyes stream forth redemption: "Is," not "means" (79). Can we not surrender Jehova? Or is all our civilisation to relapse into barbarism, like the Roman Empire? Let us try by Art to win the Folk to nobler outlooks; that would be the worthy "popularity" (81).

THE PUBLIC IN TIME AND SPACE.

Genius more than mere product of its surroundings, or why should contemporary world reject it? Sublimest instance in Jesus Christ; Giordano Bruno burnt by Renaissance monks. Tragedy of great minds their subjection to rules of time and place, whereas their birth is governed by mysterious laws of a suprasecular life (86). Plato and his political error; Dante and medieval superstitions; Calderon and the Jesuit tenets. Surroundings of Greek Tragedians rather helped, than hindered, their creative work; but attempts to place those dramas on our stage shew that we have lost the clue to something that once conditioned them in another age and country (88). Italian painters and their patrons; Cervantes starving; Frenchmen never think of writing a play that has not its public ready for it, and so with Italian Opera—e.g. Rossini. What lifted Mozart's operas above their age doomed them to live on when each condition of their performance has vanished: *Figaro*, *Don Giovanni*, but in particular the *Magic Flute* (91). Leaving aside mere local differences in present public, we come to problem of Liszt's symphonic poems: his *Dante*-symphony the redemption of the soul of the Divine Comedy from all its superstitions, but not the dullest admiration has it gained; for whom could he have written it? Plainly for an *ideal* public, conjured up by the active stir in leading minds of Paris in 1820-40.—The Public is a river rushing to the sea of Vulgarity: who aims at higher things, must steer his course against the stream (94).

RETROSPECT OF THE FESTIVALS OF 1876.

Who enabled me to erect the Bayreuth play-house and perform the *Ring* there? In front rank the executant artists; memories of the foundation-laying in '72; my artists' interest has never failed me. But a national interest? Kings and princes came to see a work they had never believed could be carried out; their condescension I owe to one untiring lady, who had to bear the same insults from the Press as had erewhile been heaped on King Ludwig's head (99). Application to Bismarck and its results. Subscriptions of Wagner-Vereins; in too many cases mere speculation on a lottery-prize. When the deficit came, I found I had really had no "patrons," and must have been crushed by the debt but for King Ludwig's intervention (102).

The designers etc. of the house and its scenery, K. Brandt, O. Brückwald, J. Hoffmann and the brothers Brückner. Minor defects and delays caused by universal incredulity: tricks played by the gas; the lindworm and Siegfried's tree (104). The performers: A. Niemann their backbone; K. Hill as Alberich, G. Siehr as Hagen; F. Betz' marvellous impersonation of Wotan, a new style of singing invented by a fertile brain (107). Hans Richter and the orchestra; the marble tablet and omitted names. Our lady-singers a model to all; two poles of the performance, Rhine-daughters and Brünnhilde's last scene. An enthusiastic will, on part of all, replaced despotic authority. A tender farewell (109).

SHALL WE HOPE?

Not to continually repeat myself, I have to presuppose acquaintance with my earlier writings, which kind friends are now expounding in these *Blätter*. I have had no occasion to change those early views; attempts to draw nearer to the burgher world in *Meistersinger*, the aristocracy in *German Art and Policy*, have availed but little. The State cannot further Art, but Life must become less barbaric (116). "L'enfer est sur la terre." Optimism and Constant Progress. Eye for the Great is rarer every day in our "widened horizon," yet no true eye for the Small; science of "atoms" and its superstitions; State with its armies and warlike industries: what hope have we from this modern world? (119). Faust and "Alone I will!" Mephistopheles would have put all his devils at my service, had I consented to rear my playhouse in Berlin; my offer to train young talents at Bayreuth fell through; it would have meant their all becoming penniless "Wagnerians": age creeping on, my "alone" grows harder every year. All I could offer in return for tons of money, would be an Example; but Germans lack the "inner must" (122). Great German masters long have striven for an Artwork national to the race itself, above our present "barbaric" civilisation: Luther translates "barbaros" by "undeutsch"; could we but found a truly German culture, we might give the whole world a new lease of life. What are our armies? The power that feeds them is German Labour, and we drive its best to emigrate! Such is our "constant progress" (125). Cromwell as recruiter; we need a spirit akin to that, to combat opinions thrust down the people's throat by Journalism; but let us pay no heed to Press itself,—not hate, the surest weapon is contempt (128). As newspaper-readers have given Press its power, so it is our own fault that we are governed as we are; our ignorance and indifference send representatives to Parliament. We must gain the strength to form fresh habits, and above all have patience; then can we "hope" (130).

ON POETRY AND COMPOSITION.

Gutzkow ascribed popularity of Goethe and Schiller to their publishers' energy: present generation seems taking the hint; printing-press at full speed, though little profit falls to the "fantastic" author; even Professors make away their stock-in-trade in low-priced pamphlets. Modern verses when read aloud! Lyrical and epical musicians; the "ballad" makes the opera's fortune. Dramas by young and old, in five-foot iambics, though naked prose has more chance with Directors; little prospect of great poets here (136). Novel-writing the most lucrative: the *narrator* is the "poet" proper; the Greeks' one poet,

Homer, and the Trouvères; seer and "finder." Was Homer an *artist*? His gift a godlike knowledge of all that lives; Greek art may all be derived from him. Dante, Cervantes and Scott have once again this "second sight"; but our moderns, who expect to turn their own experiences into romance! Cervantes saw the dual nature of the world; his Quixote and Sancho become Goethe's Faust and Mephistopheles; the seer's eye the gods have always lent to none but their believers (140). The Greek Tragedian materialised the dream-world seen by Homer, through music; when this supreme ecstasy of the Hellenic spirit sobered down, nothing remained but "techne"—no longer Art, but the arts. With the *ars poetica* Wit invaded poetry, and the epigram is the only hope of modern literature; if you can find a young Ovid, let him off the general thrashing (142). But *wit* in music! Think of a Divertissement at any of our concerts, compared with the most wit-less Symphony of Beethoven's: music can smile, but never make us laugh. The carnival of recent composers; a diploma-ed Prince of Serious Music laughing behind his mask (144). Mendelssohn's dictum: "Every man composes as well as he can"; but these maskers try to compose better; strive as they may, they never conjure up a living *shape* like Beethoven's simplest theme. Their spite at others; but the worst is, that we should pay for this cretinising of the youthful generation (147).

ON OPERATIC POETRY AND COMPOSITION.

Opera audience hears little of plot, so that young girls may safely be sent to *Figaro* and *Don Juan*; even in dialogic works, as *Freischütz*, much remains unheard; performance of operas becomes more careless every day (153). German Opera adopted Italian aria-form as sole end and aim of composer, therefore also of poet: verses had to be chopped up or partially repeated, to suit melody, and speaking-accent set awry; instances from Winter, Marschner and Weber; Naumann's setting of Ode to Joy compared with Beethoven's; moreover our best German verse is an elaborate sham (158). Mozart had raised orchestral accompaniment to symphonic characterisation of high expressiveness, but only in *opera buffa*; his followers had no pattern for *opera seria*, and tried to "melodise" everything, as the "singer would always like something to sing": cantilena, mordente, grace-notes, scales and runs, with march and ballet rhythms borrowed from abroad. Weber introduced four-part male chorus, and now whole breadths were covered by "melodic" general muster, —e.g. Marschner's *Templar* (162). And all these separate numbers must be telling in themselves, whilst the Finale must cause a tempest of delirium; if this fell through, the opera was withdrawn. Want of *style* in German Opera, even compared with French and Italian; *Euryanthe* the offspring of a Tschandala and a Brahminess; the poet-father a lady, the music in fullest sense a man! (165). No one ventured to face the problem which Weber had left unsolved; Marschner naïvely went on, till French Opera caught him too; all stood abashed by Meyerbeer's success, until my own alarmed them. Hiller and Schumann ask for help in their texts, then decline it with suspicion,—*Genoveva* and its brutal mock-chastity. What they teach at the Music-schools? Mighty little composing is learnt there (168). My "manner"? I never can compose at all if nothing strikes me; how the dramatic composer may force such "occurrences": the visionary shape begins to move, its ghostly voice breathes forth a "*motif.*" But one cannot get these inspirations from stage-dummies, or trim them by rule of three; the supply of "pretty tunes" for masque music is exhausted—had we only a Rossini!—I fear my article will not teach much: we want Examples, and for them an orchestra and singers (172).

ON THE APPLICATION OF MUSIC TO THE DRAMA.

Beethoven, so daring in his Symphonies, was cramped in his *Fidelio*; character of his instr. works not dramatic, but rhythmic. Mozart far bolder in his harmonic changes; but, approaching the Symphony from side of Opera, he missed the wonted stimulus; was he seeking for Tragedy (denied him in Opera) in the Symphony? Who shall say what he might not have done? (178). Rise of Programme-music: Berlioz' excesses nobly tempered by Liszt to portrayal of world and soul events too great for words; a development of the Overture, in other hands it fell to melodrama (180). Modern romantic-"Classical" symphonists and their toothache of the world; fallen feathers from the programme-petrel, but no Beethoven to fit them in; Chamber-music turned into symph.; little chips of clammy melody etc., labelled "Best." Programmists retain the upper hand, and turn the modern cabinet-painting into "plastic" music (182). Review of Modern Music's evolution: Unity the law of perfect artwork, and programme-music necessarily leads to so-called "music-drama" on symphonic base. No chair yet founded for my art, so I myself must give an inkling of its musical principles (184). The restraint I have striven for with increasing vigilance in modulation and instrumenting of my works; instances, preludes to *Rheingold*, *Walküre* and *Siegfried*; introduction to Norns' scene in *Götterdämmerung* only slightly richer in its treatment. Important how one commences (185). Combination of themes, e.g., Wotan's surrender of world-rule, carefully prepared by dynamic changes—such nuances neglected by outside conductors, to my own dismay; no wonder my music an abomination to "professors." Metamorphosis of motives: instance, Rhine-daughters' two-note theme throughout whole drama; such a treatment would be far-fetched in a Symphony (188). First moulding of a motive: Elsa's arioso in act i, its closing phrase impossible as symphonic theme because of its modulations, but here quite natural when performed, although a mere *reading* of it surprises one. Were I given a sacred chair in Conserv. I should make it a rule for pupils never to quit a key while they can say in it all they have to; then we might have Symphonies again (191).

AGAINST VIVISECTION.

Science, Utility and State. Societies for Protection of Animals have relied too much on utilitarian pleas, imperilling their permanence if it were proved that vivisection is a useful measure; and were it *dis*-proved, no lasting good would result to mankind while the true idea inspiring us remains unuttered. Pity, compassion, the only rightful arm against beast-torture; this Pity decried as sublimated egoism, confounded with cowardly Regret. Our Armies' idea of Pity, the abridgment of life's sufferings *en gros* (199). Science and Pity: Theology cannot find it in Genesis, yet many a humane incumbent must have learnt it in his cure-of-souls. Medical science the daily life-saviour; born physician and his eagerness to help; but our trust will vanish if doctors advocate beast-torture, for vivisection might extend to man. *Religion of Pity* toward all that lives, a Paradise regained (201). Ancient sages perceive that same thing breathes in animals as in man, and turn from animal food; in rawer climates, where that food became a necessity, the beasts were deemed belonging to a deity, to whom a part was offered; Plutarch and his "Reason in the Beasts"; Christ's atonement; legends of animals and the Saints. But the Old Testament has won the day (203). In this devilised civilised world how is our relation to animals to be made a moral one? Darwin's teaching that we descend from them, should give us fellow-feeling with them: religion of true Humanity. Many a lesson could we gain from beasts: courage and fidelity, their loving reverence of man as god (206). Bitch and litter, the mother dying when she brings the last pup safely to her master's home; self-sacrifice with no ulterior aim. Monkeys of Science scuttling up tree of knowledge in fear of their lives; Hungarian magnate's inheritance and doctors called from far and wide,—would ye but spare some portion to relieve the suffering labourer! (208). Visconti, Duke of Milan, anticipates our physiologists, in his edict against political offenders: but the people seized him by the throat, as mob has just wrecked a Leipzig laboratory. We must leave the State no peace until it *abolishes* vivisection; for man's dignity begins where he shews pity to the beasts (210).

RELIGION AND ART.

I.—The truth lying hid behind religious dogmas is revealed by ideal art; but Art was incapable of higher evolution so long as she stayed bound to fetishes. The more divine a religion, the simpler its inmost kernel; basis of all true religions a recognition of nullity of this phenomenal world, but it needed a superhuman effort to disclose that knowledge to the natural man, the Folk. The religious Founder consequently obliged to speak in parables; distinction of Christ's and Buddha's teachings, that they address the "poor in spirit"; whereas the Brahminic religion was for "those who know," and ended in philosophical casuistry (214). Christ: to believe in him meant to follow his example; this faith too simple for the rising Church, which soon heaped over it a mass of dogmas. Miracles: to the natural man none could be greater than the reversal of the will-to-live. These miracles offered ever fresh incentives to Art, whose province is revelation of the Idea. Greek statue and Nature; Greek gods and "*the*" God; but here the very shape of the Divine had taken body. Jehova, upheld by Church, but doomed by Art; whereas the "Head with wounds all bleeding" still fills us with an ecstasy of love (217). The "immaculate conception": the Will-to-live, broken before birth, becomes the Will-to-redeem; a mystery disfigured by early realistic art, but idealised by Raphael; this Madonna no icy Artemis, but Love beyond all knowledge of unchastity (219). The Last Judgment, and the Church assembling in most hideous parody the myths of each religion smirched with the belief in Hell: Michael Angelo idealises it by the glance of divine Mother, though Dante (with Poetry in general) was bound fast to dogmatic canons. But Plastic art degenerated as it left Religion for the world; portraits of crafty

Cardinals and Princes; Venus of Italian painters against the Greek (222). Art of Tone: unshackled by the words of Dogma, this art alone could give its ideal content unalloyed; a world-redeeming revelation of nullity of phenomenal world; only her final severance from Church could enable Music to save the noblest heritage of the Christian idea (224).

II.—In Historic period religions have fallen deeper, the longer their outward rule, owing to degeneration of the race. Brahminism and Buddhism; doctrine of oneness of all that lives, and abstention from animal food; an Indian famine, three million Hindus die of starvation rather than slay their domestic animals (226). Whatever convulsions of Earth may have driven aborigines to raw inhospitable climes, in History we see man's constant progress as beast of prey; cleavage between the races that returned southwards, to Indian peninsula, and those that passed north-westwards through the steppes of Asia—conquering all before them, blood at last becomes their only sustenance (228). Parsee creed, with its ideas of Sin; Greek, not shunning the awful side of life, turns that knowledge to artistic contemplation, but the noblest art must seem a mockery while violence reigns supreme. There's no blood-guiltiness this fair-fashioning race did not incur in hate against its neighbours; and so the centuries have ever brought fresh grosser forces into play, till we ourselves are fenced on every hand with cannon (231). Pythagoras and his silent vegetarian communities; among one of these appeared the Saviour: wine and bread, the unique sacrament of the Christian faith. But the Church soon sought to rule the State; for this she needed a God of jealousy and vengeance, and usurped the Jews' Jehova—strange contrast with the humble origin of the Redeemer of the *Poor*. Joshua, Gideon etc., invoked by our army-chaplains, even though the name employed be "Christ"; not unnatural, with a Church that erewhile handed her heretics to Temporal power for burning at the stake (234). Our States all founded on conquest, the right of might still holds; even sovereigns wear military uniform for grand occasions, instead of robes of Justice. Thus our whole Civilisation is un-Christian: true Culture must spring from soil of peace, but the State encourages none but warlike inventions. For *this* world men still paint and make music! (236).

III.—Theory of human race's degeneration our only hope, as it points to evils in human nature not ineradicable, results of *outer* influences. Man has survived great transformations of Earth's crust, and qualities foreign to himself may have been acquired: in any case we have proof that even in colder climates, as Russia and Japan, where grain is plentiful, the people living exclusively on vegetables attain great length of life, whilst we flesh-eaters are victims to maladies unknown to any other species (239). The true motive of Societies of Vegetarians and Protection of Animals should be the same—pity; let them join with Temperance-unions, and already a centre of force were won; Peace-societies, Trade-unions and Socialists, all might combine to win us a true Religion, not a Judæo-Christian theocracy that derives Man's fall from fruit of the fields (241). Whose memory would this community be celebrating when, after each day's work, it met to taste of Bread and Wine? Less than half mankind feeds on animal food; why cannot the lesser half migrate to kindlier climes, and leave these Northern lands to hunters of big game? (243). For all Regeneration we need the soil of a true religion. The giant force that shaped the world attained its goal in Man, for in him it becomes conscious of itself as Will; redemption through school of Conscious Suffering. The human species based on all the lower manifestations of Will: knowing them a part of our own selves, our horror turns to Pity; the actual documents of life are set before us, so let our sympathy go forth to the suffering, not the triumphant Hero,—this the lesson of the Redeemer on the cross (247). Tragedy of the world, and Art its gentle mediator; to us shall all these poet-sages once have spoken, and to us speak again. Solemn hours when the world of semblance melts into a dream and the soul of Manhood soars on high; then sounds the cry of Nature longing for redemption, and every sphere is filled with Music. Those last four Symphonies of Beethoven a revelation of the Inexpressible (250).

"Do you wish to found a new religion?" Impossible: as a working artist, it dawned on me that a happier future might befall mankind if Religion and Art were given the place now held in our social system by Violence and War (252).

"WHAT BOOTS THIS KNOWLEDGE?"

Ask the real poets of every age, ask the founders of true religions; ask *not* the State! Our statesmen all in Robespierre's plight, not knowing what to do with power won; had this knowledge been theirs, the Frankfort Treaty would have established another sort of peace, by making war impossible (255). It is hard to persuade the world of this "use," for intellect of nowadays is too clouded to perceive the genuine soil of Ethics prepared by Arthur Schopenhauer: his system as complete a revolution in our modes of thought as that of introduction of Christianity; he plainly indicates the paths to take, but leaves their exploration to ourselves (257). The Ten Commandments bear no trace of a Christian thought; only Luther's commentary turned them from *forbiddals* to commands. The new commandment of Love, whence issue Faith and Hope; compassion and recognition, with Schopenhauer, of a *moral meaning of the world* (259). It would be a great boon to the people, if someone would draft a popular version of Schopenhauer's "Apparent Design"; answer to troubled spirits: "Peace, rest and happiness dwell there alone where is *no When*, no *Where*. Yet the Folk demands a positive notion of Eternity, and this can only be given it by Art, based on religious symbols borrowed from life's exercise itself. Every path that leads to mental and moral culture must be most diligently explored; for, recognising fall of Historic Man, we believe in possibility of his regeneration (263).

"KNOW THYSELF."

It needed Kant and Schopenhauer, to revive these lessons of ancestral wisdom, "Know thyself" and "This art thou." Recent Anti-Semite agitation; yet we ourselves gave Jews their power over us, first by adopting their Patriarchs, and then by our deification of Property (267). Metamorphosis of original idea of Property, till at last the Nibelung's Ring became a cheque-book; Creed replaced by Credit; a barbarous Civilisation (269). But a reviving instinct seems to lie at bottom of movement against Jews; scarcely of Race, for present German amalgam has little purity of breed to boast—Thirty Years War destroyed that, and with it all racial *pride*, exchanged for vanity, greed and dabbling in foreign manners. The Jew is the most remarkable instance of racial stability; however he intermarries, a Jew always comes to birth (271). Our antagonism must lie deeper, in instinct of the purely Human; through this alone can the German help not only himself, but other nations. Our party-politics but a passing nightmare; let us brace our best of forces to assist the sleepers when at last they wake (273).

HERO-DOM AND CHRISTENDOM.

Besides the change in food-staple, the blood of nobler races has been tainted by admixture with ignoble, as set forth by Count Gobineau in his opus magnum. Though the globe shall disappear, and with it the human species, do we mean to go to ground as beasts or gods? Attributes of Aryan stock, preponderance of intellect over animal will, a proud obedience, and consciousness of Suffering: types in Hercules and Siegfried, repeated in History by Franks in service of decadent Roman Empire; Pride the soul of the truthful, of the free though serving; excessive possessions deemed a disgrace (278). But this code of honour vanishes with crossing of the races, and we next must seek the hero in the Saint inspired by horror at the fall. Denial of Will-to-live no act of cowardice, but always characterised by utmost energy; thenceforth the saint outvies the hero in endurance of suffering, in self-offering for others. What part does Race play here? The Saviour's nationality? The human Species' common bond, its capacity for conscious suffering, at its highest expression; the Will-to-redeem (281). The Brahminic a race-religion, ensuring supremacy of a privileged caste by the most elaborate system of ethics; religion of Christ addressed to all mankind, as his blood may be metaphysically derived from supreme effort of the Will to redeem mankind—paralleled by creation of new species. Extreme simplicity of true Christian idea; by its adoption the races might all be raised to high morality (284).

END OF THE PATRONAT-VEREIN.

Impossible to renew Stage-festivals with nothing but Patronate funds; the paying public to be admitted after first two performances; in this way the future of the undertaking is secured, while engagement of multiple caste will take the place of "School" once contemplated. Patronat-Verein should necessarily be dissolved; Bayreuther Blätter will become independent; and thus our relations with the Public will on both sides be direct (291).

THE STIPENDIARY FUND.

I can no longer entertain thought of a "School" at Bayreuth: I am no musician, of course, or I should appreciate our modern music; but even a conservancy of Beethoven's works would tire me now too much, as I am getting old. All I can undertake in future, is to superintend Bayreuth festivals, helped by the willingness of our executants. The performances being thrown open, the "Patrons" should now become "patrons of the public" by assisting needy artists to attend our festivals; this would be more practical than present scholarships with an eye to finishing lessons in Paris or Rome, for it would tend to found a *German* Art (300).

"PARSIFAL" AT BAYREUTH, 1882.

As anniversaries of Dedication of a church are celebrated by a lay feast, or "wake," inversely we had to suppose the stage consecrated, so to say, for presentation of the Love-feast of the Grail. Whatever offence the thought may give to some, we found in fact that all concerned in our performances were inspired by a reverent feeling. Rivalries impossible where six "first" singers played the unnamed leaders of the Flower-maidens: the magic of their naïve grace a type of the spirit in which all approached their tasks. Untold difficulties in *style* of the work: false pathos would have ruined all. Greatest distinctness of enunciation our first requirement; economy of breath, and artistic moderation, enabling the melodic phrase to be given as a whole: instances, Kundry in act ii. and Gurnemanz act iii. (306). The same restraint in bodily gesture, thus giving due effect to more impassioned moments. How we overcame difficulty of dialogue on the stage, without turning the face from the audience. By these and similar devices we saved the scene from ever standing absolutely still (308). Details of mounting: Klingsor's magic garden and costume of Flower-maids; temple of the Grail and simple robes of its knights; the "King's" sole distinction; a spectacular suggestion for Titurel's funeral. Only one hitch, scene-painter's miscalculation of speed of moving scenery, involving repetition of orchestral accompaniment; to be amended next year (310). The Brandts and "scenic dramaturgy": if only I could find their like in sphere of musical stage-management, to whom to bequeath my office! How much the German bandsman is capable of, when rightly led. We all were borne away from the wonted world; our grief at returning to it gives us surety of another joyful meeting (312).

A YOUTHFUL SYMPHONY.

So much gossip appears, that you [Ed. of *Mus. Wochenblatt*] may like to hear some authentic private news; a family jubilee of a youthful work. Surprise of old Rochlitz when, at the age of 19, I made my call as composer of the Symphony submitted for performance at Gewandhaus concerts: trial-trip at the Euterpe; it sounded bad; however, it was played at Gewandhaus with some good-will. Things changed when Mendelssohn assumed the reins; I pressed my score on him, and neither saw nor heard of it again (317). A year or two ago the parts discovered in my long-lost luggage; a new score put together by A. Seidl; excellent performance by orchestra of S. Marcello in Venice on Christmas-day '82, in honour of Frau Wagner's birthday. Reflections on difference in evolution of poet and musician: the young composer aims first at Melody, till he makes for self-dependence and a sense of Form through Counterpoint; then come *themes*. But nothing of the real Richard Wagner is to be found in this Symphony, save perhaps his self-confidence,—advantage of acquaintance with Beethoven's Third, Fifth and Seventh Symphonies when I took the standpoint of his Second. Nevertheless, an "old-fashioned juvenile" work (320).

LETTER TO H. von STEIN.

As preface to your series of dramatic sketches in dialogue. Your models Rémusat and Gobineau: sight, real *sight*! My experience on closing day of Paris Exhibition of '67: the school-children and their leaders; all the vices of the world-metropolis reviewed in embryo. A long deep silence; only after sight and silence may one claim a hearing (326). To speak of the things of this world may be easy; but to shew them so that they speak themselves, is given to few: parliamentary oratory mere "view," but a Shakespeare turns these nobodies' silliest speeches to a revelation. We, too, have "views," as we suffer and see others suffer, and ask ourselves the meaning of the world; the answer given by your Solon: only in this mortal life can we shape our course for that hereafter (329). And from Nature must we learn the plan: a re-foundation of Society on a new domain of earth, preceded by regeneration in the mother-land, as conceived by Goethe. To recognise and save the purer remnant of our race, and transplant it where its arrested development may proceed afresh; here hurry would be fatal; the purely-Human following the system of the ever-Natural (332).

THE HUMAN WOMANLY (*FRAGMENT*).

Importance of Marriage, in problem of Regeneration. Animals know no "marriage of convenience"; their purity of type. True monogamic unions of faithful love the fount of noble races and great characters. Buddha and emancipation of Woman (337).

INDEX

As in former volumes, the figures denoting tens and hundreds are not *repeated* in one and the same reference unless the numbers run into a fresh line of type. Figures enclosed by brackets refer to my own footnotes etc. —W. A. E.

A.

B.

C.

D.

G.

H.

I.

J.

K.

N.

O.

P.

Q.

R.

S.

T.

U.

V.

Y.

Z.